# INDIA
# OLD AND NEW

# INDIA
# OLD AND NEW
WITH A
# MEMORIAL ADDRESS

BY

**E. WASHBURN HOPKINS, M.A., PH.D.,**
*Professor of Sanskrit at Yale University*

KALPAZ

First Published in 1901
Indian Reprint in 2017

*Published by*

Kalpaz Publications
C-30, Satyawati Nagar,
Delhi – 110052
E-mail: kalpaz@hotmail.com
Website: kalpazpublications.com
Ph.: +91-9212142040

**Cataloging in Publication Data—DK**
Courtesy: D.K. Agencies (P) Ltd. <docinfo@dkagencies.com>

**Hopkins, Edward Washburn,** 1857-1932, **author.**
India old and new : with a memorial address / by E. Washburn Hopkins (M.A., Ph.D.).
pages cm
"First published in 1901"—Title page verso.
Chiefly on the Rgveda, Sanskrit literature, and religions of India.
ISBN 9789351284598 (HB)

1. Vedas. Rgveda—Criticism, interpretation, etc. 2. Sanskrit literature—History and criticism. 3. India—Religion. I. Title.

LCC DS436.H67 2017 | DDC 954 23

# PREFACE.

Of the eleven separate papers here brought together, three have previously been published in full, — that on Guilds in the Yale Review, May and August, 1898; that on Land-tenure in the Political Science Quarterly, December, 1898; and that on Gods, under the title, "How Gods are made in India," in the New World, March, 1899. The editors of these journals have kindly granted me permission to republish the articles. I am also indebted to the editor of the Forum for the same courtesy in respect to the political paragraphs in the account of the Plague which, excerpted from the unpublished original, appeared in the Forum, August, 1897. The essay on Land-tenure, owing to Mr. Baden-Powell's last book, has been changed in some regards; and, as editor of the Journal of the Oriental Society, I have given myself permission to add to the article on Gods a complementary paper, which was published in the Journal the same year under the title, "Economics of Primitive Religion." The rest of the volume consists of addresses delivered before sundry general audiences during the last two years. One, that on Christ in India, was first read before a small club in 1898, and afterwards expanded to its present form as parts of lectures delivered at the Harvard Summer School of Theology and the Yale Divinity School, in the summer of 1900 and spring of 1901, respectively.

Since this book is not intended for a special public, I have made no attempt to give a scientific transliteration of Sanskrit letters, except in the rare cases where a whole text is cited. There seems to be no reason why a popular exposition should retain diacritical signs which are meaningless to the reader, or mark quantitative values in Sanskrit vowels any more than in the Greek. Since we write Athene and Electra, we may properly write Rama and Krishna, as the confusion of quantities will scarcely disturb the specialist, and will disturb the non-specialist still less. My simple rule has been to give the simplest form; but in the index, and here and there in the notes, to satisfy a possible curiosity, I have added to this popular form a more precise rendering of its phonetic values. Anglo-Indian terms like *cherry-merry* have been kept as they are written in Anglo-Indian, — that is to say, as they are sometimes written, for the same book or newspaper will frequently transcribe the same original in two or three ways. As Sanskrit *c* is pronounced like *ch* in church, I have preferred *k* in such words as Kutch; but in other respects I have not tried to be pedantically consistent at the cost of clearness, and have, for example, written Poona, as it is usually written, not Puna, as it logically should be written by one who, out of the Anglo-Indian versions of the word for town, *pore*, *poor*, *pur*, selects the one nearest to the native form. The Sanskrit sonant aspirates *bh*, *dh*, *gh*, are pronounced as in *abhor*, *adhere*, *leghorn;* the corresponding surds, *ph*, *th*, *kh*, as in *uphill*, *at-home*, *oak-hall*.

OCTOBER, 1901.

# TABLE OF CONTENTS.

# MEMORIAL ADDRESS

IN HONOR OF

# PROFESSOR SALISBURY.

## EDWARD ELBRIDGE SALISBURY.

THE subject of the following memoir was born April 6, 1814, in Boston, Mass. He was the son of Josiah and Abigail (Breese) Salisbury. On his father's side he was of English ancestry; on his mother's, of Huguenot descent. He was graduated from Yale in 1832. He passed four years thereafter in study, particularly theological study, at New Haven. In 1836 he married his cousin, Abigail Salisbury Phillips, daughter of Edward Phillips of Boston, and immediately afterward went to Europe, where he spent nearly four years in the study of Oriental languages. He was a pupil of de Sacy and Garcin de Tassy in Paris, and of Bopp in Berlin. Soon after his return to America, in 1841, he was appointed Professor of Arabic and Sanskrit at Yale. He accepted the appointment, but did not at once assume the duties of the office, as he wished to spend another year in study. He therefore went to Germany in 1842, and spent a winter reading Sanskrit with Lassen in Bonn and Burnouf in Paris. He surrendered his Sanskrit work to his former pupil, W. D. Whitney, in 1854, at the same time establishing the Sanskrit professorship by making a permanent provision for the chair. The Arabic chair he retained till 1856, when his official connection with the University ceased. The years 1857 and 1870 he spent in travel in Europe. Professor Salisbury's first wife died in 1869. In 1871 he married the daughter of Judge Charles J. McCurdy of Lyme, Connecticut, Evelyn McCurdy, who survives him. Professor Salisbury died in his eighty-seventh year, February 5, 1901. He was a life-member of the American Oriental Society for nearly sixty years. From 1846 to 1857 he was its corresponding secretary, and president of the Society from 1863 to 1866, and again from 1873 to 1880. This memorial was presented February 16, 1901, at Yale University.

# MEMORIAL ADDRESS IN HONOR OF PROFESSOR SALISBURY.

It is fitting that on the death of a man who has lived revered we should pause in our busy work and for an hour at least make piety our occupation. Whether such a token of respect mean anything to him we honor, we cannot know; but for ourselves it is a gratification to pay the tribute, though this be merely to recall his past. Yet what better tribute can we offer to the memory of any man than with thankful thoughts to look back upon his life, knowing that he has spent it well and that not age alone has made him venerable? For so his life becomes its own encomium.

But to review completely the career even of a contemporary is not easy, and it is more difficult in the case of one who has labored chiefly during years so long gone by that they seem to belong to an epoch already far distant. To envisage such a life, to recognize its true value, we must begin with seeking to understand the environment in which it started.

Let us, then, consider first of all the conditions under which Mr. Salisbury rose to be the leader of Oriental scholarship in this country. For in awaking and directing the energies of those under him, as in opening to his colleagues in America vistas of which they had been practically ignorant, he well deserves this title of leader. It was a time when the intellectual activities of the country, in so far as they concerned themselves with the Orient at all, were busied almost exclusively with missionary work abroad and with the wisdom of the Hebrews here. Indian and Arabic literatures were ignored well-nigh completely, and Persian antiquities interested none. There was no medium of communication between

Oriental scholars, neither a society for mutual intercourse and exchange of ideas nor a journal for the propagation of new knowledge. Such a thing as a Sanskrit professorship was unknown in this country and scarcely known elsewhere. It is true that Oriental scholarship had already been placed upon a firm basis, and that, for example, our own President Woolsey studied Arabic abroad in the twenties. But there was no one in this country who had entered *con amore* into the newly blazed path of study, nor was there yet, even in Europe, any general recognition on the part of the Universities of the intrinsic value of Hindu and Iranian literatures. To wake an interest at home there was required some one who should primarily appreciate the value of Oriental research, and then, quite as important a point, make others appreciate it.

The man was needed and he came; a scholar by instinct, who, self-impelled, sought his own training and got it from the best masters. To do this, as is clear from the conditions I have just outlined, it was imperative to seek teachers abroad. When he returned, after he had acquired from Bopp, Garcin de Tassy, and de Sacy the knowledge he had sought, he came back the only scholar of his kind in America.

Let me not be misunderstood, however, for I would not seem to exaggerate. Mr. Salisbury was at that time the only scholar of his kind in America, but he was not a Rama comparable only with Rama, in the sense of being a great specialist, a recognized maker of science. He himself would have smiled gently at the ascription of such futile praise. He never tried, for example, to take the place later occupied by Mr. Whitney. His work was not such as to control the course of scientific inquiry; but he was leader, and at first unique leader, not only in being best fitted, but in actively calling others to Oriental work. Moreover, his taste was literary and historical rather than philological in the narrower sense. But when our philological work is completed, then the old knowers of literature will appear more clearly than now as precursors over this new province, and we shall not ask what strictly linguistic work Mr. Salisbury accomplished, or whether he edited any Sanskrit texts; but we shall wonder the more at the ripe scholarship which understood and appreciated Sanskrit literature, and not only Sanskrit but Arabic literature; which scholarship, as a labor of love or duty, did even edit Arabic texts; while also, in a missionary spirit, it expounded Persian cuneiform inscriptions; and yet found its chief pleasure not in such work as this, but in absorbing through the medium of the literature the life and thought of antiquity — so thoroughly that it was able to give a clear synopsis of special linguistic work; so broadly that it comprehended with appreciation the characteristics of two great and dissimilar nationalities. "Professor of Arabic and Sanskrit," — that is a title as incongruous to our modern ears as would be professor of Greek and Chinese. He who bore such a title bore more than our specialists would venture to assume, even in name; but he bore it in reality, worthily, conscientiously, as he did all things, and despite the increasing weight of the intellectual burden, though he eventually abandoned both titles, he ever retained his interest in these two fields and took note as far as it was possible of what was doing in both.

Mr. Salisbury, though not a specialist, yet shared, as I have said, in the more recondite labors of his profession. And I would emphasize the fact that in so doing he never failed to be scrupulously scientific in his method; nor did ever the genial plea of "having a more general interest in the subject" serve him as excuse for slovenly work. But there is more to add, for Mr. Salisbury not only entered into abstruse subjects, but, standing midway in age between President Woolsey and Professor James Hadley, he joined with them in that uplifting of professorial aims which leads the scholar to look on investigation and the publication of the results of study, not merely as works of supererogation, but as a requisite concomitant of his professorship. But what at that far-distant day was this elevation of aims? It was nothing less than the creation in America of the University ideal in contrast with that of the school and college. So I think it is no little glory to him that, favored by fortune to be beyond the need of toil, Mr. Salisbury should not only have devoted himself to unremitting labor from the outset of his career, but also have been foremost in publishing the results of his special studies in stimulative essays; and it was no accident, but the logical outcome of this, that, to his own honor, but also to the honor of Yale, he virtually made himself the first "University Professor" in America; for such from its inception was really his academic position.

Among the cherished possessions of my library is a volume, the Miscellanea published by Mr. Salisbury between 1840 and 1876, from the age of twenty-six to sixty-two. I prize it, not as a mine of information, but again not merely because of personal associations; for it is at the same time an index of the growth of Oriental studies during the last century, and a reflex, not without its lesson, of the mind from which these essays sprang. There are here no technical studies, no statistics, almost no investigation in the confined sense we give to that word to-day. The articles are in general descriptive, *résumés* of knowledge, maps of thought. Mr. Salisbury's scientific bent was, as I have said, pre-eminently historical. He loved, moreover, to survey from the height the road made by others, rather than dig at that road himself. For this reason he has left little in the way of subtle monographs, but many comprehensive reviews. Yet just this attitude of mind, when such a mind devotes itself to instruction, is especially valuable, not only in giving a fascinatingly broad view at the outset to the student who is to toil upon the road of progress or the field of research, but in revealing to him, as he advances, the bearing of each form of work toward every other.

But you must not think that Mr. Salisbury, in rather avoiding the technique of science, lacked a just estimate of this side of scholarship. His was not the complacent mind that boasts of breadth and betrays its narrowness by belittling the word of the specialist. In fact, from Mr. Salisbury's Inaugural Address I think it is clear that he intended to devote himself as a duty to details of study; but this would have been impossible in his case even had he possessed the temperament. For when the appointment to the professorship of Arabic and Sanskrit was made, that bipartite province could still be controlled by one man. But almost synchronously with the appointment began to appear in both fields a series of studies so special and elaborate, each province besides became so enlarged, that no single scholar could longer command it. A general knowledge of what was going on in each was all that any one could attain unless he sacrificed one of the two.

I should like, however, to read you an extract from this Inaugural of 1843, when the young scholar of twenty-nine years was just entering upon his life-work, and I think you will admit not only that he had a generous conception of scientific work, but also that he intended to exercise all the functions of a scholar. After "sketching the department of Sanskrit and Arabic literatures," he says: "You perceive, gentlemen, that my field of study is broad and requires much minuteness of research in order to know it thoroughly. I profess only to have set foot upon it, to have surveyed its extent, to have resolved to spend my days in its research, believing as I do that it may yield rich and valuable fruits, and to do what may be in my power to attract others into it, though I am aware I must expect to labor, for a time, almost alone." And let me add, as characteristic of the modesty and breadth of the true scholar, the words that follow these: "I would earnestly ask of you all to bear with my weaknesses, to be patient with my slowness in doing all that I ought to do to honor my place, and to allow me to find refuge from the feeling of loneliness and discouragement in your sympathizing recognition that each department of knowledge is kindred with every other, — the sentiment which should pervade every great Institution of learning, — and which I would myself cultivate, while I shall eagerly seek to add brightness to my flickering lamp from the shining lights about me."

In a note to this address, besides the arguments adduced in the Inaugural itself, an additional reason for the study of Sanskrit is offered in the missionary's want of proper native words with which to present the claims of Christianity, a want that can be filled better by scholars in this country than by the busy missionary in India, "and thus might one at home with his Sanskrit serve the living God." On the side of Mr. Salisbury's character which is shown in his simple Christian spirit I have no competence to speak. This is the part of those who have been privileged to know him longer and more intimately. But it was so much in and of him that I cannot ignore it altogether even in speaking of his position as a scholar, and this quaint note on serving God with Sanskrit is perhaps sufficiently expressive to show how to him a useful life was inseparable from one of religious endeavor.

The year after this Inaugural was written, the young professor, then just thirty, read at the Meeting of the American Oriental Society held on May 28, 1844, a long paper on the history of Buddhism. He had "heard a Memoir on the Origin of Buddhism read by M. Burnouf before the French Institute in the spring of 1843," and fresh from this personal impression made by the great foreign scholar, he who had heard Burnouf attempted the task of inspiring others with his own interest. Such independent observations as are strewn through this long study are thoroughly sound. They show, not new knowledge of detail, but insight. Many of them are such as to pass unnoticed to-day, but that is only because we know more than was known in 1844. Of this sort, for example, is the remark that Buddhist doctrines are an outgrowth of Brahmanism, a statement which only subsequent work could verify. Another point touched upon is in the refutation on four formal grounds of the theory that Buddha was the creation of a philosophical mythology, a discussion which anticipates by decades recent investigations and theories.

The studious care of the writer of this article is shown in the many references to works consulted by him, German,

French, and English, up to the time of its delivery. Some of these works are now classics; at that time the young scholar had just seen them fresh from the press and thought they "promised to be valuable." It is of this paper that Mr. Whitney said that it was the first really scientific paper presented to the Oriental Society.

How wide was Mr. Salisbury's interest in the Orient may be seen from his painstaking study on the Chinese origin of the compass, read before the Connecticut Society of Arts and Sciences in 1840. It is an abstract from Klaproth's letter to Humboldt, but it involves a careful investigation of an intricate subject. Again, in 1848, in a report of the Directors, which is virtually a recommendation to the Oriental Society, Mr. Salisbury urges the importance of Egyptology and the desirability of making excavations at Nineveh; while in the same recommendation occurs the following notable paragraph, which I think will be of especial interest to all classical students: "But as an indispensable condition of this advance of knowledge, the writings of the Greeks and the Biblical records relating to Assyria and the data of the newly-discovered Assyrian monuments, must all be brought together, for mutual explanation, and to supply each other's deficiencies. . . . The concentration of oriental and classical studies has shed light upon many obscurities, and is destined to do this still more in the future. There is then an evident propriety in oriental and classical scholars being associated together, for the more successful prosecuting of those investigations in which they have a common interest, and accordingly this Society embraces classical members, besides such as interest themselves in oriental researches, specially considered.

"But something more seems necessary, in order that these two elements united in our association may be brought to a reciprocity of action. It has, therefore, been proposed [i. e. Mr. Salisbury proposes] to create within this Society, a special organization for the promotion of classical learning, in its various bearings upon oriental [sc. subjects]. The simplest method of executing the proposition in question, would seem to be to create by election from among the members of the Society a Classical Section, to have in view especially, and to have charge over, the classical side of oriental subjects."

I have read this long extract, not only to show you Mr. Salisbury's catholicity, but because I think it of peculiar interest that he who has done so much for Orientalists should also be the one to initiate the founding of the Philological Association. For our present Philological Association is but the later growth of the Classical Section which Mr. Salisbury herewith brought into existence. It is perhaps to be too curious to ask whether the Modern Language and Dialect Societies, or again the Archæological Society, all offshoots of the Philological Association, may not be traced to the same source; and it must, of course, be admitted that the creation of a philological society, either as a Chapter of the Oriental or as an independent body, could not have been long delayed, and that such an association as we have now was not dependent upon the action of the Oriental Society. All this is true, but the fact remains that all these societies, historically considered, sprang from the Report to the Directors of the Oriental Society, which was accepted at the Quarterly Meeting on January 5, 1848, twenty-one years before the Philological Association became incorporated; for till then the latter remained, under the name of Classical Section, a minor at home with the parent society.

Although Mr. Salisbury's title was "Professor of Arabic and Sanskrit," he included in his studies, with his usual breadth of vision, Persian as a close relative of Sanskrit, and in the fourth part of the first volume of the Oriental Journal he published a remarkably clear and correct essay on the Identification of the Signs of the Persian Cuneiform Alphabet (1849). The writer, to repeat his own words, will only "communicate results obtained" by other scholars, and the paper is not a contribution of original material; but it deserves mention particularly because it shows that Mr. Salisbury had already worked his way through Lassen, Burnouf,

Rawlinson, and the more recent *Beiträge zur Erklärung der Persischen Keilinschriften* of Adolph Holtzmann, *Die Persischen Keilinschriften* of Benfey (1847), and to have known of Oppert's *Lautsystem des Altpersischen* (1848), although, properly speaking, the whole subject lay apart from his official field of research.

On the Arabic side, Mr. Salisbury was particularly active, publishing first a Translation of unpublished Arabic Documents, with introduction and notes, first read before the Oriental Society in October, 1849, an independent but not the most original work presented by him; since in 1852 he read a critique of the genuineness of the so-called Nestorian monument of Singanfu. Here he had to give a digest of the views of Abel-Rémusat, Neumann, Ritter, and Neander, and then "exhibit the true state of the evidence," which he does clearly and concisely.

Another paper on the Science of Moslem Tradition (read in 1859 and published in 1861) is one of his most scholarly efforts, being "gathered from original sources, either only in manuscript or so little accessible as to be nearly equivalent to unpublished authorities" (referring to Delhi lithographs). The first of these documents is a manuscript in the de Sacy collection, which was now in Mr. Salisbury's possession. This was soon followed by a paper on The Muhammedan Doctrines of Predestination and Free Will, from original sources. These were, I think, articles especially agreeable to him to write, essentially historical, and in that one of his two fields in working which he took perhaps the greater satisfaction.

The same year, however, in which was published the former of these papers, appeared in the New Englander an article apparently written in 1858, printed by especial request of the editor and entitled Sketch of the Life and Works of Michael Angelo Buonarroti, in which Mr. Salisbury gave a popular account of the great artist, quoting at the end with especial admiration the words of the sonnet composed by the poet in his old age: —

"Nè pinger nè scolpir fia più che queti;
L'anima volta a quell' amor divino,
Ch' aperse a prender noi in croce le braccia."

Mr. Salisbury, it may be observed, had more than a reading knowledge of Italian, and though he never prided himself upon possessing linguistic attainments, yet it is worth recording, especially in view of the fact that such ability was very rare in the first half of the last century, that he not only read Sanskrit, Persian, Arabic, and Hebrew, besides, of course, Greek and Latin, but spoke German, French, and Italian. Spanish he knew but slightly, and I am not sure whether he could speak it.

Another historical article was published in the same magazine — then one of the leading literary journals of the country — in 1876, on some of the Relations between Islâm and Christianity. But in the meantime Mr. Salisbury had published in the Journal, to which he contributed, in all, thirty-two papers, his most extensive scientific article, a "Notice of the Book of Sulaimân's First Ripe Fruit" (read at the Meetings of May and October, 1864), a revelation of the mysteries of the Nusairian sect, the article being a critical interpretation of the titular work (which had appeared that same year in Beirût), according to copies forwarded by Dr. Van Dyck, the able local missionary. This very original tract was written by Sulaimân 'Effendi, who appears in it as a zealous convert to the Christian religion. But this was by no means the first time that Sulaimân had undergone the mental distraction of conversion. Starting out as a Nusairy, but soon growing dissatisfied with this religion, he soon became a convert to Judaism. This faith, however, also failed to content him, and he converted himself again, this time becoming a Moslem; after which, for he had not yet found peace, he became converted to his fourth religion and entered the Greek church. His fifth religion was his last, and as a member of the Protestant Christian church he reviews the iniquities of his original faith in the diatribe translated and published by Mr. Salisbury. Such a work would be considered by many a find to exult over, and had it been discovered recently we should doubtless have had the Sunday papers advertising the odd facts therein chronicled, such as the present existence of Syrian moon-worshippers and of "trinitarian Muhammedans." But forty years ago such methods were unknown, as they were ever inconceivable in connection with the dignified scholar who quietly published his most extraordinary discovery in the current number of the Oriental Journal, knowing that, though never noticed by others, it would be seen by those whose opinion seemed to him of worth.

This last essay was published after Mr. Salisbury had retired from his professorship. It is a tradition that his prediction of loneliness was in so far fulfilled as to give him but two students. You know, however, what the lion said: "I have only one child but he is a lion." Mr. Salisbury at least reared two lions. In 1851, the elder of his whilom students, James Hadley, had already succeeded Mr. Woolsey as Professor of Greek, and to the other Mr. Salisbury in 1854 resigned his Sanskrit work. The teacher's influence is clearly perceptible when we read that Mr. Hadley was not only versed in the classics, but acquainted with Hebrew, Arabic, Armenian, Sanskrit, and Keltic; and of Mr. Whitney it need only be said that when as a youth, after studying Sanskrit for some years by himself, he sought in 1849 for one to guide him further in his studies, his adviser, who, it is pleasant to add, was our own venerable Dr. Day, then Whitney's pastor in Northampton, naturally referred him to Mr. Salisbury, as the only man in the country who could teach him.

After the publication of the last article to which reference has just been made, Mr. Salisbury's mind turned to new fields of investigation. To him is due the very complete sketch of the Trumbull Gallery in the Yale Book of 1879; while in 1877 he had read before the Art School a lecture on the Principles of Domestic Taste, which was printed the same year in the New Englander — parerga of a scholar; but Mr. Salisbury, for many years one of the Elective Members of the Yale Art School, was always interested in art, nearly as much so as in the Orient, and allowed none of his faculties to become atrophied, so that when his eyes could no longer peruse texts his active mind could still work in other, yet not unfamiliar fields.

The studies of his later years were, however, still of historical sort. In 1875 he read before the New Haven Colonial Historical Society a paper, full of minute investigation, on Mr. William Diodate and his Italian Ancestry (printed in 1876). Thereafter genealogical research was his chief occupation, especially as fast failing eyesight precluded further Oriental study, whereas in genealogical work he had the skilful and devoted assistance of his wife. In 1885, when over seventy years of age, Mr. Salisbury published his (own) Family Memorials; and in 1892, the Family Histories and Genealogies (of his wife), in several large volumes, sumptuously prepared, and edited with such attention to details that he is said to have ordered a whole volume reprinted because of one typographical error.

Mr. Salisbury says of his own contributions to Orientalia that he published his papers in the Journal of the Oriental Society "more as an amateur-student than as a master with authority." But, as we have seen, there was real and rigid scholarship in all that he presented. Moreover, though not perhaps "master with authority," his abilities were fully recognized by learned confreres, as bears witness the fact that he was elected a member of the Asiatic Society of Paris when he was twenty-four years old (1838); of the two Academies of Art and Sciences of Connecticut and Boston in 1839 and 1848, respectively; a corresponding member of the Imperial Academy of Sciences and Belles Lettres at Constantinople in 1855; a corresponding member of the German Oriental Society in 1859; and of the Antiquarian Society in 1861. He was twice given the degree of Doctor of Laws, once in 1869 by his Alma Mater, and again in 1886 by Harvard. It is characteristic of his modest estimate of his own ability and of his love of truth that he refused to accept the latter degree until the terms (employed in bestowing it) in praise of his own services to science were so modified as to make it possible for him to admit that they might refer to himself. In 1869 Mr. Salisbury was strongly urged to accept the chair of Arabic at Harvard, but no inducement could tempt him away from New Haven.

In the sketch I have given of Mr. Salisbury's more important writings you have seen what he was as a scholar. But the energies thus early devoted to philology were not allowed to remain selfishly employed. The young professor was appointed in 1841, and after studying abroad a second time, with Lassen in Germany and Burnouf in France, as previously he had studied with Bopp in Berlin and Garcin de Tassy and de Sacy in Paris, he assumed the duties of his office in 1843. The year before this, chiefly in the interest of missionary work, had been founded the American Oriental Society (1842, three years before the organization of the German Oriental Society). Into this opening for new labor Mr. Salisbury, on his return from abroad, flung himself with ardor. To him it was to be a society which should concentrate activities till then scattered and unorganized. There are few living who know how much Mr. Salisbury has done for this Society. As has been said by one of his colleagues in a recent review of his life: "No notice of Professor Salisbury would be complete without an emphatic recognition of his invaluable services in the development of that Society by the unstinted expenditure of time, labor, and money." For Mr. Salisbury not only supported the Society, but he contributed besides the constant spur of his own example in offering memoirs, in suggesting improvements, and last but not least in being present as a duty at the meetings of the Society. For eleven years he was its corresponding secretary (and practically the editor of its Journal), filling an arduous and thankless office with constant fidelity and self-sacrificing devotion; and for ten years he was the Society's honored president.

Of his own work in behalf of the Society he himself says merely that he "labored to make its Journal the vehicle of some valuable contributions . . . as well as for the general prosperity of the Society — not wholly without success, due in large measure to the co-operation of learned American missionaries" (Class-book of 1832),— a characteristically humble appraisement. But let us add this to it, that of his long service in behalf of the Society, an active membership from almost its beginning to his death, nearly three-score years, is itself witness. Nor does that testimony stand alone. Just ten years ago Mr. Whitney, who knew well what Mr. Salisbury had done for the Oriental Society, and was the best judge of its value, wrote as follows: "Professor Salisbury, by his own writings and by the active correspondence which he kept up with American missionaries, . . . provided most of the material for publication; he also himself procured a number of fonts of Oriental type — mostly the first of this kind in the country, and still in part the only ones — for use in printing the Journal; and, not less in importance, he met the expenses of publication of volume after volume. . . . For some ten years, Professor Salisbury was virtually the Society, doing its work and paying its bills. He gave it standing and credit in the world of scholars, as an organization that could originate and could make public valuable material" (April, 1891).

Such also is the testimony of a younger colleague, Mr. Lanman, who, six years ago in his address in memory of Mr. Whitney, alluded to Mr. Salisbury as the "life and soul of the Society," during the period of its earlier growth.

Nor has the Oriental Society, either individually or as a body, ever forgotten him, and when by good chance its meeting fell on his birthday, as has happened twice within the last few years, it has been with a sense of personal gratification, even on the part of members who knew him only by his works, that this Society honored itself by sending him a congratulatory telegram. In reply to one of these despatches, sent two years ago, on his eighty-fifth birthday, Mr. Salisbury responded by sending his own congratulations to the Society "on what it has grown to be from its small beginnings of more than fifty years ago," — and there was none that heard the answer who did not add to these unassuming words, "Thanks largely to him that sends the message."

To appreciate fully what Mr. Salisbury has done for Yale University is no easy task. Nearly sixty years ago, in 1842, he gave considerable sums for the erection of a library building, and subsequently for the erection of East and West Divinity Halls, and for the income of the Art School. But aid for building, great as was that, was the least of his numerous benefactions. For it was through him alone that two of Yale's most distinguished professors were permanently located where, in the case of one, it was most proper that he should be retained, at the seat of the labors that had already made him famous; as in the case of the other it was most fortunate that the University could thus secure for itself the promise of his future greatness. Gladly would the University have been first to induce the one to remain and the other to come, but on neither occasion when the need arose were funds available for the purpose. In each case the prospect was that Yale would fail to gain its end. But Mr. Salisbury was here, and quietly, unostentatiously, as he did everything, he said, "Let this be my office." And not once but twice, out of his own means, he accomplished for the University what the University left to itself would have been unable to do. What glory remains to Yale in the names of Dana and Whitney,— and the measure of a university's renown is not in the number of its students, but in the reputation of its teachers,— this glory as an abiding possession is due to him whose memory we are here assembled to honor. "It is a thought that may interest us all," said President Dwight in his Memorial Address on Professors Dana and Whitney (June, 1895), "that the two men were alike secured for our University by the generous interposition of a friend of the institution, one and the same friend, whose liberal gifts made the remaining here possible for them. This friend, now in his serene old age, survives them both, having witnessed with deepest satisfaction the rich fruits of their work. His scholarly life within the University for many years, and his benefactions bestowed during the long course of half a century, have accomplished much for its well-being in many ways. But the student of our history will ever recognize with a peculiarly grateful feeling, as he traces the progress of this institution for the last forty years, the service which was rendered by this benefactor when he gave these two generous gifts, and the names of Professors Dana and Whitney will be closely associated in his mind and memory with the name of Professor Salisbury, their honored friend and ours."

There is another factor in the totality of a university's completeness. The foundation of its scholarship lies in its library. A university without books, the best and latest, is like a factory filled with workmen but without works. Against this deficiency Mr. Salisbury supplied the University out of his own store, first of books and then of ever-present assistance. The treasures of learning accumulated by the great Orientalist de Sacy were bought at his death by Mr. Salisbury, who thus more than sixty years ago laid the foundations of the unrivalled Oriental library of which Yale boasts to-day. For he did not wait, as many would have done, to leave this collection to the University, but robbing himself of his treasure gave it thirty years ago to Yale. Nor has there ever been a time since then when in furthering the good work thus begun he has failed to respond most generously to appeals for aid. Only two years ago a collection of Oriental books was offered for sale and there was no chance of the University being able to purchase them. I went to Mr. Salisbury and laid the case before him. The sum demanded was large. "I can scarcely afford it," he said, "but," he added, "Yale must have the books and I will pay for them." This was his spirit always, and as long as he lived he continued to give annually for the support of the library. Without show or exploitation, almost secretly, he aided continuously for more than half a century, by his munificence as well as by his sage suggestions, the development of this University.

Thus as scholar, as member of the Oriental Society, and finally as benefactor of Yale and of the Society alike, Mr. Salisbury lived his noble life, — a life of fulness to himself and of much benefit to others, not only in material things but also in the mental stimulus imparted by it until its very close. Such is his record as a public character. But to us who knew him there was more than this, the charm of his personality. For he himself, the aged scholar, was ever crowned with such a gentle dignity and antique stately courtliness that even to meet him gave great pleasure, as to know him was an intellectual gain. But of his kindness and of the love felt for him I may not speak, lest I come too near the heart of some here present; yet even in the case of those not of his family the reverence felt for him was indissolubly associated with affection.

In the ancient burial service of the Rig Veda it is described how the survivors of a dead man must raise at his grave a wall, separating the living from the dead, and sing these words: "Now are the living sundered from the dead; (there lies the dead) but we go on" (to life). Fortunate is it that the living can thus turn again to the varied interests of life; but fortunate also are they who, in thus turning, feel that not all which once was theirs is sundered from them, but that through the dividing wall of death there still extends, in memories linking together the present and the past, an impulse that does not die with the dead, but is still a vital force among the living.

# INDIA OLD AND NEW.

# INDIA OLD AND NEW.

## THE RIG VEDA.

More than a generation has now passed since the work called Rig Veda, that is, Verse-Wisdom, was first completely published in print. The first half appeared just forty years ago, and the second half followed two years later.

But although the Rig Veda has been in the hands of scholars for so long, there is no unanimity on their part as regards either the time and place of origin, or the character of this Verse-Wisdom. There are, however, already at hand certain data the consideration of which should tend to solidify opinion on these points. Some of these can be explained without bringing in technical details, and the general problem may easily be stated in such a way as to be comprehended by any student accustomed to deal with the history of literature.

In a narrow sense the Rig Veda is one of four Vedas; yet since two of the other three are merely the Rig Veda itself, arranged for chaunting, *sāman*, and for a sacrificial liturgy, *yajus*, while the fourth is also a collection of verses, many of which are simply taken from the older Rig Veda, we may say that in a wider sense, for historical purposes, there is only one Veda, that is, a body of hymns composed separately in remote antiquity and afterwards brought together and arranged in various groups called "Collections." But in this wider sense the Verse-Wisdom of ancient India is itself a heterogeneous combination of old hymns, charms, philosophical poems, and popular songs, most but not all of which are of religious content.

As the starting-point of our critique we may take the admission made in the Vedic literature itself that the various Collections known to us are parts of a more primitive Veda. Something more than philosophical and religious interpretation is contained in this statement. It holds a bit of literary history, and the view here advanced is supported by a careful study of the structure of our extant texts. For not only is it true that the three oldest Collections are merely various arrangements of Verse-Wisdom, in the main the Collection or Rig Veda, but it is also indisputable that this Rig Veda Collection itself is a composite consisting largely of the same material disposed in various ways. The same whole verses and a still larger number of parts of verses are found repeated in different hymns, while in almost every hymn occur phrases which are used elsewhere in other situations. All this points to the fact that the hymns are founded on older material, the wreck of which has been utilized in constructing new poetic buildings, just as many of the temples of India are to a great extent built of the material of older demolished temples. The extant Verse-Wisdom Collection, then, far from being a group of primitive hymns, is probably in part the later remnant of older hymns (which in course of time were changed both in substance and in form), while in part it is merely more modern imitation of these hymns.

By such re-handling of older material literature has in fact always been preserved in India. We need look only at the later form of hymns of the Rig Veda Collection as they appear in the Atharva Collection to see that in order to be intelligible the poetry of the ancients had to be brought down to date, so to speak; or, again, at the verses of the Upanishads that still preserve archaic forms, as they in turn are passed along through the medium of the epic, with the sense kept but with the outer form remodelled to suit a later age.

It is for this reason that attempts to discover dialectic differences in the Rig Veda have as good as failed completely.

Some few traces of a primitive dialectic divergence in the use of certain grammatical forms have been thought to be perceptible, but they are mostly imaginary; that is, the divergence in any one case is too small to establish a dialect upon, and all the supposed traces taken together fail to show any special dialectic difference between the different parts of the Veda. This is true both in regard to other dialectic distinctions and in regard to a distinction between priestly and popular language. All that has been shown is that some of the hymns are nearer than others to the norm of the later language, that is, are themselves later. The reason why the Veda Collection was made at all was doubtless the very fact that the form of antique hymns was continually changing. As the Athenians wished to preserve the tragedians, so the priests of India made at last an authorized edition of their hereditary material, as it had been handed down in their different families by that much belauded Hindu memory which has foolishly been supposed to be always infallible, whereas, in point of fact, wonderful as it was when so trained as to absorb all other intellectual powers, by nature it was untrustworthy; for in citing older material by memory the Hindus, as I have just shown, are constantly unreliable as far as regards the exact reproduction in stereotyped form of the verses they repeat. And this must have been the case always till the Vedic material began to be felt as something ancient enough to be divine. Previously there is no reason at all to suppose that the repeaters of old songs were themselves very nice in this regard, or that they were estopped from making individual alterations in the text. On the contrary, we must believe that the hymns with other poetic tradition of older Verse-Wisdom were at first handed down in just the way in which the later hymns and other poetic literature were handed down in the Upanishads and epic, — that is, modified, transformed, freely altered. On this point, as on many others, a study of what has actually happened is far more likely than *a priori* argument to direct historical research rightly. In regard to the Vedic verses, the very case taken to preserve them exactly as they were, the extraordinary machinery invented solely to this end, such as dislocating the complete words and repeating the parts separately, saying them again by an overlapping process, and finally repeating them forwards and backwards — all this anxious solicitude shows not only, what has often been commented upon, that the priests held the text in veneration, but also, what is more important and is not sufficiently recognized, that they were sure the text would continue to be corrupted, modified, modernized, as without such precaution it had been changed in the past.

From what I have already said it follows that hymns of very different periods originally, but reduced pretty much to one linguistic level, will be found in the Verse-Wisdom, which, at some time in its natural development, was thus arrested. For the older hymns, as they passed through generations of reciters, would have been steadily modified, not indeed to the very level of the reciters, but, so to speak, to within easy reaching distance. We see the same thing exactly in our successive editions of hymn-books. The quaint old hymn loses its oldest, perhaps incomprehensible or repugnant features, but it is not reduced quite to the same form as those written in this generation. Sufficient antique flavor is preserved to conserve its sanctity, as it were, but at the same time sufficient change is introduced to make it appeal to the intelligence and sympathy of the modern worshipper. How far this has gone in the actual Veda Collections has been shown by Professor Aufrecht. The evidence is valuable; but before there was any such Collection the same process must have resulted in the linguistic and syntactical modification of the older hymns of the Verse-Collection.

The present Rig Veda Collection consists of ten groups, which may be roughly divided into three main divisions, indicating two earlier groups and a later (completed) Collection; the first comprising the second to the seventh book inclusively, the second containing additions set round the older group, and consisting of the first to the eighth books (inclusive), and the third, or final redaction, consisting of the former groups with the addition of the ninth and tenth books. These two last added books differ more in character than in age from the preceding, though generally speaking the latest hymns (linguistically judged) are found in these two books. But as the books differ in character they contain also a great deal of old material, which had not previously been incorporated because it did not correspond to the character of the earlier books. While, therefore, the books ii-vii are the oldest group and books ix-x the latest books, i and viii being intermediate, some parts of the latest group are nevertheless probably earlier than the earlier groups as such; and likewise the eighth book does not quite suit the character of the first group, and may for this reason have been preserved apart before it was finally tagged on to it. But since its vocabulary is distinctly later than that of books ii-vii, as its rhythmic arrangement is more refined, it is most likely that it really is a later product; nor is there anything in its content similar to the antique content of certain of the hymns of the tenth book to counterbalance the lateness of vocabulary, style, and arrangements. The most important book chronologically is the ninth, which has a character all its own in that it comprises nearly all the Vedic hymns to Soma; that is, it is exclusively occupied with a cult that is pre-Vedic, and yet as a part of the Collection it is clearly a late addition to the first two groups; and the individual hymns, some of which must in their original form have been among the oldest hymns of the whole Veda, are in their group-form all reduced to the same linguistic level, which in general is that of the end rather than the beginning of the Collection.

The time when the Verse-Wisdom Collection was made cannot be much earlier than the sixth century B. C., and may be considerably later. That the individual hymns of which the Collection consists are in their original form older than this is unquestionable, and scholars have referred the date of the hymns, in distinction from the date of the making of the Collection, to the tenth, twelfth, fifteenth, and even thirty-fifth century before our era. The last date is the result of certain astronomical factors supposed to be valid as determinants and applied with much ingenuity to the solution of the problem. But the premises on which rests this theory of the date are scarcely admissible and the theory neither has had nor is likely to have the support of other critics, though the inventor of the theory is himself an extremely able and sober-minded critic. But it is a well-known fact that when one makes what appears to be an important discovery one's critical faculty is almost sure to be unduly influenced by one's enthusiasm for the idea, — very fortunately, for otherwise there would be no advance in science, since caution would so check as to palsy invention.

As to the other dates proposed, they have no other basis, as may be seen by their fluctuating nature, than the vague belief that a certain, or uncertain, number of centuries must elapse before a thousand hymns of varying chronological value can be written and explained; for other data of change require no very long period. But the chronological values are based not so much on the number of hymns and elucidations (for no one knows how many authors were concerned in the making of the Veda, and the number of elucidations, Brahmanas, does not represent time so much as schools) as on sundry allusions of the poets themselves to older poets and hymns, and on an assumed difference in age between some of the hymns, which have a more antique vocabulary and grammar, and those that come nearer to the later standard.

It is obvious, then, that the first factor may be admitted and yet largely discounted by the admission of only a few generations of poets, not more than two centuries. Nor are the linguistic differences so great as to make it necessary to assume anything like half a dozen centuries for their formation. Again, the chief reason for believing that circa 600 B. C. is the date of the Collection as such, is that the older explanatory Brahmanas do not show any acquaintance with such a Collection, whereas the later do, as do the early philosophical Upanishads. Now the linguistic changes arising between the time of the Brahmanas in their oldest form and the Upanishads which belong to them are not much less than those between the Brahmanas and the hymns, and there is no reason whatever for supposing that all the changes between the oldest hymns and the Upanishads of the first and second period (the old prose and verse Upanishads) could not have been effected in the course of two centuries. Two hundred years are a long time in the course of a language unrestricted by written literature, and even when handicapped by the drag of writing, which naturally impedes change, it needs but this to turn the language of Cato into that of Quintilian; nor does the language of the Upanishads compared with that of the Rig Veda show greater changes than those that mark the language of Milton when compared with that of Chaucer, two centuries earlier. Further, as I have said, the development of the literature is not so great as to oppose this narrower limit, nor are the ethical, philosophical, religious, and sociological factors of the sixth century B. C. such as to preclude the probability that they represent the evolution of six generations, without revolution of religion or state, after the earliest hymns were written.

On the other hand, there is a very important factor which tends to restrain the assumption that many preliminary centuries are essential in this reckoning. As long as Zoroaster was indefinitely remote all similarities between Veda and Avesta could be explained on the basis of an indefinitely remote relationship. But now that Zoroaster's date is fairly well determined, we must face anew the fact, which has never been denied, that the language of the Avesta and that of the Rig Veda are too closely related to admit of the possibility of any great chasm in time between the two works. But the Avesta, as Professor Jackson has shown, cannot be referred to a period much earlier than 600 B. C., and as we are probably safe in saying that in part of the seventh century even the Gathas of Iran were still unsung, so we may well believe that the earliest hymns of the Rig Veda were not much earlier. A couple of centuries would meet all Indic requirements and be as much as can be granted in view of the religious and linguistic affinity with Iran. One thousand B. C. is, then, not the lowest, but the highest limit that we can reasonably set to the Rig Veda, and 800 B. C. is probably nearer the mark, as far as the bulk of the Rig Veda is concerned.

The home of the Rig Veda has been located in almost as many places as Paradise. Now it is by the Caspian Sea, now it is in Kandahar, but the Punjab is the favorite place, and quite naturally; for the poets are familiar with the Punjab, sing of it, talk of crossing its rivers, and in many ways show that they occupied, in part at least, the country stretching from Peshawar to Delhi.

Only, in this ready solution there is one fact which arrests the attention of those who know India from seeing it, as well as from its ancient literature. When one traverses the district just mentioned, one crosses in going from east to west, from Delhi to Peshawar, from the extreme limit of the monsoon's influence, over a bare sandy plain, remote alike from the effect of seasonal rains and from the view of any mountains. And then one remembers, at first with wonder, that the climatic conditions of the Rig Veda are quite different from those of the Punjab; that the poets are continually extolling the furious battles of the storm-gods and live ever in sight of the great mountains. As I have written on this subject elsewhere,[1] I will here merely sum up what I have said previously. Apart from a few hymns where the Indus and streams west of the Indus are mentioned, the life of the Vedic Aryan, as depicted in his earliest literature, reflects not so much a wandering life in a desert as a life stable and fixed, above all, a life in sight of mountains and within the influence of the monsoon storms. Further, the poets sing of having crossed the very last river of the Punjab, and between this and any possible abiding-place there is only a plain that is practically a desert. But when one retraces his steps and, turning east to the old "limit of India," Sirhind, passes still east of this, one arrives for the first time at a

[1] Journal of the American Oriental Society, vol. xix, p. 21 ff.

district where monsoon storms and mountain scenery are found, that district, namely, which lies about Umballa or Ambala, south toward Thanesar, Kurukshetra, between the Sarasouti and Ghuggar rivers. In this district noble mountains are visible, which recede from sight as one approaches Thanesar. Here the monsoon still breaks in violence, while the Punjab has only showers and dust-storms. Here are softly sloping hills and verdant pasturage, such as the Vedic poets besing. It is here that, in accordance with these facts, the Rig Veda as a whole, as I think, was composed. In every particular this locality fulfils the physical conditions under which the composition of the hymns was possible, while it explains the lyrics of the priests in regard to the crossing of the Punjab as having been composed after the event; whereas any other assumption carries us west of the Punjab, for only here do we come again upon a mountainous and storm-beaten country.

One point more. In the usual sunset in India there is a sudden red glow followed by a dull copper-yellow, which soon fades. At sunrise there is the same quick succession of colors reversed. Only in the Punjab can one see a really beautiful sunset, or a sunrise such as is marked by bright yellow, gradually deepening into rose, and this continuing with a long, slow flush of crimson.

Now why is it that among the oldest hymns of the Rig Veda we find such beautiful Hymns to Dawn, and why is it that this erst so well-beloved Damosel of Heaven, who is especially invoked to give "good paths to the sojourner," is entirely neglected in the later Vedic and liturgical literature? First, because Dawn was dawn indeed only in the watery northwest, with its cloud-making atmosphere. When the sun leaps at a bound out of cloudless night and makes dazzling day, as it does generally in India, there is no dawn to speak of, much less to sing of. And second, because she who is especially invoked to give good paths is the right leader of those whose journey begins with the first light in the east. Then Dawn is invoked by those who still live to the west of the great rivers, otherwise she would not be addressed as one who "in shining light before the wind arises comes gleaming o'er the waters, making good paths." Again, those that tend their flocks upon the great plains are they who are most apt to keep in religious reverence the God of the Sky. He too, Varuna, was a great god to the early poets, but the bulk of the Vedic Hymns pass him over in favour of the Rain-and-Storm-god, Indra, a new creation, for the Punjab has no place for him. Varuna and Dawn belong to the Punjab; Indra to the East. Varuna and Dawn are more antique than Indra, as the Punjab is the older habitat of the Aryans. But the bulk of the Rig Veda belongs to Indra and his cult.

The Vedic poets always represent the rivers as rising suddenly in consequence of Indra's slaying the demon of drought. This applies to the rivers above Umballa, but not to the Indus nor to the Punjab rivers, which rise long before the monsoon breaks (in June), in consequence of the melting of Himalayan snow. Consequently, when in one of the Vedic lyrics we find Indra addressed as the god that makes the Sutlej rise, we must remember that this lyric was composed to the east of the Punjab and long after the event. The poet credits Indra with having the same power over the Sutlej as over the rivers he himself knows.

The implication made in the distinction here suggested between the mass of Vedic hymns and the few that belonged to an older age and more western habitat will not be acceptable to those who hold that all the Vedic hymns were composed in the same ritualistic environment. But such a view is as yet merely a theory, and though it is a popular fad of modern criticism,— for criticism has its passing fashions, — it should not be accepted on that ground, but be held subject to the facts we can control. But it fails to conform to the data. For not only does it take no note of a difference in the religious attitude of the various poets,— evidence of any such difference is with magnificent scorn said to be due to "merely subjective" criticism,— but it assumes, what is not true, that all the hymns show traces of having been "made for baksheesh" and mechanically ground out to subserve the purpose of a ritual essentially the same as that of the later Brahmanas. Historically this claim is about on a par with a theory which should start with the assumption that because the Psalms are rubricated they were all written for the use of the Church. It is even more daring, for all the Psalms are rubricated, but not all the hymns find a place in the later ritual. The absurdity is increased when it is necessary to dispose of hymns that were clearly never meant for any service at all, or such as have been violently twisted out of their original meaning to subserve the purpose of the very ritual which this facile theory declares was in existence when the hymns were composed, as when the later ritual distorts a burial hymn into a service for a burning-ghat. If the theory means only that when the Vedic hymns were composed there was a Soma-sacrifice, sacrificial grass, and Kavis, or seers, all this is not a new idea but a platitude, for we know that such was the case when the Indo-Iranians were one people, before the Iranians drew back from the Punjab (into which as far as the Beas they probably at one time had penetrated). But if it claims, as it appears to do, that the service of the later Brahmanas was identical with that of the earliest hymns, and that all these hymns were composed simply for that service, then in view of the facts just mentioned it may be dismissed as sufficiently unhistorical to break with its own weight. No theory which holds that every one of the thousand disconnected hymns of the Rig Veda is as late or as ritualistic as every other deserves serious consideration. Such a view represents merely an extreme, and therefore incorrect, reaction against the previous exaggerated notion of antiquity and simplicity, traits ascribed to the Rig Veda as a whole by earlier scholars. But the Rig Veda is neither very naïf and primitive nor wholly late and ritualistic. Differences of time may be almost obliterated linguistically, for the reasons which I have already given. But differences in thought and belief are still so marked as to demand an explanation; nor does the only other solution suggested, that a monotheistic trait in Varuna was a loan from Semitic sources, seem so probable as that the Rig Veda itself contains different strata. The chief reason given for believing that the later ritual underlies all the Vedic hymns is that the ritual frequently explains the hymns. But it is an unwarranted induction that therefore all the hymns, whether reflecting the later ritual or not, and even those which stand opposed to that ritual, must have arisen in the same ritualistic environment. If in separating the strata and differentiating the elements it is impossible to be sure of judgment in detail, it is better to make mistakes in detail than to err in one's general estimate.

An objection that might be urged against what I have said about the Punjab is that, whatever the Punjab is now, it may have been quite different in ancient times. Its rivers may perhaps have run in different courses and there may have been more of them, for it is difficult to-day to see why Seven Rivers was the original name of the Punjab (that is, Five Rivers). But this name, Seven Rivers, may have been, as it was an older name, the designation of an older group of rivers; while the Vedic poets often allude to the "desert," so that the country was probably much as it is now, especially as it is improbable that the monsoon has backed away from its former scene of operations.

In short, as far as we can judge on the evidence, there seems no reason to doubt that the Verse-Wisdom of the Hindus dates in general from about the eighth or ninth century, and, while a few hymns come from further west, was composed near Umballa, where finally, about 600 B. C., the different hymns were made into what is now known as the Verse-Wisdom Collection, in which, however, we may detect three redactions, made at different times. This Collection as a whole contains some old and some more recent material, the former more or less levelled to the style and language of the latter, as it floated down to the later period, much tampered with before being caught up in a collection, and still tampered with till after the final redaction, when greater care began to be exercised in regard to preserving all the hymns; for there is no reason to suppose that the first collection was due to a desire to preserve the form, but only the matter. The idea of a sacrosanct form is much later. The title "Hymns" may serve, as it has served in the past, to designate the Collection of the Rig Veda; but that work contains not only the mechanical hymns of a later day, but the spontaneous songs of an earlier period, as it contains worldly poetry, heroic lyrics, epic beginnings, and philosophical studies.

## THE EARLY LYRIC POETRY OF INDIA.

FOR some mysterious reason our handbooks of Sanskrit Literature, after describing the Vedic and epic periods, come at last to a separate division called Lyric Poetry, to which is given as an initial date circa 500 A. D. This date is wrong by more than a thousand years. It ignores all the background of the classical lyric. Of this background or foundation or forerunner, as you will, I purpose now to speak.

The lyric poetry of India is of four kinds and belongs in general to four epochs, although with one exception each precedent variety glides into the next following without sharp interval. To follow the onward course, the slow development, the persistent reversions, to note the final loss of the early strain and the inception and growth of a new sort of lyric, unknown to the earliest period, is a fascinating employment, though in some regards a sad one. For as nothing reflects the singer's heart like lyric song, it is melancholy to discover that the good growth which died is the heroic, while the self-ingrafted weed that finally choked out the heroic strain is the sentimental, erotic, neurotic, religious-erotic lyric, poisonous as it is fair. But before we examine particularly the earlier forms, let me sketch briefly the course thus indicated that you may have at hand an outline of the whole.

There is first to be noticed the lyric of circa 800 B. C., partly altogether religious, partly altogether worldly, while heroic themes in some examples are united with a religious element. This may be called for convenience the inspired lyric, to distinguish it from the religious lyric of a later day, for only the earliest poetry is regarded as divinely inspired. After this there is an intervening strain of devotional lyric, which appears here and there in the early philosophical essays of circa 400 B. C., but it is so sporadic in its outgrowth and so scrappy in its nature that it may be grouped with the same sort of poetry found a little later in the epic, only that here there is added the new strain, the sentimental element, but the two together may be called the devotional and sentimental or epic lyric. Third in time and kind is the simple love-lyric, which begins in the drama and appears as an independent genre in the later classical lyric. There is also, besides the descriptive lyric which runs through the inspired and epic periods, some descriptive lyric of fragmentary inscriptional character; but this last may be passed over as a prelude to the higher artistic perfection of the poets of 400–800 A. D. Last of all there is the complex love lyric of the later poets. This is a fusion of erotic and religious elements, and in distinction from the simple love lyric may be called the mystic lyric. In this last form it is sometimes difficult to say whether the poet is more influenced by amorous passion or devout piety, or whether both are as strangely blended in his spirit as they are in his words.

The earliest form of lyrical expression is in the main religious, and of this religious mass, — that is, the Vedic Hymns, — the general content may be described as joyful laudation mingled with a canny sense of the usefulness of gods when properly praised, as in these verses, which I cite from a previous translation:[1]

> 'T is Indra all our songs extol,
>   Him huge as ocean in extent;
> Of warriors chiefest warrior he,
>   Lord, truest lord for booty's gain.
> In friendship, Indra, firm as thine
>   We nothing fear, O lord of strength;
> To thee we our laudations sing,
>   The conqueror unconquerèd.

And so on, in laud of "Indra, the doer of every deed, the lightning-holder, far renowned," whose gracious acts are men-

[1] The Religions of India, p. 20.

tioned as being without number, though the poet alludes especially to his greatest deed, slaying the demon of drought and helping his own worshippers in their raids for cattle; until the song, which in no wise reflects the sacerdotalism that pervades so many of the Vedic hymns, concludes with the stanza:

> Indra, who lords it by his strength,
>   Our praises now have loud proclaimed;
> His generous gifts a thousand are,
>   Aye, even more than this are they.

Indra is the war-god, and most of the hymns addressed to him portray him as leader in battle as well as slayer of the demon-dragon, who holds pent the longed-for rain. The spirit of these hymns is exultant, often jovial, and not seldom almost brutal; while, on the other hand, grace and dignity are respectively the characteristics of the religious lyrics addressed to Dawn and Heaven. Dawn, the path-finder, the gentle maiden-goddess of the early Veda, has but few hymns, but these are such as to make one wish for more:

> As comes a bride, hath Dawn approached us, gleaming;
>   All things that live she rouses now to action.
> A fire is born that shines for human beings;
>   Light hath she made and driven away the darkness.
>
> O near and dear, keep them afar who hate us,
>   And make secure our cows' wide pasture-places.
> Keep harm away, but what is good, that bring us,
>   And send the singer wealth, O generous maiden.

Varuna, the Heaven, whose spying eyes are the orbs above, who sits upon his golden throne and sees even the thoughts of men, is the most majestic and loftiest conception of the Vedic poets:

> Bearing a garment all of gold,
> In jewels clothed, is Varuna,
> And round about him sit his spies;

Him whom th' injurious injure not,
Nor they who men deceive, deceive,
Nor foes attack, a real god.

Far go my thoughts to him, as go
The roaming cows that meadows seek;
I search for him, the wide-eyed god,
To whom, beloved by him of old,
I bear this honey-sacrifice.
Then let us talk again, we two!

O would that I might see my god,
See his great chariot sweep the earth,
And know that he accepts my song!
Hear thou my cry, O Varuna,
Be merciful to me to-day;
I need thy help. I turn to thee,
For if thou art both wise and king
Of everything in earth and heaven,
Then must thou hear, and grant, my prayer.

These verses are arranged in stanzas of three verses each. Their metre is but roughly approximated by the iambic English version, which is true to the original only in the number of syllables given to each verse, though the general cadence of the model also is iambic. But the latter has the pyrrhic and trochee as well as the spondee and iambus, so that the combination may be a choriambus, — ◡ — — ◡ — ◡ —, ◡ — — ◡ ◡ — ◡ —, — — — ◡ ◡ — ◡ —, to give the cadence of one stanza of the above as an illustration: Come an' united once again | To thee bringing a honey-feast | Let us talk as of old, the two.

In the same metre, and also arranged in groups of three verses each, a combination which by the way afterwards fell into desuetude, another poet sings to Pushan, a divinity who also fell into desuetude as time went on. Like Dawn, Pushan is the path-finder, who is invoked to conduct the Aryans as they push on in their journeys; a function that was not so useful after they became settled along the Jumna and Ganges, but was indispensable while they wandered through the desert:

Go, Pushan, on the road with us,
Take every danger from the way,
And lead us forward, shining god.

And, Pushan, if a wicked wolf
Or evil doer threatens us,
Him truly smite from out our path.

Whoever lurks upon our path,
The robber, or the doer of ill,
Drive him afar from out our way.

Past all pursuers lead us well,
Make easy all our pathways thou,
O Pushan, give us wisdom's strength.

Such poems as these, set in verses the articulation of which, it must be confessed, bears in many cases a painful resemblance to that of Midas' epitaph, though for the more part they are merely lauds of gods, play between the objective and subjective. Thus they often reflect the singer's animosities, his hate not only of wrong, but of special wrong-doers; his desire for converse with the gods, his sorrow for sins committed by himself. Other Vedic poems have a lyric-dramatic setting and give lamentations, or again, they portray erotic feeling in situations more or less alien to modern taste. One unique hymn addressed to Soma is lyrical in so far as it expresses the singer's longing for a happy life hereafter:

Where light that never fades is seen,
To the world, where heavenly radiance shines,
Thither, O Soma, bear me hence.
Th' immortal world, that never ends,
Where Yama is the king, within
The innermost part of yonder sky,
Where everlasting waters flow,
Make me to be immortal there.
Where as one wishes one may go,

In the third vault of the threefold sky,
Amid the luminous worlds of light,
Make me to be immortal there.
Where every wish is gratified,
The highest place the sun attains,
Where longings all are satisfied,
Make me to be immortal there.
The place of joy and mad delight,
And all intoxicating bliss,
Where all desire's desires are stilled,
Make me to be immortal there.

Of quite worldly content, on the other hand, is the following poem, which may be reckoned as a personal lyric, since the poet, in uncovering the source of all human activity and finding it in greed alone, exhibits, or pretends to, his own inner feelings, as well as those of other men, even of the priest, who, he implies, performs his sacrifices merely to get the drink of liquor which goes with them; just as the carpenter or wagon-maker seeks a smashed vehicle to mend, and the smith prepares to work, not for love of it, but for the money he will earn. All work, even that of the poet, is done for pay, and "we are all, as it were, pecuniarily inclined," *ánu gā́ iva tasthima.* It is a late production, belonging, like the last, to the close of the Vedic collection, but the bard must have had a powerful mind, for his explanation of the reason why the Vedic poets composed songs at all is precisely that of a certain school of Vedic criticism of our day. Perhaps, however, this late mocker, who represents the end of Vedic poetry, was incapable of understanding the spirit of the older poets. But at any rate his criticism, if not very deep, makes an interesting bit of satire:

Aye, various plans (of work) are ours,
  And different are the ways of men;
The carpenter desires a smash;
  The doctor, wounds; the priest, a drink.
With brush-wood dry (to build a fire),
  And feather-fan (to make it hot),

And glowing stones (as anvil used),
  The smith a man with money wants.
I poet am, my dad 's a quack,
  The mater grinds the flour — and yet,
Whate'er our work,[1] we all seek wealth;
  For after money run we all.

In any lyrical production, the rhythm is so essential an element that I will not apologize for pausing here again to explain the structure of the Indo-Iranian eight-syllable verse as it is found in this so-called anushtubh stanza, which at a later date became stereotyped as the çloka verse. The pankti form just employed has an additional verse, but otherwise it does not differ from the anushtubh, which is the prevailing stanza of the octosyllabic verse. Like the gayatri, or three-verse stanza, it admits light or heavy syllables in almost any part of the verse, and though there is a slight difference in the frequency of iambic cadence the two forms are not essentially different. I have spoken above of pyrrhic and trochee, but in fact the verse is not divided into feet of this sort, and the classical nomenclature is merely convenient in describing it mechanically, syllable by syllable, whereas for the equivalent of our notion of "foot" the verse of eight syllables must be taken as a whole. This frame is very difficult to render into English, but I shall try to give one exact equivalent of the anushtubh, reproducing for that purpose without regard to anything else the precise quantities found in this Vedic measure, which it is evident no one name will describe and no one English rhythm can do more than caricature. The vowels in this English version, as I have here ignored the stress, are to be measured by classical rules (except that *y* is *ĭ*). The specimen will at least show how varied is the cadence of the different verses in a single stanza:

[1] Literally, plans or thoughts. No matter how we plan to attain it, we all have the same objective, is the sense. Dad and mater imitate the poet's jocose use of *tatá* and *nanā́* (papa and mama) for the more dignified words for father and mother.

Praise his great might, Indra the king
  Of earthly kings, the fear of all,
Bright Indra ruleth e'en the gods
  In glory, ever, as of old.[1]

Indra our army always leads,
  Lofty his home above the earth ;
Great is Indra, the lord of wealth,
  In worlds on high, the mighty one.
Extraordinary ruler, he !
  Indra wisely, the chief of heaven,
Reigns o'er all worlds, the lordly king,
  Whose priest gains wealth on earth, in heaven.
It is Indra rules ăbove there,[2]
  Yon proud Indra, adored of all ;
Raise up a chorus all to him
  In a band joined to worship well.

As indicated here, the iambic cadence is not always that of the end of the verse, and sometimes we find trochee and spondee fairly ousting the iambi from this their strongest position. The chief difference between this and the subsequent çloka style is in the later adjustment of the half-stanza to make one period, in which the first part (or quarter of the whole stanza) shall end in an iambus and spondee (trochee), the second in iambics only or iambic-pyrrhic (⏑——⏓ *versus* ⏑–⏑⏓). This arrangement was already growing popular in the Vedic age, and subsequently it became the rule.

But this metre, perhaps on account of its confined form and rather choppy rhythm, was not that chosen to give full play to intense feeling. Hence we find that the most spirited effusions of the first lyric poets are couched in more dithyrambic verse. This verse was one of the two oldest forms which the Vedic poets shared with the Iranians; for at the beginning of the first millennium B. C. the Indo-Iranians were probably living together near the Indus. But the former

[1] Compare the verse *dasmásya vásu rátha á*, not so common a combination as some of the others.

[2] Compare a verse of this sort in the poem above, *járatībhir óṣadhībhiḥ*.

had already modified the metre from the inchoate form it had at first, a mere counted string of eleven syllables, short or long. On the other hand, as compared with what this metre became afterwards, the Vedic trishtubh (as it was called) was still very free; for later the length of every syllable became nearly stereotyped, and the cæsura too tended to be cut after the fourth, so that there was little variety in the verse, and the regularity with which a choriambus occurred in its middle gave it the appearance of two or three similar groups, ∪ – ∪ –, – ∪ ∪ –, ∪ – ∪ (–). In this, the classical form, the middle dactyl has quite altered the old Vedic trishtubh, which admits a dactyl only as one of many variations, so that in the latter there is no constant choriambic effect, and consequently the equipoised middle group disappears altogether. Therewith we get to the one characteristic Vedic feature, not a choriambic middle, but a ditrochee close, which is in fact about the only limitation upon the form, except that the poets do not, of course, use a whole group of precedent long or short syllables. So this lyric measure in the Vedic age, as opposed to the classical form, may be expressed by almost any combination of seven syllables followed by – ∪ – ∪. All sorts of variations are admitted, not only in the middle, but at the beginning; while instead of eleven or twelve syllables (the classical form also admitted the latter) ten may stand for a verse, giving a double pentad.

Nevertheless, despite the occasional exercise of great freedom, which, especially at the beginning, makes the sharpest contrast with the diiambic opening of the classical poets and shows verses beginning with a trochee or even a choriambus, the Vedic poets were already tending toward the classical norm, and on the whole the measure they employ is iambic and anapæstic in movement. Very often we get a decidedly anapæstic form, ∪ –́ ∪ ∪ –́, ∪ ∪ –́ ∪ –́ ∪. The swing of the verse, as compared with the trot and amble of the classical poets, is that of a gallop, often falling into a sharp canter, so suddenly changing that it is impossible to suppose that the poets had in mind any "regular" form, according to which they composed. The general run of the verses, ignoring these frequent breaks, is, indeed, not without a common ground-plan, which may be given by the two schemes,—

⏒ –́ ⏑ –́, ⏑ ⏑ –́ – ⏑ –́ ⏑,  
⏓ –́ ⏑ –́ ⏑, ⏑ ⏑ –́ ⏑ –́ ⏑,

He went to war, as a man goes to marriage,  
He went to battle, as a man to marriage.

The occasional lengthening of the ninth syllable, and the frequent shortening of the eighth, when it makes part of a word and implies a light cæsura, deserve special remark, as shown by the variation,—

He went to battle, as ever, a hero.

A second cæsura sometimes gives to the last part of the verse the forms ⏑ ⏑ –́, –́ ⏑ –́ ⏑; ⏑ ⏑ –́ –, ⏑ –́ ⏑; ⏑ ⏑, –́ ⏑ –́ ⏑; ⏑ ⏑ –́, ⏑ –́ ⏑. But these are all very general norms, as may be seen by comparing with them many other varieties of the verse, alternating in the same stanza, some of which, as shown in the list below, would correspond to the English, "Hail to the chief, who in triumph advances," if only we accented the second syllable of triumph, for example, if it were Hail to the chief who is ours, proudly going; while others would reflect the form, Hail to the chieftain, proudly goes the chieftain; and still others, At last he comes, whom in old state advancing, or, O behold him, as upon earth a god he, or, He came as a chief, as a lord to rule us, and so on. For example, in the first heroic lyric, that of Viçvamitra, translated below, though it has only twelve stanzas, of four verses each, there are twenty-two different arrangements, those that occur most frequently being ⏑ –́ ⏑ –́ –, ⏑ ⏑ –́ ⏑ –́ ⏑, and ⏑ –́ ⏑ –́, ⏑ ⏑ –́ –́ ⏑ –́ ⏑. Some idea of the variety of forms, used side by side in the same stanza, may be got by comparing the following varieties, not half of those actually employed in this one short lyric: ⏑ ⏑ ⏓ ⏑, ⏑ ⏑ – – ⏑ – ⏑; – ⏑ ⏑ –, ⏑ ⏑ – – ⏑ – ⏑; – ⏑ – –, ⏑ ⏑ – – ⏑ – ⏑; ⏑ – ⏑ –,

⏑ ⏑ – – ⏑ – ⏑; ⏑ – ⏑ – ⏑, ⏑ ⏑ – ⏑ – ⏑; ⏑ – – ⏑,
⏑ ⏑ ⏑ – ⏑ – ⏑; ⏑ – – –, – ⏑ – – ⏑ – ⏑; – ⏑ ⏑ ⏑,
– ⏑ – – ⏑ – ⏑; – ⏑ ⏑ – –, – ⏑ – ⏑ – ⏑.

This varied metre is employed, however, not only in the heroic lyric, but also in the usual laudatory or descriptive verses, the primary object of which is to ascribe general praise to the gods.

The pentad form, as shown in a complete poem, may be illustrated by this extract from a little lyric addressed to the storm-gods, who follow the lightning-god, Rudra. In general plan the cadence is here iambic, but not infrequently it is spondaic, and even the whole group, as in the turn "in brightness brightest," may consist of heavy syllables:

> Who knows, to name them, the host fraternal,
> The pride of Rudra, on gleaming horses?
> Of them the birthplace no man can tell us,
> They only know it, their common birthplace.
> With wings expanded they sweep each other,
> Like falcons fighting; wind-loud is the sound. . . .
> In speed the swiftest, in brightness brightest,
> With beauty join they the fiercest power.

Here "wind-loud is the sound" apes lamely – – ⏑ ⏑ –, another substitution found in the original; where one group has even a dactylic form, *mā́ vo durmatír.*[1] The whole song, being set before another in trishtubhs, ends with a connecting verse of that measure.

Another well-known hymn, which is enveloped in only so much sacerdotalism as is implied in the final verse, "Let us honor him with an oblation" (perhaps of milk, or it may be of grain or of Soma), I have translated in my Religions of India,[2] literally, though not with very close attention to the Vedic verse-structure. But I will repeat it with little alteration here, to show how marked even in the earliest lyric is

[1] But in *dhúnir múnir iva* there is a grammatical correction of the older *va*, which undoubtedly stood there originally (the Pali form).

[2] p. 88.

this element of pure description. The hymn is otherwise interesting; since Vata (*vāta*, from *vā*, blow), to whom it is addressed, is Ventus, the wind-god, perhaps the same with Woden, who here, "keeping the order" of time, brings the monsoon water-clouds in due season. The first sentence is an ejaculatory accusative without any verb:

Now Vata's chariot's greatness! Smashing goes it,
And thundering is its noise. It touches heaven
And makes the clouds; skims earth, the dust uprearing —
Then follow after all the forms of Vata,
And haste to him as women meet a lover.[1]
With them conjoined, together rushes onward
The gleaming god, king of this whole creation.
Ne'er resteth he, when on his many pathways
He goes through air, the first born friend of waters,
Who keeps the order. Where was he created?
And whence arose he? Spirit of gods, this bright god,
Source of creation, courseth where he listeth.
His sound is heard but not his form. This Vata,
Wind, with an offering let us (duly) honor.[2]

Yet it is rather in recounting the great deeds of their own past than in describing the gods that the Vedic poets show their strongest lyrical power. In the first lyric following I have reproduced not only the cæsura, but also the exact syllabic equivalence of the first three verses,[3] though as this had to be united in English with stress (the Vedic accent is musical), in the following stanzas I have given simply a stress-equivalent of the quantity, not according to each verse, but not introducing any form for which the poets do not use a quantitative equivalent. The translation itself is as nearly literal as it was possible to make it.

[1] Literally, Come to a rendezvous.

[2] This phrase is stereotyped.

[3] That is, as in the study above, assuming the classical rule for the length of vowels before two consonants. But to unite this successfully, with stress and sense also even for one stanza, was difficult, and the fourth verse conforms only by pronouncing Beas and torrent as trochees.

This first specimen of the heroic lyric is a poem that needs little explanation. I give it complete, except for a stanza in another metre which has been tagged on to it by a later hand. The priest Viçvamitra, the son of Kuçika, is represented as having come to the two rivers Sutlej and Beas, which run together in the present Punjab. They block his way. He bids them obey the mystic might of the priestly word, which is holy, *somya*, and powerful. The rivers in amœbic strain refuse to obey. They obey only god Indra. Viçvamitra sees his mistake. He then addresses them humbly, and in a stanza of laudation to the god acknowledges Indra as their master. Therewith he wins their approval, and as a favor they sink in their channels, and Viçvamitra leads over the booty-seeking host of Bharatas.

## HOW THE BHARATS CROSSED THE BEAS AND SUTLEJ.

### AS SUNG BY THE PRIEST VIÇVAMITRA.

THE POET SPEAKS:

From out the hills' heart, as if horses, eager,
  Tumultuous, in a race, newly loosened,
As cows a calf lick, lapping earth, the fair streams,
  The Beas, Sutlej, in a torrent hasten.
By Indra loosed, and his impulse beseeching,
  Ye, swift as war-cars, to the meeting hurry,
Where streaming together, with thick'ning billows,
  Each enters the other, ye lovely rivers.

VIÇVAMITRA SPEAKS:

I 've sought the Sutlej, the stream maternal,
  To Beas, broad-flowing and kindly, come we,[1]
These two that together, like cattle licking
  A calf, hasten on to the destined union.

[1] These words "seek" and "come to" imply not only that the priest has come, but that he comes demanding something (that he has not only sought but, like Latin *peto*, besought), a common Vedic idiom. This the Rivers recognize in their reply.

The Rivers speak:

With thickening waters, we floods together
  Flow on to the union the god prepared us;
Ne'er to be checked is the impulse that urges us;
  What wishes the bard that invokes the rivers?

Viçvamitra speaks proudly:

Ye streams, that flow, duly in season rising,
  Stand still, obedient to my utterance holy.
My will on the flood hath a might compelling.
  Your aid invokes Kuçika's own descendant.

The Rivers speak reprovingly:

Indra, who beareth in his arm the lightning —
  He dug our broad channels; he slew the dragon
That held us confined; it is Indra rules us;
  Fair-handed he leads us; his might we follow.

Viçvamitra lauds Indra:

Be praised forever that deed heroic,
  The act of Indra, who destroyed the dragon.
With bolt of lightning all your jailers slew he;
  Out rushed the streams in a wide course rejoicing.

The Rivers speak approvingly:

Thy song, O bard, never shall be forgotten,
  That future ages may acclaim thee always.
In songs exalt us and never, 'mid mortals,
  Seek to defame us. We bow before thee.

Viçvamitra speaks humbly:

Hark to the bard, if ye will, sister rivers;
  He comes from afar with wagon and chariot.
If so ye will,[1] give me an easy passage;
  To th' axle alone, O ye rivers, flowing.

[1] Here the repeated word *su* is used for the first time, meaning "if you please," "kindly" (*pūjā*).

THE RIVERS SPEAK:

Now to thy words give we good heed, O singer.
  Thou com'st from afar with wagon and chariot.
I will bow down, e'en as a loving woman;
  As maid to a man will I bend before thee.

VIÇVAMITRA SPEAKS:

When all of the Bharats have crossed beyond thee,
  This host of raiders that is led by Indra,
Then forth let flow in a wide flood the waters.
  I beg for the grace of the holy rivers.

ENVOI.

The Bharats have crossed now, the cattle-lifters,
  The singer is blessed with the rivers' favor.
Now streaming unceasingly fill the hollows;
  Run full to the brim, and be kindly ever.

One such "hymn" as this — the original word, by the way, does not mean hymn at all, but simply something "well said," a good thing in poetry, eulogia in a broad sense — is sufficient, I think, to prove that lyric poetry in India did not begin with the bon-mots of the fifth century after Christ, but is at least as old as the oldest Greek lyric. As a matter of fact, the truest Hindu lyric is just this old Vedic heroic song, in which (as will be shown still better in the next example) the poet pours out his feelings in hearty praise and curses, rather than the gem-wrought bits of daintiness of the "lyric period," in which the poet seldom appears to be in earnest, but plays with his loves and hates as he plays with his delicate fancies, making exquisite poetry, but poetry which, like all exquisite things produced by man, is thoroughly artificial. Elaborated passion, pretty conceits often done up in complicated verse, that is the decadent lyric of the so-called classical period. The lyric of the Vedic period is rough in comparison. The poet has mastered neither his passions nor his verse-form; he is mostly rude in expression, as he is usually rude in feeling. His poetry is seldom the elegant amusement of a blasé gentleman and never the morbid blend of erotic and religious sensuousness, which we find later, but the straight and rather rough talk of uncurbed emotion.

In the last specimen of Vedic song the poet Viçvamitra sings his lay of triumph. But a still greater song was sung by his rival, Vasishtha. It appears that the latter at some time ousted the former from his place as Purohita, or priest of the Tritsu king, Sudás, and that Viçvamitra in anger went over to a band of allied kings who planned a destructive campaign against Sudás. It is a famous battle, and is known in Vedic poetry as the Battle of the Ten Kings. Instigated by Viçvamitra, these kings and their armies came against Sudás, who opposed them with only the help of Vasishtha, the river itself, and god Indra. Suddenly, as they had entered the Ravi, then shallow and fordable, which lay between them and Sudás, the hosts of the ten kings were overpowered by a flood sent by Indra, — one of the sudden risings common to all the great northern snow-fed rivers, — and so found death where they had hoped for booty.

This overthrow is sung with biting sarcasm by Vasishtha. The lyric abounds in jeering puns, of which I reproduce only a few. The one most used is a play on the name Viçvamitra, which is literally "friend of all." What sort of a friend he was to those whom he led to death is described in taunting phrase by his rival. The play on the name of Lion (of the Punjab!) is more obvious than the one connected with it and contained in the etymology of Tritsu, which is literally the "piercer." As (the horn of) a goat pierces, so, says the poet, with Indra's help, but otherwise undefended, the Piercer smote the Lion. I omit the formal introduction, which simply asks that Indra's good-will may continue in the future as in the past; as also a receipt for the reward gained by Vasishtha for composing this triumphal ode, which, after the manner of the times, was appended to the ode itself and sung on other occasions, to please the family of the royal donor. It is evident that the reward was not given till the song had had its effect, so that it has nothing to do with the real lyric. The place of this sort of verses is such as might have been that of an additional stanza composed by Pindar as a thank-offering for the reward of his services to the Syracusan and subsequently sung as part of the whole. In the translation of the ode I have generally followed the interpretation made by me some years ago, but with two or three changes suggested by more mature consideration.[1] I also omit one stanza containing the names of some of the foes.

The river Ravi (Parushni, so named at the beginning) is called at the end of the poem *yamunā*, the received explanation being that after Sudás had conquered at the Ravi he withdrew to the Yamunā (Jumna) and there fought a second battle with Bheda. But this seems very improbable, as there is no indication of any such change of position. I interpret *yamunā*, therefore, as a name of the Ravi (afterwards transferred to the eastern river). The word means "twin"-stream and may as well be applied to the double channel of the upper Ravi as to the Jumna. Nothing is more common in India than the transfer of a river's name to another stream. On the other hand, though "Bheda's" defeat is mentioned elsewhere, the Rig Veda knows nothing of his defeat at the Jumna.

## THE VICTORY OF SUDÁS, KING OF THE TRITSUS, OVER HIS ALLIED FOES.

### AS SUNG BY HIS PRIEST VASISHTHA IN HONOR OF GOD INDRA.

Sudás to aid, Indra hath turned to torrents
 The shoals (regarded as an) easy fording,
And Çimyu, the Lion, the god-defyer,
 Our god hath made as the flotsam of rivers.

[1] Journal of the Oriental Society, vol. xv. p. 261 ff. In the opening stanza the sense is not, as in common with others, I formerly thought, that Indra made the river easy to cross for Sudás, but that, for Sudás' sake, he turned the shallow river into the torrent (which drowned his enemies).

Of them the leader was Turvas, the Yakshu,
  Whom followed for pillage the Matsya people,
The Bhrigus, the Druhyus; while o'er the river
  The Friend his friends guided on — to destruction!
Friend of the Aryan!" Friendly proved his leading —
  Like cattle they came to contend with heroes!
Sinners they, seeking to make her miscarry,
  Who witless parted the Ravi, the boundless.[1]
But he, so sage, who of wide earth was master,[2]
  Embraced earth well — as a scared victim lay he.
On bootless quest Ravi they sought for booty, —
  Not even the swiftest e'er home returnèd.
To brave Sudás, as in wild haste they scattered,
  All weak and *friendless* now, god Indra gave them.
Like kine on a meadow without a herdsman,
  In crowds they scattered, the Friend surrounding,
But brilliant the herd and a brilliant downfall,
  As horse and foot they the leader followed.
Indra, our hero, he who loveth glory,
  Cut down Vikarna's best chiefs, one and twenty,
And strewed them around as a handy reaper
  Mows down in a moment the grass for th' altar.
Thou Indra, who bearest in arm the lightning,
  Didst drown their renownèd ones, Druhyu, Ailush;
But we, who elected as Friend the true Friend,
  Revering thee, shouted thy name in triumph.

The Anus, who came on a raid for booty,
  The Druhyava heroes, their sixty hundred
—Or six by the thousand, 't is six and sixty——
  They have fallen asleep and the glory 's Indra's!
Like a pent flood loosened we Tritsu people,
  By Indra guided, descending whelmed them,

[1] Or the divine, *aditi*. The river is a goddess. This stanza has been interpreted to mean that the allies tried to divert the course of the Ravi by digging canals. But *sriv*, miscarry, may be used figuratively as fail; while *vigrabh*, sever, separate, part, may possibly have its simple epic meaning, attack.

[2] That is, lord and master, husband? Or: Strongly he encompassed earth, a lord: scared lay he, a sacrificial victim.

—For evil their Friend — till to pieces shattered
To Sudás they abandoned the joy of pillage.
The ranks of the mighty, the boastful, sinful,
Who knew of no Indra, them Indra vanquished;
He, stilling the storm of the wrathful stormer,
Their lord in truth, tore them apart, dispersed them.
With few to assist him, this deed did Indra, —
With a goat(-horn) smote he a certain lion;
The foeman's spears, clove he with only needles;
To King Sudás gave he the joy of pillage.
All thy foes, O Indra, have bowed before thee;
Smite thou him, whoever will boast of rending;[1]
Aye, strike unto earth with thy sharpened lightning
Whoever hereafter thy praiser injures!
Aid to Indra gave the twinned stream and Tritsus;
Then despoiled he throughly the (helpless) render.
The Ajas and Çighrus and Yakshu peoples,
They gave as a tribute their slaughtered horses!
But, O Indra, not in an age of long days
Can a man, counting, tell thy wealth of kindness;
Each foe that has fancied himself a godling
Thou smit'st from on high, as thou Çambar[2] rendest.
But they that have always rejoicing loved thee,
And worshipped thee truly, as has Vasishtha,
Will never forget thee, the Friend and helper, —
So bright be the days of my lord[3] forever.

You see that even to the end the fierce anger of the old bard plays on his defeated rival's unhappy name, as he again echoes the statement that Indra is the true friend.

Despite the roughness of the form, made still rougher by Englishing, I think you will admit that this lyric well deserves to be handed down through the ages. Its vigor and bitterness as well as its stirring description give it a high

[1] The true "render" is Indra himself, as in the second stanza below ("rent from on high"). "Render" may be the name of one of the foes, the idea being "make the render surrender."

[2] The demon of drought.

[3] My lord, the king Sudás.

place, not only in the antique collections of India, but among all lyrics of its time.

But now I must leave the Vedic lyric and pass on to the next stage.

The early phases of religious philosophy after the Vedic period are deeply colored with emotion. Not in Buddhistic works alone, but in the Upanishads also the wonder at the new-found religion is profound and often bursts forth in lyrical verse, as may be seen in the following:

As God of all, All-God, maker of all things;
  As He that in the heart of man abideth,
By the heart alone conceived, by mind and fancy,—
  Who thus know God, they have become immortal.
Within His light, nor night nor day existeth;
  Being, not-being, — all is He, the Blessèd.
He is the treasure sought by Vedic poets,
  From Him was born all knowledge and all wisdom.
Above, below, across or in the middle,
  None hath grasped God; nor is there any image
Of Him whose only name is this, Great Glory.
  His form invisible is and always must be,
For He in mind and heart abides. Who know Him
  As their own soul, they have become immortal.

Though there is here, perhaps, more fear than joy, "In fear I come before Thee," says the poet in the verses following, yet there are other passages which reflect the joy imparted by this new-found religion, as, for example:

The Soul in all things is the one Controller,
  Who makes His one form manifold in many.
The wise that Him as their own soul acknowledge,
  They have eternal joy; but not so, others.
Among the transient He is the everlasting;
  The only wise one He, among the foolish;
The one of many. Him perceive the sages
  In their own souls and feel a peace eternal.

The sun shines not, nor moon, nor stars, nor lightning,
Nor earthly fire, within the All-soul's heaven;
For He alone is the Light that all shines after,
And by His light is all the world illumined.

But such passages rarely attain so finished a form, and they may be omitted here as of too fragmentary nature to require more than a passing notice. Nor is epic poetry the place to expect fully developed lyrical expression, though in the frequent hymns to the gods this is often attained incidentally, and even the descriptions of the godhead are at times lyrical, not only in their intense striving to express the poet's adoration of Him who is the All, but also in the employment of more elaborate metres, as in this: [1]

Beginning, and middle, and end of all beings,
Both doer and deed He, creator and creature;
The worlds, when the age ends, absorbing, He slumbers,
Till a new age beginning He wakes as creator.

Rare too, because of the epic form, is any expression of feeling as regards nature. Descriptions of storms and other natural phenomena come down from the Vedic period, as I have shown, and are found also in the epic; but there is little in these that reflects the poet's own feelings even in so small a degree as is perceptible in the hymns to the gods, where at least human desires play about the divine person thus besung. Perhaps, however, one of the few descriptions of nature found in the great epic (they are more common in the Ramayana), may prove interesting, and as it presents the emotions incident on the coming of the rains, it is not without a touch of the delight which we know that the poet himself must have experienced when the monsoon at last broke:

[1] sa ādih sa madhyah sa cā 'ntah prajānām, sa dhātā sa dheyah sa kartā sa kāryam; yugānte prasuptah susaṁkshipya lokān yugādāu prabuddho jagad dhy utsasarja.

Then came the time that ends the heat
And bringeth happiness to all.
Black clouds loud thundering covered space,
And ceaseless rained by day and night.
By hundreds and by thousands piled
They hid the glorious sun, themselves
With stainless lightning glorious made.
Up sprang the crops and all the earth,
Bewatered, full of peace and joy,
Was filled with happy creeping things.
Then 't was impossible to say,
So deep the flood, if level ground
Or heights or rivers lay beneath.
Like hissing snakes, impetuous, swept
E'en through the forests, waters wide,
And made new beauty in the wood ;
Where boars and birds, all forest things,
Drenched with the rain, exulted loud.
The peacocks, kokils, catakas,
Circled about and danced for joy,
And mad with pleasure croaked the frogs.

As we shall see, the same motif is copied again in the later lyric of the classical period. And this gives to the epic lyric its historical value. We cannot separate it sharply either from the pre-epic or from the classical lyric, although the latter has a new growth superadded. Even the form in its simplest shape, that of the çloka, is still the medium of much of the classical lyric, not to speak of the fancy metres in the epic, which, as inscriptions show, may have preceded any classical specimens. But, of course, as the very expression epic lyric seems like a misnomer, so the lyric in the epic may be more or less intrusion, especially as it often makes scenes apart from the main action, or is found only in epigrammatic collections which were inserted whole into the epic. To ignore these altogether, however, is to lose links from the chain that really runs from the Upanishads of perhaps 400 B. C. to the classic age of 400 A. D. and later.

As an example of a lyric scene set apart in the epic, I will take one specimen describing the feelings of Arjun, the hero of the great epic, when as he was carried to heaven he looked back on earth, where he had been dwelling on Mount Mandara, the Blessed Mountain of antiquity. The poem is remarkable not only on account of its description of nature's beauties, and the happiness of dwelling in the open life of forest and mountain vale, but also because of its unique anticipation of the discovery that the stars, though they look small, are really large bodies placed farther away than the sun, huge worlds which shine by their own light, a light less than the light of God only. This discovery is vitiated from a scientific point of view by the addition that these remote "self-luminous" worlds which "on account of their distance men on earth think to be small as lamps" (I cite the very words of the text) are at the same time the souls of departed saints and heroes; but that is an idea which even in our own age is accepted by many good people. I will give an almost complete version of this whole passage, except that I have exchanged the last verse for another which, though implied in the original, is not expressed there; but it is expressed soon after and makes a better conclusion, for the original text continues with a further description which is too long to include. The metre is that of the last selection, but I have here allowed myself a rhymed form. The translation, however, is literal. The date is about 200 B.C.–200 A.D.

When Arjun, loved of Indra, came to leave the Blessèd Mount of earth,
On the god's chariot wreathed in flame he rose to heaven, but still the worth
And beauty of that sacred hill retained his heart, and as above
The Mount he soared, his spirit still returned, while thus his reverent love
He voiced: "O home and sacred shrine, where holy pleasures never cease,
Farewell! I leave, no longer mine, this fair abode of perfect peace.

Thy rocks and caverns, springs and streams, how often gladdened
they my sight;
With fragrant flowers thy forest teems, and purest water cools
thy height,
Like nectar and ambrosia sweet. As a child upon its father's
breast,
How oft I found in still retreat upon thy bosom balmy rest,
Which followed joyful toil. Each day I heard the chaunts of
pious men,
And songs of happy nymphs at play, loud echoing from thy rocks
again.
Yea, blissful ever did I dwell among thy vales and ridges." So
To the Mount the hero bade farewell, Arjun, and rising, straight
did go
Upwards upon that gleaming car, high as we mortals see, and
higher,
Where self-made glory shines afar, o'er sun and moon a loftier
fire.
For on that super-solar height, though still below the plane of
God,
Beamed many a self-illumined light, which mortals, standing
upon earth's sod,
Look up and see but fancy small as lamps, because the distance
vast
Belittles those great worlds; but all are bodies huge and brilliant,
cast
Through space supernal. These he saw, marvelling, and knew
them not; but they
Are souls that by the heavenly law, passing from earth, so sages
say,
Shine evermore as stars on high, beneath the height of God,
whose light,
Radiant as are in the upper sky those orbs, is yet beyond them
bright.

The Hindu drama, to which I now turn for a moment, introduces us to the third form of lyric, little stanzas of description and love, all centred round and sung by the actors, who are their own chorus. A detailed examination of these roundelays belongs rather to the history of the drama. In this sketch of lyric development it will be necessary only to point out that here in the drama is one of the lyrical stepping-stones from the old heroic, religious, sentimental, and descriptive poetry to that which, passing out of the dramatic environment, becomes in the treatment of later poets an independent phase of literature. Independent, yes, for Bhartrihari of the seventh century needs no dramatic setting for his exquisite lyric gems, whereas such little stanzas do not appear alone in the works of the dramatic poets; but not independent in the sense of a new creation, for all these phases hold together. Most clearly is this seen in the philosophical and — save the mark — didactic lyric of Bhartrihari. For that monkish philosopher composes with equal grace his Herrick-like songs of love, morality, and religion. But when he drops from more artistic versification into the çloka, his sententious and didactic muse is exactly the same old lady who successfully conducted the epic poets through thousands of similar verses; nor is there really any more lyric therein than in Hesiod. For example, the Hitopadeça, a late Book of Propriety, cites a çloka from Bhartrihari, "He cannot be said to be really born through whose birth his family is not elevated;" just as it cites in the same metre the epic, "fruitful is a gift given to a poor man," and we may call lyric the one as well as the other, or more fittingly neither. But, on the other hand, truly lyric strains are found in the same metre in the epic as well as in Bhartrihari. So this poet links his present to the past, as did the epic poets themselves.

But apart from the didactic stanzas, the model of Bhartrihari's truer lyric may be found, as I have already said, in those bursts of song which are ever escaping the lips of the *dramatis personæ* from the time of the fourth and fifth century after Christ. Thus when the king, in Kalidasa's drama of Çakuntala, sees the hermit's daughter, whom he straightway loves, and finds her shy, he says reflectively: "These children of the forest are always inclined to be rather timid, but —

Her eyes she drooped as she stood before me,
  She laughed and pretended another reason.
Nature itself, her love concealing,
  Even in hiding it played her treason."

Take out the environment, leave the stanza, and you have the kind of verse in which Bhartrihari delighted.

But before Bhartrihari played lapidary to the Muse, and Amaru, his rival, made the fine mosaic work for which he is famous, Kalidasa had brought to perfection another side of lyric poetry. I have just read you from the epic a selection, complete in itself, describing Arjun's journey from earth to heaven, wherein we saw that the poet succeeded pretty well in weaving in a bit of description of earth and uniting it with a religious turn in describing the upper spheres. I think the Cloud-Messenger of Kalidasa may properly be regarded as a more modern working out of the same theme, though the motif is quite different. Here the poet makes a captive husband address a cloud and send by it a message to his wife. This gives opportunity to describe what the cloud will see on its journey, and with this description, especially in the first part of the poem, must be compared as historical prototypes not only the scene just referred to from the great epic, but the frequent scenes of nature-description found in the Ramayana. Even the second half of the poem, which describes the beloved wife's distress, must be looked upon as merely an historical evolution from just such scenes in the latter epic. So one by one, for example in descriptions of autumn and the other seasons, on which Kalidasa has left us a beautiful poem, we may trace back the factors of the later lyric as they show themselves to be refinements of the older poetry. But as compared with the older epic they have more of the erotic element and more extravagance of description in portraying the charms of nature and of woman. In this as in other regards the Ramayana stands between the great epic and classical poetry.

But I have already over-passed the limit set by the title

of this address, which should confine me to the early lyric. Perhaps, however, as I have alluded so often to Bhartrihari, you will allow me a few moments to show you, before I close, what I meant in speaking of his gem-like poems and dainty conceits. But I do not cite from him merely for this, but rather to show you how far hitherward stretches the older lyric as it appears in its various forms. There is, however, no reason to exceed Bhartrihari's time, for the still later mystic erotic type is not a projection of Vedic thought, as are many of the other phases found in the classical lyric. Bhartrihari is not an isolated figure, but among the host of later lyric poets he stands conspicuous both for the versatility and the perfection of his genius. All that we have of him is contained in an artificial grouping of Three Centuries, or collections of miniature poems according as they are amorous, moral, or religious. As I have said, the latter divisions are not always very lyrical. On the other hand, some of the selections called moral might as well have been grouped under the head of amorous, or immoral, as Bhartrihari in his repentant moods regarded the other division. For he was an interesting character, who flitted from a monastic religious life out into the world and back again, not once, but as often as he was moved to do so. When a monk he wrote verses to show that love was folly, and when in love he wrote verses to show that a monastic life was folly. He was a man of emotions, and lived according to their leading, a child of the moment. You will liken him to Anacreon, when you read

> The god of love a fisher is;
> Woman, his line; his bait, desire;
> And man 's the fish that soon is caught
> And cooked in passion's fire.

You must pardon the off-hand roughness of the translation after all I have said about exquisite polish; but I have spent no time on Englishing these specimens, knowing that I could not give you any idea of the form. They are chosen from here and there — and translated perhaps all too hastily —

merely to give you an idea of the content and to show you the difference between the lyric of the seventh century A. D. and the lyric of perhaps the same century B. C. or earlier, such as I illustrated from the Rig Veda.

Bhartrihari's Love-Century must of course ring the changes on one subject; but it is pretty to see how many are his quaint conceits:

> Women have honey on their lips,
>   But only poison in their hearts, no doubt;
> Hence one the mouth of women sips,
>   But squeezes them to get the poison out.

If you think this too shocking, please remember that it was written by a clergyman. But perhaps I had better draw my next selection from the Conduct-Century, or moral apothegms, a bit that may be familiar to you if you read German:

> She whom I love loves one who loves her not,
>   She whom I love not, she must needs love me,
> Then whom I love and who loves her, and she
>   Who loves myself, with Love himself, and me,
>     May cursèd be.

But why this stanza should be called especially moral it is difficult to see. The next is of course put into another division:

> There is a sickness falls on man:
>   The heart grows faint, the eyes roll round;
> 'T is madness that no drug may calm,
>   To heal it is no doctor found.
> Such sickness every man hath had;
>   The god of love hath made him mad.

The god of love, armed with five arrows, is native to India, but he is not a little cupid. In fact, it is hard to define him except as an archer, for he is invisible, immaterial, "limbless Love," as the Hindus call him.

I said that Bhartrihari glides easily from adoration of woman to most monastic horror of her, though oddly enough the following selection is found in the Love-Century. It is the only one of its kind I shall read, and I trust, though you will of course see what is coming, that you will regard it as only another form of poetic nonsense and let it pass without incriminating the translator. But even this slur must not be taken seriously, for it is meant to be only amusing, as may be seen in its rapid and comic changes of metaphor:

Who made this monstrous combination,
This whirlpool full of doubt's gyration,
This home of wrong and town of terrors,
This garden of tricks and store of errors,
This bar that shuts the gate supernal,
This entrance to the door infernal,
This basket full of all delusion,
This poison-honey's deadly fusion,
This snare which catches every human,
This strange machine — who, pray, made woman?

But Bhartrihari was no coarse and constant railer at women. He believed in love and the wedding of hearts:

Separation still is union if the hearts united be,
But if hearts are separated then divorce should set them free.

What again could be more perfect than this version of a sentiment which we are not wont, I think, to regard as more than a thousand years old:

The fruit of love on earth is this, one single thought of two souls wed,
If those made one have twofold thought, 'tis but the union of the dead.

This, by the way, is a çloka, identical with the epic verse, in which rather unlyrical setting appear, as I have said, many of Bhartrihari's lovely stanzas, for example:

Though lamps may glow and the hearth be bright, and stars and moon I see;
Yet fail the light of my love's eyes, this world is dark to me.

To paint a situation with a stroke is the ideal of the poets of this age, and though Amaru is cleverer in this, Bhartrihari is a close second in his skill:

She talks to one and to another sends
Provoking glances; while a third her mind
Finds in her heart; whom loves she of her friends?
(She loves one hidden, yet to all is kind),

is the natural answer.

The moral specimens are, as I have said, not always such as we should group under this head, but here is a stanza which illustrates the poet's similarity to the teacher in the didactic parts of the epic:

One moral law all codes proclaim —
Kill not, steal not, do not defame;
Speak truth, be generous, modest, pure,
Compassionate to all. Endure
This law and all its rules obey,
So hast thou found salvation's way.

More characteristic is this little stanza:

God made for ignorance a guise,
With which to hide its nakedness
And give its wearer fame;
Worn in the presence of the wise
'T is e'en an ornamental dress,
And Silence is its name.

Here, too, is another moral stanza, beautified by poetic imagery:

The fruitful tree inclines its branches low,
The cloud that bears rain's blessing sinks to earth;
Virtue cares not proudly on high to go,
And they are humblest who have greatest worth.

Science too is drawn into Bhartrihari's net. It is true that the physical explanation which serves his turn in making a pearl the solid deposit of water in an oyster-shell may be criticised as a wild guess and not a scientific fact, but that is of no consequence, while on the other hand his assertion in the face of the old philosophy, which taught that "all we are is the result of what we have thought," that we are all merely the result of our *sansarga* or environment, adds historical as well as poetical interest to this stanza:

> The drop of water on hot iron steams,
> Evanishes and leaves no trace behind,
> But falling on a lotus, pearl-like gleams,
> And if its way into a shell it find
> Becomes, that water-drop, a pearl in sooth.
> Its altered self by what it meets is lent;
> So all man's qualities in very truth
> Arise in him from his environment.

I almost hesitate to introduce among these light fancies or even among the moral and speculative thoughts the graver wisdom of our poet. But here too we see that he is running back along the grooves of change, and we must recognize in Bhartrihari's religious poems the same lyric, though in more personal form, as that which glowed forth centuries before in the rapturous words of the Upanishads and echoes again through the great epic. One stanza only of this, and I have done:

> Thou descendest to hell, thou ascendest to heaven,
> Hither and thither thou rushest, O heart,
> Unstable, uncertain, in courses uneven.
> What willst thou? That bliss which thou seekest apart
> Is God's; God is thine. From all else, then, cease,
> For only in God the heart findeth peace.

## SANSKRIT EPIC POETRY.

In few departments of literary activity is there a greater chasm between Greece and India than in epic poetry. The Iliad, as we look back to it, remains for us the one stately structure that closes the vista of Greek literature. In India, on the other hand, the epos is a relatively modern building, placed late and midway down the avenue that leads us to the first temple built by the Hindus, the Vedic edifice of hymns to the gods. Between these two, the Veda and the Mahabharata (the elder of the epics) stand other buildings, representing centuries of verse and prose, a whole civilization in various stages of slow development. The very metres with which epic poetry is adorned — I do not mean the metres of the mass, but occasional embellishments — are late forms of versification. There is much that is primitive in this poetry, but, taken as a whole, it reflects ages of culture, philosophy, and religion. If comparable with any western form of epic, that of India should then be set beside the Rhodian and Roman epic, or perhaps more fittingly beside the mediæval romances of France and Germany.

But in any such parallelism there is danger, and each of these illustrations is faulty. Apollonius and Vergil copy older models; the Hindu epic is original. The romances of the middle ages are, again, more romantic than one of the Hindu epics and less ornate than either of them. But, in general, we may say with von Schroeder that the earlier of the two Hindu epics, the Mahabharata, answers for rough comparison to the Nibelungen, the Ramayana to the Parcival.

As was to be expected in poetry such as this, the wisdom of antiquity is engrafted upon it. But we find more than this, for in the Mahabharata — the Ramayana has something of the same sort, but it is too clearly a modern addition to discuss — there are interpolated tedious sermons, tractates on morality, philosophical essays, religious discussions, interminable laudations of the supreme gods, all set into the poem as distinct pieces, having nothing to do with the action, some of them clearly differentiated by metre from the poem itself.

We must, then, if we would get at the original epic, discard this alien mass, and in many cases it is easy to see how the first poem has been distorted by it. In fact, the greater epic, as it stands to-day, is so heterogeneous that only the most unhistorical type of mind could view all this heap of goods and rubbish as the product of one uniform source. Such a theory has indeed actually been suggested, but it was too fantastic to find support, and has awakened only a passing interest.

If we compare the two epics, we shall find quite a difference between them. The huge Mahabharata is seven times as long as the Iliad and Odyssey put together; the Ramayana is but a quarter as long as the Mahabharata. The Ramayana is more symmetrical, more homogeneous, and lastly it is more refined, both in its visibly polished metre and in its social atmosphere. A further distinction is to be noticed. The Bharata poem belongs to the west, the region about Delhi; the Ramayana, to the east, to Oudh, the region north of Benares. Nevertheless, the style of the two epics is in so far related as to be formed to a great extent on identical phraseology. Both epics have the same proverbs and know the same stories. All of this shows that the ancient tale of the northwest has been transplanted into the new seat of culture about Benares, and that the Mahabharata was completed where the Ramayana began. In the course of this brief survey I cannot go into the further reasons for this assumption, but I may add that all the literary indications point to this explanation, such, for example, as that the tales woven into the later epic are almost always set about the lower Ganges.

To turn from the finished product to the origin of these two poems, which arose far apart but ended in the same literary environment, of the source of the Ramayana there is little to say, for it is attributed as definitely and regularly to Valmiki as is the Æneid to Vergil, whom the Hindu author preceded by several centuries. Now, tradition ascribes the great epic also — that is, the Mahabharata (which means the great Bharata story and so may be called simply the Bharata)— to a certain Vyasa; but this Vyasa is a very shadowy person, to whom is ascribed also the arrangement of the Vedas and other works, his name meaning merely arranger or disposer. In fact, his name probably covers a guild of revisors and retellers of the tale. Moreover, there is internal evidence that the poem has been rewritten. There is, in a word, no one author of the great epic. It was handed down piece-meal at first in ancient lays. These became recitations and, united with heterogeneous material of all sorts, were at last bound together as one loosely connected whole.

The manner of presenting the primitive lays out of which arose the first epic stories was as follows: At a certain point in the performance of a sacrifice the ritual demanded that two or three singers should step forward with lutes or lyres in their hands, and, to quote verbatim from the antique directions given for the ceremony: "They shall then sing the king or some other brave hero," and the subject shall be "This king fought in such a battle," "This hero won such a victory." Here we have recorded in a formal rule of the ancient ritual the very same conditions, barring the sacrifice, as those which gave rise to the Greek epic, the *κλέα ἀνδρῶν*, the rhapsode singing them; and so, later on, we find that in India, also, the song changes to recitation. But in India, epic recitation never became a mere reading, except to the learned. It was dramatic, the reciter of the epic scene flung himself into the description with immense fervor, and it was not long before the various parts were acted, for the chief heroes of the epic were deified, and so had the scenes of their earthly life represented as a religious service. The very earliest mention of such epic-dramatic plays is in connection with the chief hero of the Mahabharata, and his godly exploits.

I should be glad to give you a description of one of these mediæval mystery plays — mediæval means in India about 200 B.C. — as it is preserved to us in the account of a native scholar, who by the merest chance, as he is explaining an involved point of grammar, illustrates what he means by quotations from the life of the day, and in so doing gives us a pretty clear idea of the play which serves him as illustration. The painted actors, the masks, the dramatic killing of the foe of the divine hero, are all plainly put before us by this happy accident. But the details would take too much time and they belong rather to the history of the drama. They show, however, that the extant Hindu epic may have come in part from the drama. We must, in fact, enlarge our definitions of epos and drama in dealing with India. The lay once recited became therewith dramatic. There was thus drama before the drama, and these drama-recitations, instead of simply repeating old material, added to it and so created new epic scenes. For probably there were always such plays of demigod-heroes, just as we find them in village life to-day, as they were depicted 200 B.C., and as they are referred to in Buddhistic works.

To sum up what we know in regard to the origin and growth of the two epics. Various considerations show that while the Mahabharata as a completed whole is later than the Ramayana, in origin it is older. The former, for example, is the epic first mentioned in the literature. It is impossible to assign exact dates to either epic, but while the lays on which the Mahabharata was based probably revert to a much older period, in its present shape even the narrative part cannot be older than the second or third century B. C., and its didactic masses are still later. Apart from the didactic fungus that has grown upon it, the great epic is derived both from lays and dramatic legends (recitations), worked together by various revisors. It has no one author. The

Ramayana, on the other hand, is the work of a poet familiar with the older epic style, which he improves upon, for Valmiki was the first writer of what used to be called elegant poetry. The Hindus call it Artistic Poetry, Kavya, in distinction from the rougher epic, which is simply Akhyana or Tale. Valmiki himself was very likely a contemporary of Apollonius, though the material he used was undoubtedly older.

Finally, one word about the metres. Both poems, as I have already said, have embellishments or fancy metres sometimes added to, rarely inserted in, the different sections of the poem. But the staple metres are a development of the Vedic octosyllabic measure, called çloka, for example:

kathaṁ samabhavad dyūtam bhrātṝṇāṁ tan mahātyayam
yatra tad vyasanam prāptam Pāṇḍavāir me pitāmahaih,

and besides this the trishtubh, a verse of eleven syllables, having in most cases the rhythm of Horace's verse, *trahunt que siccas machinæ carinas*, but much more plastic. In the use of these metres the Ramayana varies but slightly from the later classic usage of Kalidasa, whereas the Mahabharata is very much freer and in part admits the older license found in Vedic verse.

But I think by this time you will incline to hear something of the epic story itself, rather than of its setting.

The plot of the great epic, the Bharata, is simply this. The old royal house of Kurus, living at Hastina on the northern Ganges, become jealous of the rising fame of the house of Pandus, who are the cousins of the Kurus, living at Indraplain (Delhi), and the Kurus plot to overthrow the Pandus by unfair means. For this purpose the king of Hastina, called the Invincible, avails himself of the magic power of Çakuni (*i. e.* the Hawk), who knows how to play dice better than any man living. Nowadays we should say simply that the Hawk played with loaded dice, but in those times he was said to cheat by being a magician and by keeping the demon of the dice under his control. He challenges the Pandu emperor (Battlestrong) to gamble, and as an Aryan knight the latter cannot honorably refuse to accept a challenge either to fight or to play. This Pandu Battlestrong has just been crowned emperor, "All-conqueror," and his rank is higher than his cousin's, the king's, but he comes willingly to Hastina on his cousin's invitation, and very bravely loses everything he has, and is banished with his wife and four brothers. Then the Pandus plot and plan and at last get allies and have a great war and kill all the wicked Kurus, and so live happy ever after. Into this poem has been woven, as I have already said, a mass of tales, such as that of Nala, and pious discourses, such as the famous Bhagavad Gita; but I must pass by these accretions and, to show the character of the real poem, I will translate one specimen. There is nothing in this extract, I think, that needs explanation. It gives the gambling scene at the beginning of the epic. You know that an Oriental despot may sell or gamble his family into slavery. I have already said that the dice are governed by a demon (called Kali) whom the wicked Hawk, Çakuni, has under control. The dice are called Kali's eyes or heart and are made of cowrie shells. The scene opens as the sly king of Hastina sits down to play with his cousin, the noble-hearted Battlestrong, his emperor. Of the brothers, who are gambled away, none is so conspicuous as Arjun, the Silver Knight, who is the ideal and perfect warrior of the epic. Krishna the heroine (in so far as this epic may be said to have a heroine) is the polyandrous wife of the brothers; but this feature is repressed as much as possible and in fact Krishna appears as the best loved wife of the emperor. The only verses here paraphrased freely are those explaining her position, as it is explained in the original not only here but in other passages. The extract as here given shortens the original somewhat, but otherwise follows it closely, though it is not always quite literal; but it reproduces the scene as exactly perhaps as the Occident can at times imitate the Orient.

Now when the dawn awoke the earth and glory filled the sky,
As out of Night's dark prisonhold the great sun rose on high,
Then came the lords of Hastina and sought the gaming-hall,
Where two by two the elders sat — long rows about the wall.
The Hawk stood in the midst of them, beside him lay the dice,
Within the hand of Battlestrong rested a pearl of price.
"Now, Çakun, name thy stake," said he, "for here in hand I hold
A pearl, whose mother was the sea, set in a ring of gold.
It hath inestimable worth. Name thou the counter-stake."
Then quickly spoke the Invincible: "This compact first we make:
Çakun shall play, but mine the stake; his loss or gain for me;
My crown of gold against thy pearl, whose mother was the sea."
"Strange compact this," said Battlestrong, and lingered ere he played;
But in his hand he took the shells. "What odds to me," he said,
"Who throws the dice in an honest game? Much skill have I of heaven.
Stake but enough and play me fair; I seal the compact given."
He flung the shells, down leaped the dice, their master's heart they knew;
With trembling haste they hid their best, their worst remained in view.
"Now mine the throw," false Çakun said, and took the dice in hand.
The heart of Kali shook with fear to feel his soft command.
The dice, obedient to his will, rolled on the table tossed;
The Hawk looked up at Battlestrong: "Lo! emperor, thou hast lost."
"My chariot next," said Battlestrong; "eight steeds thereto, well loved,
And gold piled in, against this pearl that traitor to me proved."
The dice upon the table rang, by magic turned and crossed,
They rattled false from Çakun's hand. "Again, great king, and lost."
"I have at home," said Battlestrong, "a treasure-house of jars,
Unnumbered jewels in them each, with each a hundred bars
Of heavy gold. Now thousands stake and wager like a king."
Quoth Çakuni, "Our Hastina against the stake ye bring."

Twice rolled the dice. "Thou losest yet," said Çakun, "try once more."
"A thousand maids," cried Battlestrong, "the fruit of joyful war,
With jewels on their bosoms hung, in costly raiment clad,
Adorned with anklets, fair to see,—these for the jars I had."
Again he threw the trembling shells, again cried Çakun, "Lost."
"Now, by the gods," said Battlestrong, "and if it kingdoms cost,
I yet will win. As many men I pledge, each man a slave
Fit for the retinue of a king, — these for the girls I gave."
Twice rolled the dice. "Lost, emperor, lost." But now an angry frown
Settled upon the emperor's face. "What fortune weighs me down
To check my skill? My cattle all, three hundred thousand kine."
Twice rolled the dice. The Hawk looked up, "Lost, emperor, all are mine."
"A thousand elephants of war, four thousand warlike steeds, —
This for my kine." The Hawk looked up,— "Lost, emperor! Now, who needs
The chariots that those chargers drew? Stake those." "Aye, be it so,"
Said Battlestrong, "a thousand cars of war, and swift to go."
The dice won all the cars of war. "What, still?" cried Battlestrong.
"But sixty thousand Aryan knights to Indraplain belong.
I stake the knights." "And lose them, sire," cried Çakun, "Now the rest,
For every knight retainers hath, and human stakes are best."
Or fear'st thou further play?" he sneered. "Fear?" said the emperor, "all
I stake, till nothing more remains, my riches great and small,
To win whatever I have lost. Can emperors be afraid?
Nay, never have I shrunk from man, whatever casts he played."
The Hawk's eye smote upon the shells like sun on quaking frost,
Again they trembled, rolled, and turned,— "Lo! all is played and lost."

(Except his own family, Battlestrong played everything he had on the last throw.)

Then spoke aside to the Kuru king his counsellor Vidur,—
"Forbid the play; stop while ye may, for sorrow, be ye sure,
Will follow on the track of gain. This Hawk is false at heart.
What mean ye, then, to leave your kin? What think ye? Will they part
Thus calmly from the greatest throne god Indra looks upon?
Now hearken to a wise man's words, for all your wits are gone.
Ye stand above a precipice, and see not to your feet;
Your gain is loss; your winnings, death; for Justice's steps are fleet.
What though our Aryan law prevents yon knights from speaking now,
And if until the emperor stop they still must smile and bow
Before the madness of their king? Think ye, when once 't is done,
That they will hand ye Indraplain? 'T is no man's skill hath won.
What if these honest fools at last see straight? Stop while ye may,
Or long shall Hastina lament the playing played to-day."
Up flared the wrath of Hastina: "Whate'er we Kurus do
Is nobly done. Go, leave the hall; my crown is small for two.
Who made thee king of Hastina? I rule myself alone.
My will shall be my counsellor. Leave thou the Kurus' throne."

(I shorten somewhat the dispute here. The emperor's brothers stand gathered about the gaming-table.)

"All hail the great All-conqueror," the Hawk said, "much is won,
And all is lost; so now, methinks, the emperor's game is done."
"Lost, all is lost?" said Battlestrong. "Who mocks an emperor's game?
And who will check me when I play for victory and for fame?
I play — my crown? Nay, that I lost. But much is left to me.
Eldest am I, their emperor, too; my brothers still are free."
He spoke, but stumbled in his speech. Then cried the Hawk again,
"Now, bravo, true All-conqueror, behold, we play like men.

Here's Nakul, worth a host of slaves, for him the dice be tossed."
The dancing cowries touched the board, the prince was played and lost.
"The next of age," said Battlestrong, "and he is good and brave;
Aye, virtuous and obedient, he, my pledge is Sahadev."
The dice won all the virtues of Sahadev the good.
Loud laughed the Hawk and stroked the dice: "Long gaming have we stood.
Thy youngest brothers now are lost. It is a heroes' fight.
And so, once more, the next of age, play thou the Silver Knight."
A horror seized on Battlestrong; he felt his brain grow weak;
But drunk with gaming was his soul, he forced himself to speak:
"I play the Knight and all he hath," he muttered to the Hawk,
But on the table held his gaze lest aught his fortune balk.
He trembled like the writhing dice; he dared meet no man's eye.
The Silver Knight in speechless pride stood motionless thereby,
Too loyal to his brother's throne to question or to doubt;
His life and freedom were the king's till the king's game was out.
Into the air they flung the dice for the high-hearted knight,
For his great bow Gandiva and for his horn of might.
The eyes of Kali won the Knight and all that he held dear,
The great horn Devadatta, whose sounding sendeth fear,
The bow Gandiva wrought in heaven, the steeds th' immortals gave,
And Arjuna the Pandus' pride became the Kurus' slave.

(So then the next brother is played and lost.)

"Is there yet more," cried Çakuni, "a brother or such thing,
Or has he now in truth no more, who lately was our king?"
"King am I still," cried Battlestrong; "I have myself to lose.
I Battlestrong play Battlestrong, no challenge I refuse."
Once more upon the table's groove danced Kali's eyes aflame;
Once more the Hawk looked laughing up: "Th' All-conqueror hath his name.
All else is lost. Oh, foolish stake, there being aught beside,
To play thyself, forgetting her who still remains, thy bride.
Then stake thy Krishna, win with her all that is lost and mine.
'T is but a little pledge to lay, this youthful queen of thine.

We hear she hath the lucky signs, a favorite of the gods;
It were not wonderful if she, so wondrous, changed the odds."
Now as he spoke, the wily foe, and waited for the word,
The cheeks of the four brothers blanched; they trembled as they heard.
For what themselves as slaves might meet was what brave knights may bear,
But Krishna was the sacred love of all, not only fair
Beyond all fairness known on earth, but hers this heavenly dower—
To bind unwilling every heart with more than beauty's power.
For lovely she, and well beloved, yet not for beauty loved
So much as for her winsome grace, which all men strangely moved,
And for the gentle kindliness that crowned her more than queen,
And made her perfect in all eyes as none had ever been.
Still paused the king. The crafty words were buzzing in his brain.
"'T is but a throw of dice," he thought, "and all is mine again."
"A little pledge?" he muttered low, "nay, Krishna's form is tall.
How stately she, how beautiful to hold man's heart in thrall!
Her eyes like autumn-lotus shine, her form surpasses praise,
Welcome as autumn welcome is after long summer days;
Gentlest and fairest, dearest— Nay! If all save her is gone—
Lo! I am Battlestrong and king and cannot yield. Play on."
The dice for Krishna's fate were flung,—again the emperor lost.
"Joy!" cried the king of Hastina, "now let their arms be crossed;
Strip off their silks, these new-made slaves." The voices of the old
Quavered across the gaming-hall and some were overbold
And cried out "Shame!" but sternly spoke th' Invincible to all:
"This is no people's conference" (he said), "and kingly hall
Is built for kings; let no man speak." Then shrank they back dismayed,
While the dull light of evil thought o'er their lord's features played.
"Bring forth," he cried, "this whilom queen." To her of noble birth
Prince Hardheart ran. The Pandus five bowed them in shame to earth.

But to the woman's inner court sped fast that soul of sin,
And burst into queen Krishna's room, who sat half-robed within.
"Thy lord will see thee in the hall, now come without thy veil."
She looked at him with wondering eyes; her heart began to quail.
She drew her veil across her face; she turned to him again:
"Prince, go and ask of Battlestrong if I be seen of men."
Before her virtue cowered the prince, but answered: "Say'st thou so?
Thy lord is king of Hastina, he speaks and thou must go;
For Battlestrong staked first himself upon the cowries' cast,
And when that maddest throw had failed he staked and lost thee last."
Then answered she, "Not lost am I whom Aryan law will save,
If Battlestrong before he threw had made himself a slave.
For slaves possess nor gold nor child nor wife; then how could he
Who first enslaved himself at dice, possession claim in me?
Back, Hardheart, to the elders go, and say thou com'st again,
To know if I be slave of slave or queen of Indraplain."

(The point raised here, in strict accordance with the law that a slave could not own a wife, plays a great part in the later development of the epic.)

He bore her question to the hall and not an elder spoke,
They were as mute as docile cows beneath the wagon's yoke.
But taunting cried th' Invincible: "Who ruleth here, good prince?
Thy king hath spoken, thine to act; or does brave Hardheart wince
Before the tongue of servile shrew?" Then angry back he fled.
He seized fair Krishna by the arms and raised them o'er her head,
He stripped the covering from her face, he tore her linen down,
He bared her body to the waist and left her half a gown.

(I omit part of the description here.)

But at the door fear mastered pride; her lips with terror shook,
"Not this," she cried, "oh, prince, not this; how may I living brook

The eyes of men beneath a robe that is but nakedness?"
"What odds," he cried, "what slaves may brook or what a slave's distress?
Thou art the common wife of slaves." Then said she nothing more;
But Hardheart grasped her by the locks and dragged her through the door.
"Now let us see this beauty rare," exclaimed the Kuru king.
"Is this the Pandus' famous spouse, of whom the poets sing?
Ill suits her such a wretched garb; tear off that ragged dress,
And let us see this half-hid form if it have loveliness."

Base Hardheart clutched her by the waist and would the knot set free
That men her unprotected form from head to foot might see.
But she that was so pure of heart, who ne'er had offered wrong
To modest thought or wifely due, stood up before the throng
Helpless, while on her stricken lords fell her despairing eye.
She saw them helpless as herself; then rose her piercing cry
To God in heaven, "Save, Vishnu, save, help Thou the Pandus' queen.
If ever I have loved Thy law and ever constant been
In thought and speech and action true — hide Thou my form and face.
God, save Thy loyal worshipper, and spare me this disgrace."
Then lo, a wonder sent from heaven — for ere her garment fell
A cloud-like veil in countless folds enwrapped her close and well.
But fear came on them as they gazed, beholding how she stood,
By man forsaken, saved of God, in stainless womanhood.

This is not the end of this scene, but it is too long to complete, and what I have given will suffice to show that the great epic of India is not without a certain dramatic interest. Before passing on to the Ramayana I would add that this scene, which is the beginning of the real epic, is prefaced by an invocation to the Divine Bard, who tells the whole tale, an invocation (the text is given in part in the çloka above on p. 71) which reminds us of the opening of the Iliad, in that the game of dice is brought at once into the foreground as the cause of woe. The poem is related to the descendant in the third generation:

What caused the game, that fatal game,
  The Pandus' grief and overthrow,
Wherein my father's sire took part
  And won for winnings only woe?
What kings, O thou divinest bard,
  Assembled there to judge the game,
And who beholding it rejoiced,
  And who to hinder sorrow came?
This story would I hear thee tell
  In full, O thou of heavenly birth.
For this was that destruction's root
  Which grew to overwhelm the earth,
What time the emperor Battlestrong
  Rested in Indraplain at ease,
When he the All-conqueror's name had won
  After long wars and victories.

The Ramayana, like the Mahabharata, has a later prefixed book of *les enfances*, after which the real drama begins. The plot of this poem also, like that of all good epics, is simple.

Daçaratha, King of Oudh, having grown old, gives up, after the custom of the country, his royal power to his heir, who is naturally Rama his eldest son and also the son of the eldest wife. But Kaikeyi, a younger wife, has a son Bharata, who is next of age. Now Manthara, a dwarf serving-maid, persuades Kaikeyi to plot against Rama and put Kaikeyi's own son on the throne. The opening part of the epic explains how this plot is effectually carried out. Manthara, the maid, hears the rumor that Rama is to be consecrated that very day and rushes in to her mistress, queen Kaikeyi, with this startling information.

I begin at this point, condensing the first part somewhat, but otherwise following the original.

"Hast heard the news," she cried, "the dangerous news?"
"What news?" Kaikeyi asked, but Manthara swift
And angrily answered, "News? why, news of kings.
Awake, my queen, awake, for 't is proclaimed
That Daçarath thy lord (who loved thee once),
Resigns his throne this very day to Rama,
That son he truly loves." To whom the queen
Unmoved replied, "Truly 't is unexpected
That this should come so soon, but long expected
That this should happen; either now or then —
What matters when? Why wake me for such tale?
Could this not wait? Nay, I rejoice to hear
The happy news, for Rama Bharat loves,
And Bharata loves him, nor see I aught
Of danger here." Then wrothful cried the dwarf:
"O foolish queen, a rival's son to love
More than thine own, who sure is nobler far,
And were himself made king, being next born
After this Rama, did nor Rama live
And bar his way to royalty, — but now
Bharat must live inglorious." — "What, thou fool,"
The queen replied, "and is it then disgrace
To be a younger son?" "Nay, queen, in faith,
'T is not a shame," she answered, "yet if Bharat
Could set his fate aside and reach the throne,
'T were so much more a glory. O my queen,
Act, ere the time be past." Now speaking thus
She stirred the queen, within whose eyes a fire
New-lighted burned, and thus Kaikeyi spoke:
"Thy wit is keen. If any way I knew
To compass this, be sure I should not falter —
But how leave Rama out? Aye, if the gods,
Remembering all that I have done for them,
Had but in turn proved kind, some lucky hap
Might well have changed the scale; I know not what,
Rama's rash bravery or his father's whim,
One of the thousand oft-appearing turns
That mar young princes' fortunes — but to-day
I see no hope." "Yet I," cried Manthara, "I,

Who love thee well, had I but known before,
Had soon devised a plan, and even now —
Listen, my lady, did'st thou not one day
Tell me, aye, surely thou did'st tell me, thus:
The king was in thy chamber, as I think,
And dallying with thee. Was there not a boon
He granted thee, not named, but to be claimed
Thereafter, as thou would'st? 'T was years ago,
And yet methinks I still remember it.
Recall the boon. 'T was not a simple promise
Such as men make to women and forget,
But sworn to by the gods and by the soul
Of him that promised. Claim that boon to-day.
Tell Daçaratha he is bound by oaths
To grant the boon, and say: 'This boon I ask:
Let Rama banished be for fourteen years,
To roam the woods that south of Ganges lie,
And Bharat in his stead be king of Oudh,
Till Rama doth return,'— if he return.
Distrust it not, the plan will work the cure.
For Daçaratha is a weak old man,
Else had he never thus surrendered power;
And well he knows he stands upon the road
That leads direct to the gods, the gods he swore by.
A younger man, stronger and far from death,
Might disregard those deities. Short of murder,
Which were a crime to overpass his strength,
He will not break his oath. Remember, lady,
That ancient proverb, which all men repeat —
'Man reaches perfect joy but once in life.'
Seize now thy joy. And here 's another saw:
'The water 's gone and now he builds the dike.'
Ah, queen, or e'er the water of success
Be utterly gone, bestir thyself."

Then spoke
With rapturous haste Kaikeyi: "O dear dwarf,
Let others call thee hideous, but to me
Most beauteous thou for this thy beauteous thought.
I do believe thou read'st the king aright,

For he was ever most intent on gods,
Pious past all belief, and now so old,
Weak as thou say'st — aye, truly, 't is a chance.
I shall risk much; but if the trick succeed,
Then ask *me* boons. Go, Manthara, call the king,
Tell him I'm sick and in the chamber of wrath
Have hid myself and lie upon the floor
In uncontrollable weeping. Strip my arms
And bosom of jewels, fetch my saddest robe;
Go call the king; tell him thou knowest not
Wherefore I weep, but thrill his heart with fear
Of some vague trouble, bid him hasten. Go!"
She spoke, the maid obeyed, and, as they planned,
Kaikeyi, stripped of all her jewels, lay
Fair as a goddess on the chamber floor,
With heart aflame but wrapped in seeming grief.

I omit here a Sarga, wherein is described how the hunchback executes her mission. She calls the king, and the latter comes to the chamber of wrath, — a boudoir or sulk-room, — finds the queen, Kaikeyi, prostrate on the ground, and at sight of her beauty and wretchedness feels himself smitten afresh with the arrows of love. He asks her very gently why she is angry. The poem continues: —

Then spoke the queen Kaikeyi to Daçarath,
The aged king whom Love still pierced with darts:
"Thou hast not vexed me. 'T is not anger holds
Thy queen to sorrow, but my heart 's a wish
Not yet accomplished, therefore lie I here,
Grieving. So now, if thou indeed dost love,
Fill this desire. But never ask, dear lord,
For what I long; which I will then reveal
When this my wish is granted. For so much
I have it at heart, that only this one thing
I make that boon, which, as thou wilt remember,
Long given I ne'er have claimed."

Thereat the king
Looked tenderly upon her as she lay
In the beauty of tears and fingered her long hair
Loosenèd in supplication, while he spoke:
"O doubting heart, and wilt thou never learn
How Daçaratha loves thee? On this earth
There is none dearer unto me than thou
Excepting Rama. By his head I swear —"

You will notice here that we have a case of real "dramatic irony." The epic has in fact the very form and action of a drama in these vivid scenes.

"Excepting Rama. By his head I swear
To grant whate'er thou askest, aye, by him
My dearest son, the pride of my proud race,
In whom I live, whom not to see were death,
By him I swear. From out my bosom pluck
The heart if 't is thy pleasure; take what else;
But doubt me never; e'en as I trust thee,
So shouldst thou trust thy lover. Have thy wish.
The boon is granted and I renew the bond."
When thus the king lay fairly in her net
Up sprang the queen and spake:
"Shouldst thou refuse
Now thou hast sworn, lo, I myself will die,
And this shall be foul murder on thy head.
So hear my wish. Thou consecratest Rama.
Bid that this consecration cease, and turn
The holy rites to Bharata, my son.
But as for Rama, for nine years and five
Let him be banished unto the forest dark
Of Dandaka, that south of Ganges lies.
In deer-skin clothed, a hermit let him live.
But king of Oudh before the sun goes home
Let Bharat be proclaimed. Behold, the boon,
Granted already, thus I name; which thou,
As thou lov'st truth and honor, consummate,
Or be forever that accursèd thing,
A king that breaks his oath."

So Kaikeyi;
But while she spoke, as were he in a dream,
The king upon her gazed. So looks a deer
One moment shocked to stillness as he sees
A tigress crouch. Then like an angry snake,
Which, fury-blind and raging, but encharmed,
Still helpless writhes, within its circle bound,
Whence no escape, he hissed: "Thou traitress vile
What ill hath Rama done thee? What have I?
Like his own mother hath he treated thee,
Thou poison-hiding viper that unknown
I deemed a thing divine. What, Rama, Rama?
My best loved son, my soul, my very self,
My life, my all? Nay, surely 't is a trick
To test my love for Bharat. What, no trick?
O oath that I have sworn, O beast that hold'st
My heart within thy fangs, what prayer can move
Thy savage spirit? Is any bitter means
Of self-abasement open? As for me,
I shrink at naught that promises me shame,
If but that shame protect the son I love.
See me, Kaikeyi, as before the gods
Suppliant I lie, who never begged before.
Be pitiful, queen, unsay the spoken word.
The king of Oudh I kneel, a poor old man,
Entreating only mercy. Take thou all
I have; my realm from east to western ocean
Extends its wealth to thee. Take all save this.
Look where I lie beseeching, I, the king —
My tears are on thy feet."

So, whelmed in grief,
Babbling his woe, lay the great king of Oudh.
But him the queen Kaikeyi, full of scorn
And wrath, addressed:

"Ask mercy of the gods
If thou dare break thine oath. Hark, Daçarath.
Thou hast lived long, and ever 't was thy boast
To honor truth and virtue. Was all this
But idle words? And shortly, when thou seest

The gods in heaven, what wilt thou answer them,
If they shall question — 'She to whom I swore
Sits cheated of her oath'? O shameless king!
Nay, having promised, thou art bound. Why whine
Like a base beggar, crouching here for alms
He ne'er will get? Shall I surrender now?
I yield no single particle of this oath.
Hear, all ye gods, who witnessed what he swore,
Ye gods to whom this impious wretch would lie,
Witness for me if Daçarath keep his word
Or prove a perjurer in the face of heaven.
Behold! They hear me, all the heavenly host,
Who know thy oath. Thou dar'st not break the oath.
'T is mine, 't is mine, I claim the boon intact.
Bharat shall reign." But as she spoke, the king
Sank at her feet and fainted where he lay.

You must not imagine, however, that the whole epic is carried out in this intense fashion. The scenes immediately following are, it is true, also dramatic. The king revives. There is a fine scene where he tells Rama what has happened, and Rama, despite the entreaties of his mother and the urgent request of his brother and friends that he should resist, declares that he will carry out to the full the letter of the oath, even when Daçaratha dies of grief, as happens soon after. The virtuous Bharata, when he learns of the circumstances, will not consent to reign. Finally as Rama insists on fulfilling the king's promise and leaves the city with his young wife Sita, Bharata consents only to act as his viceroy during his absence, and as a sign of submission to Rama, he wears the latter's sandals on his head, a protest against his own elevation. But after these city scenes, which are more or less dramatic, the poet or poets who rewrote the epic give a long interlude which is less dramatic than idyllic. Rama's wife and his faithful brother Lakshman go with him, the latter as a fidus Achates, and they pass several years in hermit life. The situation is rather difficult, for as the poet has to indicate a long lapse of time ere begins the war which ends the story, there is little for him to say except to describe an occasional feat of Rama's, and so he spends a good deal of time in reporting the conversations between Rama, his wife, and his brother. It is especially these scenes which make the Ramayana a romantic epic in contrast with the heroic style of the older epos. Sita is a charming creation, an unaffected innocent and devoted young wife, eighteen years old, who worships Rama; but she often appears as a mere lay figure, listening while Rama makes love to her or explains the beauty of the scenery. There is a great deal of sentimentality, but most of it is contained in descriptions of nature. At Citrakuta, for example, one complete Sarga (with only a few repetitive verses omitted) is as follows:

There dwelt he long and for the mountain felt
A true affection. And oft his wife to please
And his own mind distract, as might the king
Of all the heavenly gods show to his spouse
The joys of heaven, so Rama showed to Sita
The mountain Citrakuta, saying: "Lo,
Not loss of rank nor absence from my friends
Distress my heart, who view this lovely hill.
See how this mountain rises toward the sky
With glittering peaks and bright with various birds.
Here silver white the rocks, red, yellow, there,
Some crystal and some topaz, some like flowers;
Some gleam like mercury or a distant star,
Gemming this glorious mountain, through whose shade
Wander the wild beasts, tigers, bears, hyenas,
And deer they harm not. Many too the birds;
And see again the trees, whose flower and fruit
And wealth of leaves are here displayed — the mango,
Pippal and tamarind, with the great bamboo,
Love-apples, fig-trees, citrons — all are here,
While bright cascades leap broken down the hill.
What man but joyed to smell this cave-born breeze
Laden with scent of blossoms? Many autumns

With thee, O perfect one, and Lakshman here,
Devoid of sorrow could I live. I love
This beauteous mountain filled with flowers and birds.
And dost thou, Sita, too rejoice with me
To dwell in Citrakuta, seeing all
These various things that make for our delight,
The rocks of many colors, red, green, black,
The plants and shrubs that gleam a thousand fold
On every side, the glittering peak above?
All here is loveliness — here let the years
Glide past us, quickly numbered, as we bide,
I, thou, and Lakshman in this dear retreat.
For living here with him and thee
Joy will be ours and greater fame,
The oath my father swore be kept,
And honored be our name."

The last stanza I have rhymed and set in a different metre to show that the poet here, as he very often does elsewhere, changes the rhythm in the final stanza of the canto. The rhyme itself does not actually occur in this place; but in many other passages we find not only the weak rhyme of assonance, but a pure rhyme, sometimes extending over several of the rhythmic periods.

But to continue: After a time, while Rama is away, Sita is carried off by a giant. Her recapture forms the plot of the latter part of the epic. Here we have a very interesting analogy with the plot of the Iliad. Just as Helen is carried to Troy, so Sita is carried to Lanka, and her outraged husband with his faithful brother forms an alliance with the ruler of a South Indian kingdom (where the men, to the higher Aryan type of the North, appear like apes and are actually spoken of as such), besieges Lanka and wins Sita back. A whole book is devoted to the battles that take place on the plain which surrounds the city. As in the Iliad, the king of Lanka comes out on the city walls and inquires the names of the different heroes, though the conventions of Hindu social life do not permit Sita to appear, as does Helen in the Iliad. She is kept in the women's part of the city, and it is a spy who has gone and returned that tells the king. And as Achilles could be wounded only in the heel, so Ravana (but he is here the ravisher) cannot be killed except by a mortal's hand. This has led some scholars to suppose that the Hindu epic was influenced by the Greek model. But such similarities are not striking enough to prove right this audacious attempt to deprive India of her native epic. For my part I should be glad to believe it, for just as soon as this turn of affairs takes place we are plunged into a series of endless battles and fighting-scenes which, to say it with the fear of the Greeks before my eyes, are just as tedious as are the fighting-scenes in the Iliad. I shall give you no specimens of this kind of epic writing, which is common to both Indian epics. You know it already, how one hero fights till he dies and then another fights in just the same way, the warriors being described in the same old phrases, and doing the same impossible things. The Hindu genius is, however, more extravagant than that of the Greek. For here we have not only giants who think nothing of picking up a mountain and hurling it on a foeman, but even foemen who, though to be sure really shocked by the mountain falling on them, yet bravely survive. But as in Homer, not only do they not die when they ought to, these interminable heroes, but even after we have conducted them through several cantos of myriad darts and crushing mountains, and have at last with a great sigh of relief reached the place where the poet lets them expire, we find presently, to our dismay, that without any warning or explanation of where they come from, they pop up again on the battlefield, as fresh and lively as ever, and have to be killed all over again. This is monotonous and tiresome. It is, however, according to the taste of an earlier age, and we should be as foolish to criticise adversely such battle-scenes as to condemn fairy-stories. There is only one thing to do, let them pass unread. We of this later age and western world are more for thought than for action. The ancients regarded character sketches as ancillary to a spirited tale, and if they rejoiced in giants, genii, apes, and devils, and we do not, it is our fault if we fail to appreciate their pleasure.[1]

The end of this long contest brings us face to face with another example of the difference between Occidental and Oriental notions, this time unhappily where it affects the chivalry of Rama. You must remember that Rama was robbed of Sita when he was away from his hermitage. He has only Sita's word for it that she was carried away unwillingly. She has been a long time in the ruffian's palace. When she is rescued, Rama, who has been described throughout as most devotedly attached to her and has really never doubted her innocence, thinks it incumbent upon his good name to prove that Cæsar's wife should be above suspicion. With apparent sternness he therefore bids her begone, well knowing that she will appeal to the fire-ordeal, and that her innocence will be proved to all the world by the god of fire himself. "For otherwise," he says, "the world would speak ill of my pure wife." Sita herself proposes the fire-ordeal, and after invoking the proper gods who witness truth, especially the fire-god, walks into the flame. Needless to say, she soon walks out again unharmed, to the great joy of all the bystanders, and falls into Rama's arms; nor has she any reproach to make for his putting her to this test, so I do not know that we are called upon to blame him, though the scene certainly detracts from the effect of the finale.

The poem ends here. The fourteen years are over. A kindly deity wafts the party back from South India to Oudh. Bharata is found still acting as viceroy, only too glad to relinquish the throne to Rama; and all ends well.

But now I must cut short this glimpse into an antique life, distant in space as in time, a life of desire and hope, intrigue, brutality, if you will; an unfamiliar life, where it is a point of knightly honor to accept a challenge to play as well as to

[1] Since this address was given (Jan. 1901) a very interesting study of the demonology of this epic has been published by Angelo de Gubernatis, who, in his Su le orme di Dante, has shown the possibility of indirect borrowing on the part of the Italian poet from Hindu sources.

fight, the life of a far-off people loving strange gods; but at the same time thoroughly human, and noble withal, where women are loved faithfully, where even a king may not break his oath; full of passion, but filled also with a very modern appreciation of the beauty of nature — a glimpse, I trust, not without value for us all.[1]

[1] It is of interest to notice that some of the quaint touches in the ancient epic are not unparalleled in the life of modern Hindus. Thus the episode of Bharata carrying Rama's sandals on his head may be compared with the action of Ranuji Sindia, who, about 1700, "carried the Peishwa's slippers, to contrast his original with his subsequent condition," as is narrated by Grant Duff, in his History of the Mahrattas, vol. i. p. 480. The dramatic epic has never lost its charm for the Hindu, and instances are known in modern times where military operations have been suspended that the chieftain might attend the performance of one of the Kathas, or dramatic epic recitations. Perhaps the last formal epic written in India is the long "religious metrical drama" of Padre Francisco Vaz de Guimaraes, in thirty-six cantos and containing sixteen thousand verses, representing the mysteries of the incarnation, passion, and death of Christ. It is called a Puran, or History, and was written in the corrupt Marathi dialect of Bombay, in 1659. A specimen of this Christian imitation of the favorite Hindu Katha is given in Da Cunha's Origin of Bombay (1900).

# A STUDY OF GODS.

WHAT is the origin of gods? Herbert Spencer says that they are originally ghosts, even the sky-gods and storm-gods of India. The comparative mythologist replies that all gods, even ghost-gods, are derived from a more primitive group of gods, which at bottom are personified natural phenomena. On the other hand, the interpreter of modern folk-lore asserts that the earliest gods are fairies and "spirits," and regards the ghosts of Spencer and the divine natural phenomena of Max Müller as merely magnified forms of gnomes and giants.

In this matter India is beautifully fitted to be the object of scientific research, for while Greece and Rome are, as it were, museums of the remains of dead gods, India is a divine menagerie where, still alive, are to be found all the gods or kinds of gods we read about in classical antiquity. Nor do we have to grope through literary remains for slight indications of the processes which gave rise to divinities; each process is clearly revealed in present conditions. Since, however, there is, besides this, another advantage in the fact that the still fertile folk-lore of to-day can be traced directly back through a literature more than three thousand years old, we may hope to find some light on the problem of divine origins in studying the present beliefs of the Hindu, and comparing them with his theological annals. It will, for instance, be a distinct gain if we can separate the confused mass of Hindu gods into categories distinguished by certain marked features. It will be a still greater advance if we can determine whether these categories have existed since the earliest times, and discover which gods are likely to survive a change of home.

GODS OF PHENOMENA. If I begin with the gods of personified natural phenomena, it is not from a wish to lay undue weight upon this category, but because these divinities occupy the most prominent position in the oldest records. From the hymns of the Rig Veda we learn that the first gods of this class were Dyaus, that is Zeus; Ushas, that is Eos, *aurora;* Agni, that is *ignis;* and Soma, the moon-plant, Persian *haoma.* They who deny the primitive character of sky-gods are compelled to assume that Father Sky was an imitation or transfer from another class. But this is opposed to the earliest account of Aryan civilization, wherein Father Sky, or the Sky-Father, appears as a god so antique that his name is preserved in Greece, Rome, and India.[1] Other similar cases of primitive deified phenomena might be added, such as Sun and Mother Earth, but it is sufficient to establish the class. By imperceptible degrees we may pass from these gods to others, which, while they are no less personified natural phenomena, are usually grouped in different classes, even by those who postulate one origin for them all. Such are not only sun and clouds, but mountains, rivers, trees, and stones. Without any hard-and-fast line of demarcation, these, again, stand grouped with such divine beings as battle-axes and war-drums. Some of these are personified natural phenomena; and some we may prefer to call personified unnatural phenomena. But they are all alike in this, and differ in this from the gods of other categories, that they are objective phenomena, which, though devoid of recognizable individual volition, yet seem to possess the power to harm or benefit at will. To prefix the word "personified" to this general group is really unnecessary. To the early Aryan, as to primitive peoples generally, the notion that things are not persons, not the idea of personified things, would have appeared new and startling. But there is nothing peculiarly antique about this point of view. The modern Hindu villager regards everything as alive and animate. Rain and hail are not only sent by a cloud deity; they are themselves conscious and have volition. If a hail-

[1] Zeus-pater, Ju-piter, Dyaus-pitar.

stone wishes, he (to speak with the native) will injure a flower-bed; but if the hailstone sees a knife set up over the flower-bed he will turn one side to avoid it.

As late as our era, it was still the belief of the educated in India that mountains and rivers were alive, and could propagate their species. Both these divinities are exalted in the Vedas and are regarded as true gods. To-day they are still revered in the same way. The peasant prays to them, and believes they are instrumental in his welfare. Moreover, it made no difference to the Vedic believer whether the object he worshipped was natural or artificial. Thus he worshipped the sword, the furrow, the mill-stone, just as to-day every artisan worships his tool, every gardener his spade, every farmer his plough. This is, therefore, not totem-worship. It is in some cases fetish-worship; but it is impossible to draw a hard-and-fast line between fetishism and the worship of natural phenomena. The deity of a hill is the hill itself in the first instance; but in India, especially in the North, — where, to the eye, the hills pass into mountains, the mountains pass into cloud, and the cloud into sky, — the plastic nature of this belief is especially well preserved. Exactly as the peasant worships the sky-god, cloud-god, and mountain-god, so he worships the god of an uncouth rock, and the god of a strangely shaped pebble, which he may carry with him. Each is a spirit in phenomenon or phenomenon personified, for the native villager or tribesman makes absolutely no distinction in this regard.

All this by no means forbids the assumption that a deity of this class may become a deity of another class. It is curious to see that, in the most striking case of this sort in modern times, in contravention of Spencer's theory, the Vedic sun-god, who shows not a trace of having been the spirit of a mortal, but was first worshipped simply as the hot red ball in the sky, is to-day worshipped in many districts as the soul of a dead Raja, though elsewhere he still maintains essentially his Vedic position.

The chief gods in India originating in personified phenomena are those of which I have already spoken, — sky, earth, sun, moon, clouds, storm (lightning), mountains, rivers, trees, and also stars. The worship of the last is as old as the Rig Veda, but it is not so pronounced as in later times, when astrology came to aid stellar divinity. At a later period, stars were revered not only as celestial deities, but as the homes of the souls of the dead, and finally as the self-luminous souls themselves. Only in modern times and in a restricted area appears the belief that stars are the sheep of the shepherd moon. Storm-gods are early creations, and modern gods of the same sort show that they may be made independently of ghosts, although it is perfectly true that the ghosts of certain well-known people are also revered as storm-devils to-day in some localities. But apart from these there is the modern "East-wind" god, openly revered and placated as a mere physical phenomenon, and the whirlwind-god Bagalya, who is as purely physical as the Vedic "one-footed" god of the cyclone or water-spout, whichever he may be. So in the epic, Kundadhara is at the same time a "water-bearing" cloud and an intelligent godling, who bows down to the great gods and talks with them.[1]

Tree-worship has been the object of much extravagant speculation, but the true explanation has been given by the author of "The Golden Bough," who says that trees are no exception to the rule that the savage in general regards the whole world as animate. Certain trees, because they are favorites of certain gods, are particularly holy, and others are holy because they are totems and ancestors; but trees are in general divine (apart from their dryad spirits)[2] and especially any useful or beautiful tree. The same is true of plants, many holy plants being medicinally valuable and therefore sacred.

[1] Mahabharata, xii. 272.

[2] This was a point debated by Brahmans and Buddhists. The Buddhist denied that the tree itself was animate, and admitted only a "spirit in the tree." The Brahman recognized a tree-spirit, but also a spiritual, animate tree as well.

There are in Hindu literature other divinities of this class which may be called poetical gods. Such are Day, Night, Twilight, the Year, the Fortnight, and other phases of time and the moon. They are chiefly poetical or ritualistic, but some of them in a more or less veiled form are actually worshipped to-day. Thus the Year and his sister Holi, the Spring, are worshipped, and so is Nissi, Night. In Vedic times worship was paid to the remains of sacrifice, because it had been in contact with the gods. "Even a stone," it is said in the Hitopadeça, "becomes a god when set up by priests." So, to-day, the ignorant priest worships not only the stone idol, but even the iron chain which hangs in his temple. The chain itself is a real and separate god because it has been in contact with the divine. Anything peculiar in itself becomes a god; anything, again, that has been connected with a god, though not in itself peculiar, becomes a divinity. Thus from the earliest Vedic period we have the worship of amulets and talismans, partly as being useful in themselves, partly as having been associated with useful divinities, whose power they have, so to speak, imbibed and retained.

Gods of the Imagination. The gods of the next category are invisible spirits, malevolent or benevolent, which aid or injure man. Such are the giants, fairies, and sprites, which, from the Vedic period onwards, have affected man's welfare without being referred by him to other origin than that of pure fancy. Here it is necessary to distinguish carefully between ghost-spirits and such sprites as have been defined. The Rig Veda recognizes the difference. It has a special cult of ghosts, but at the same time it has a cult of fairies. "One hears strange noises and sees strange sights in the woods after dark,— that is the Maiden of the Forest." This belief in gnomes and fairies is synchronous with the worship of sky-gods. Just as to-day the peasant worships the great invisible gods, but reveres no less these invisible spirits, so he has always done, as far back as literary evidence extends. As these *numina* are all more or less alike, it is only necessary to point out that, apart from pure creations of fancy, there are demons which are ghosts. These ghost-giants, again, are sometimes confounded with phenomenal deities. A very good example of what may result from such confusion is given by the figure of Bhimsena. He is first a national hero. Then he is revered as a ghost-god. Then he is revered again as a storm-god. Some malevolent spirits of modern times are clearly and historically ghosts of well-known men, like the village gods known as Birs, Latin *vir*, that is, Heroes. But, on the other hand, there remain many spirits which are not the remains of a mortal. Again, some fairies are phenomena. Such are the Apsarasas, which, as their name shows, are "water-nymphs," scarcely to be differentiated from divine water revered as a divinity. But their consorts, the angelic Gandharvas, appear to be dissociated from all material substance, though at a late period they are identified with the stars.

Both these sorts of divinities are Vedic. Soon after, and perhaps really synchronous with them, appear the Yakshasas, beautiful genii, chiefly of the woods, creations of the imagination; the Rakshasas, gigantic fiends; and the little Bhuts, "beings," or demons whose type is Vetala, a Bhut that is to-day in process of becoming identified with the greatest god in the pantheon. The ancient Vedic spirits of this class, Daityas and Danavas, are still religiously worshipped as Daits and Danos. On the other hand, the bright Devas of the Veda, gods of natural phenomena, have now been generally reduced to the condition of Bhuts, and under the modern name of Deo are worshipped as insignificant spirits. Dyaus himself became in the epic period a sort of Hermes, famous chiefly for his skill in thieving. It is, therefore, impossible to say in each and every case that a spirit or fairy has always been what it is to-day. But, on the other hand, since in the earliest times the spirits of the dead are distinguished from the Bhuts, and the latter are looked upon through the whole course of literature as unembodied spirits or sprites and nothing more, exactly as they are regarded to-day, it is clearly not correct to identify Bhuts, on the strength of an *a priori* argument, with ghosts or with natural phenomena. So the Vedas know the "Elves," etymologically identical with Ribhus, the Vedic name of these clever artisan spirits, and there is not the slightest reason to identify them with natural phenomena, as has often been done. They and their class are transcendental, as are the fairies of our nurseries.

Another sort of imaginative deities includes the "wonder-cow," "wonder-bird," and "wonder-tree" of post-Vedic mythology. These, too, are still believed in, though they are not invoked and worshipped as they once were. No particular cow is thus glorified. The fancy plays around the concrete "giver of good things," as the cow is called, till it evolves an archetypical divine cow, which gives everything. The Vedic gods of Love and Anger, with all the later host of these divinities, are abstractions of emotions, just as the wonder-cow is the abstraction of a concrete cow. These gods, which are real and worshipped, are surely not referable to ghosts or personified natural phenomena. Again, from these to the intellectual or logical gods there is but a step. The Vedic period knows the divine, primordial giant, whose members are the universe, a crude pantheism found in several other parts of the world. Worked upon by the priestly imagination, this god becomes in the Atharva Veda the primordial Support, Skambha, who is dissected in a philosophically grotesque analysis of the universe. To the close of this Vedic age were familiar Vac (Latin *vox*), a philosophical deity; Brihaspati, the later Brahman, "lord of prayer," a religious deity, whom the "goddess Gayatri" (that is to say, the personification of a particular prayer) and a large number of similar deities follow. The god of death, again, must have his secretary, Citragupta, who is invented at a later date. There must be a special god of battle, suited to the post-Vedic age, and Skanda is imagined (whom, to be sure, some have wished to identify with "Aleksander"). We cannot go back to any literary period where we do not find alongside of the worship of sky-gods, ghosts, and demons, the worship of some abstract powers. Even Infinity,

Mercy, Wisdom (as an active, instructing goddess), and other such deities appear during the Vedic age, though probably most of these are not of the earliest period. This evidence of the past is particularly valuable as showing that primitive superstition of the grossest kind may be contemporary with the creation of abstract divinities. Conversely, as we see in the modern life of the people, the most philosophical creeds may exist alongside of the most primitive superstition. Only in the latter case the mixed national faiths have amalgamated Dravidian and Mohammedan elements with Aryan, while in the Rig Veda there is, as yet, no evidence of external influence.

It is perhaps owing to outside influence that Brahmanism in contradistinction to Vedism has so much demonolatry in its composition, but even here the effect of other beliefs on Aryan creeds seems to have been exaggerated. For the Vedic religion contains in itself the prototype of all the later demonolatry.

An important division of devils, for instance, is that of the disease-demons of modern times, many of whom can be traced back to Brahmanism. But, if we fit the beliefs of to-day into the practices of antiquity, we shall see that this kind of demon was really included in the host of divine beings of the Rig Veda itself. A very interesting example of this lies in the case of a young woman who is said in the Rig Veda to have been drawn through a round hole and cured of disease. As the hymn stands, it is merely a song in honor of the storm-god Indra, to whom credit is given for the cure. But the method of cure explains what is otherwise unintelligible. In all ages in India, just as to-day, crawling through a circle is one device to escape the demon of disease,[1] for every circle is a mystic and hence holy power. This gives the cue to the Vedic rite. The young woman was running away from the "devil of disease," and was cured by being dragged through a round hole. We have, too, at this period a host of personified "Diseases," which can be nothing but the modern disease-devils. In very rare cases is a disease

[1] Compare Crooke, The Popular Religion, i. 142; ii. 41.

attributed to the action of a great god, and only when, so to speak, the influence of the great god's power is unavoidable. Thus Varuna, a god of sky and water, possibly identical with Ouranos, is also worshipped as the god of dropsy, because the disease is clearly a water-disease. But in general all diseases are simply the outward manifestation of an evil spirit. Just as a bruise is the result of a blow, so disease is the sign that one has been smitten by a devil. When the disease itself is regarded as the body of the disease-spirit, this class of demons belongs to that of phenomena. But this is rarely the case. The devil causes the disease, but the eruption or other sign is not generally the incorporate being itself. Some exceptions seem to occur in the case of prayers addressed directly to such and such a phenomenon of disease, as in deprecation of the yellows as personified jaundice. But this class of what has been called symbolic gods is merely the result of the usual interchange of cause and effect. "Depart, O yellowness," is really to the speaker the equivalent of "Depart, O yellow-making evil," and evil is synonymous with devil.

This group of disease-devils is by no means homogeneous. Not only do the great gods, like Varuna in the Rig Veda and Çiva to-day, occasionally inflict disease, but there are also demons who are responsible for disease and yet are ghosts. Thus there is a cholera-devil who is the ghost of a gentleman who died in the seventeenth century. On the other hand, Putana in the epic and Çitala to-day are not ghosts; the latter, the goddess or she-devil of small-pox, is a pure abstraction. In ancient Brahmanism there may be found an army of these "disease-mothers," whose highest type is dark Kali, the spouse of Çiva. Some of these again are plainly reduced in circumstances, like the Great Mother of Gujarat, who is now a disease-devil and once, like Momba Devi of Bombay, was a tutelary local divinity, perhaps Mother Earth. But despite the manifoldness of their origin, though some are ghosts and some are decayed phenomenal deities, there are many which, like the devils bearing the name of the disease, can be referred only to fancy and the simple logic of disease explained above. Among these there are interesting types showing the original condition of some of the great gods who have been elevated from just such a beginning to a higher sphere. One of these present logical prototypes of Çiva is the horrible little demon worshipped to-day (as he has been worshipped for three thousand years) under the name of Bhairava, or in modern form Bhairoba, a caricature of Çiva, with whom he has long been identified.

The first grouping of this general category of gods occurs in the Vedic expression "other people," a general term for all the powers of darkness, who later are supposed to be under the dominion of Kubera, reckoned a Pluto and guardian of under-ground riches. Long after the first appearance of this god as a god, his name is assumed by mortal kings, so that in this category also the historical process, as recorded in literature, has been the reverse of euhemeristic.

Although they are not gods, yet the creatures imagined by the epic poets deserve a word here as superhuman (or inhuman) beings, whose origin has usually been held to be due to simple fancy. Such are the one-legged men and men with ears long enough to wrap about them. But I think that most of these are due to distortion of travellers' tales. In South India I chanced one day to be in company with a young Frenchman who knew nothing of Hindu literature. On seeing the earring-extended ears of a peasant woman he exclaimed, "What ears! Why, she could use them for a shawl!" As to the one-legged men, Colonel Holdich, in his Indian Borderland, tells us that in Kafirstan the favorite amusement is racing up and down steeps on one leg, "sometimes with a drop of fifteen feet." Such a tribe would easily be described as "one-legged."[1]

GHOST-GODS. Reference has already been made to a class of deities quite different in origin from those discussed

[1] The circumstance that in the epic some of the foreign allies are the "stone-throwers" may be illustrated by the fact, also recorded by Colonel Holdich, *op. cit.*, that this is the Baluch weapon *par excellence*.

above. These are the ghost-demons and ghost-gods. They may be divided into two classes, — deities that are the ghosts of certain well-known people, and the vague host of Fathers or Manes without special name. In modern times both classes are worshipped. In the Vedic period there is some doubt whether the first class was recognized at all. But there is a possibility of this in the fact that the Bhumiya, or local "lord of the field," in modern times is often the ghost of a local hero, and that, in the earliest literature, worship is given to a "lord of the field." But just as there was at a later time a "goddess of the house" differentiated from all ancestral spirits, so here the "lord of the field" may be only the equivalent of the later "lord of the corn," an abstraction and not a ghost.

But in the earliest hymns the "Fathers" are recognized as a distinct group of deities. Their position and powers are rather undefined, but the important fact stands out clearly that they are never confounded or merged with the gods of phenomena. The spirits of the dead either go to heaven and sit with Yama, the "first of mortals who died," in the vault of the sky, where they enjoy their new life in his company under a "beautiful tree," or, according to the varied beliefs reflected through the Vedic period, they stay on earth in various housings, such as plants and the bodies of birds. At a later date they become stars, or go to the moon and sun. They are generally a nameless, inconspicuous host, and the only one revered by name at first is Yama, the mythical first mortal. Then some of the great saints get identified with constellations; but, generally speaking, the soul of a dead man first becomes a Preta, or unhoused ghost, which on being properly fed with oblations is "elevated" to the host of happy Fathers in the sky. After three generations it loses its identity and is named no more at the sacrifice, becoming simply "one of the Fathers."

Yama, whom the ingenious comparative mythologists have identified with both the sun and the moon, is regarded as the "twin," or male of the primitive pair from whom men come.

He had a sister Yami, with whom he paired, originally identified with Night, though now in popular tradition she is the Jumna River, the waters of which on account of her incest are still unholy. But Yama is a ghost-god only in the view of the tradition that makes him, being mortal, a man. He may be merely a poetic image, but if a natural phenomenon this same "first to die" would make it most natural to regard him as the moon.

Other ghosts revered as terrible are the Kabandhas of the epic, headless trunks of slain heroes, corresponding to the modern Dunds. So, too, the Piçacas are a class of devils which were originally malevolent ghosts. India to-day is full of shrines raised to ghosts of this sort. But it is not at all necessary that malevolence or unnatural power should be exhibited to ensure divinity. Not a few Englishmen have been worshipped in life, and should have had shrines after their death in the estimation of the natives. Among the Hindus nothing is more common than the deification of a man, dead or alive. To speak here only of the former case, a few years ago a poor man in one of the districts of northern India fell asleep on the shrine of the local deity. He woke to find himself adorned with flowers and worshipped. The villagers persisted in accepting him as their local god in bodily form. Finding the position an easy one, he remained an *avatar* till he died, when he became a true god whose divinity increased so rapidly that he was regarded at last as the original god of the shrine. In this case a few successful cures established his cult and ousted his predecessor. Again, Hardaur Lala was a worthy man who lived in the seventeenth century. He is now the god of cholera, of whom mention has been made above. Any disease-healer or Ojha, that is, Teacher, if successful in life, becomes deified after death.

Less often is found apotheosis of literary worthies; but Vyasa, the epic author, and his rival Valmiki, are now gods in some parts of India, as are the heroes of their poems, who have many shrines and thousands of worshippers. Finally, the ghosts of "good" women, Satis, are regarded as "new divinities," to cite the expression of the Abbé Dubois, who at the end of the eighteenth century saw some of these unhappy gods in the making.[1]

MAN–GODS. Although men as divinities should logically precede ghosts, yet it is significant of the healthy Aryan tone reflected in the Rig Veda that, while ghost-gods are acknowledged, no worship is paid to a living man, though it is true that one of the poet-priests asserts his own divinity, but only in a hymn that is particularly marked by late features. Nevertheless, the germ of this disease was already at work, and shortly after the first Vedic period man-gods were as much feared as sky-gods. The first to win the power was the one who still keeps it, the Ojha or wizard. He was the Purohita, or domestic chaplain, of a king, and his incantations have been handed down in the Atharva or Fire-cult (magic) Veda. In the earliest period, indeed, any one might be a wizard; but long before the Vedic period ended the prerogative was safe in the hands of the priestly caste. In the Rig Veda itself the real "arbiter of battle" is said to be not the warrior king, nor even the great gods, but the priest who controls the armies through his magic rites. In the great Indian epic the real office of the domestic chaplain is to "slay evil magic" and invent evil magic of his own.

But long before the epic age, the whole caste of priests had gradually acquired through the superstitious fears of the kings the same power originally got by the Purohita (equivalent to *cohen*). And in fact the ordinary ceremonial of the sacrifice was not very different from the witchcraft of the despicable Ojha. Through this power over the sacrifice and over the gods, the priestly caste arrogated divinity to themselves, and before the Vedic age closed proclaimed themselves "gods upon earth," a claim legally sanctioned in the native law-books. This pretense they have always upheld, and to-day all the disgusting service of Gosains and Gurus, the pontiffs of modern

[1] Satis (suttees) are women who allow themselves to be burned to death on their husband's pyre, and are hence called *satis*, "good." Dubois relates that their divinity began when the procession to the pyre was formed.

sectarian bodies, is based on the same notion that the priests are actual gods.[1]

Another division of man-gods is that of heroes, spiritual or military. Occasionally such men are deified in life, but generally it is their ghosts that are worshipped. Buddha, Rama, and Krishna are good examples. Rama was so clearly a man that even in his own epic he is represented as not knowing that he was a god till he was told of it. Both he and Krishna were originally local chieftains of Northern India, though to-day they are both *avatars*, that is, "descents" (to earth) of Vishnu, the Supreme Deity. A quite modern instance of a military leader becoming a god is that of the Mahratta chieftain, Çivaji, whose disciples are to-day, for political purposes, urging his cult in the Bombay presidency. The common people cannot quite decide whether he was a god or not, as they still remember what a demon he was in life. But his devilry will, in the ordinary course of things, soon be merged in his divinity. A shrine and offerings are enough to establish a god.[2] Even professed monotheism, as in the case of the Sikhs and modern reformers of this century, is not enough to prevent the deification of the high priest of the order, withal, before he dies. Chunder Sen too was deified by his followers, and long before her death the Queen-empress to many Hindus was a great divinity.[3]

[1] The *jus primæ noctis* is assumed by some of these pontiffs on the basis of this claim. The bride is "purified" by preliminary intercourse with the priest.

[2] This may seem to be putting the cart before the horse, but it is not said unadvisedly. The Hindu worships what he does not understand, and may even take a Mohammedan tomb as a temple and add his flowers (given to a deity) to those placed there in remembrance only. I saw a Hindu peasant do this in Lahore, and had him asked why he did it. "They are all great and powerful, those in the tombs," was his simple reply. Again, to start a new god on a successful career, it is necessary only to build a shrine, and say, "Here is a god." The worshippers collect at once. All they need is a sign, and the new shrine signifies a god.

[3] It must be remembered that the ascription of godhead to a man is in India not quite what it would be among people not believing in metempsychosis on the one hand, and pantheism on the other. As any very good man may become a god at death, the transition in life is only a prolepsis. And the

The Abbé Dubois, who spent his life in India and knew the people thoroughly, reports that a respectable Hindu once said to him: "My god is the headman among my field-laborers; for as they work under his orders, he can, by using his influence, do me much good or evil."[1] Here, applied to man, is the same cause of deification, which, as we have seen, underlies the worship of phenomena that are lifeless. On this point also the learned Abbé in the same passage says in regard to idols that "idolatry in India has for the object of its worship the material substance itself. It is to everything which they understand to be useful or hurtful that the Hindus pay direct worship." He adds that there is a more refined idolatry, where the divinity in the idol, not the idol itself, is worshipped, "but that which has for its object the actual substance itself is more common."[2]

In the early literature, both the father and the mother are declared to be divinities to their children, but this is little more than a phrase, expressing the absolute control which the parents had the right of exercising. The marital god, however, is a real divinity, though he has only one worshipper, for the wife must renounce all other gods if they oppose the husband-god. A favorite tale in Southern India tells how the wife flouted the Guru, or priest-god, and disobeyed all the other gods in the pantheon, because the priests told her that the great gods had commanded her to do what her husband had forbidden. She died in the odor of great sanctity, for "a wife's god is her husband," as he has been, both in proverb and in Hindu law, for the past twenty-five hundred years. Absolutely to obey and "worship her husband as her only god" is the wife's one religious duty, though she may invoke other deities if not forbidden by her husband-god.

fine old saint of Benares (since dead) answered, when I asked him in 1897, in the course of a friendly conversation, how he could adore his own image, "As I worship you too, both being portions of God." But, though deified, I was not a god.

[1] Dubois, Manners and Customs, ii. p. 556.

[2] *Loc. cit.*

ANIMAL-GODS. Whether animals, which make a new category of gods, were worshipped as such by the Vedic Aryans is extremely doubtful.[1] With the exception of the lion, which is not referred to as divine, the animals now most dreaded were not then known. The tiger and perhaps the elephant are not mentioned; the crocodile is not alluded to till the second period of Vedic literature. The wolf and the wild hog were not then deified. The divine cow of the later age is at this time, and even for centuries thereafter, regarded as better to eat than to revere.[2] The only animals, indeed, that appear in this period to be hedged about with any sort of divinity are snakes and monkeys. But it is centuries after this when we find any trace of the mediæval and modern worship of snakes as protective deities and totems. The difference is very well marked in Brahmanic worship, where sacrifices and witchcraft against snakes come before the recognition of deified snakes. Of the latter, the Nagas are not snakes, but idealized serpents and dragons. One of them upholds the world. They have human faces, and are no more real serpents than Centaurs are real horses. It is highly probable that Naga worship was introduced into Aryan theogony from the aboriginal tribes, as the latter revere serpents both as gods and totems. At the present day the native peasant worships snakes both as dire fiends and as ancestral ghosts. The latter are the house-snakes, which are propitiated and looked upon in somewhat the double light with which Æneas views the serpent on his altar: —

> Incertus geniumne loci famulumne parentis
> Esse putet.

[1] That they were sometimes worshipped as spirits of the dead is probable. See below.

[2] Down almost to the time of our era beef-eating (at sacrifices) was common, as is shown by passages in the national epic. It was even said by some of the ancients (though I doubt it) that *goghna* meant guest (it really means "cow-killer") because the "fatted calf" was killed in his honor. To-day no sacrilege is so heinous as the "murder" of a cow. The fact that beef was eaten in the epic period has sometimes been noticed without the all-important addition that the cows killed to be eaten were at this time killed only for sacrifice.

Other animals also are credited with being ghosts or wizards in beastly form. Totemism has been made responsible for many divinities of this sort, but reflection brings prudence here also. It is now quite generally admitted that, as Mr. Crane and Mr. Bull do not imply a totemistic stage, so many clans have descended from men who bore nicknames of beasts. An early instance is the Tortoise clan of the Vedic age. Unless in fact the descendants are known to treat an animal as a totem, that is, refuse to eat it, totemism is not even probable. In many cases, even when the animal of the clan or family is regarded as sacred, it may be only a subsequent enlargement of reverence, due perhaps to a belief that the nickname implied a real descent. This is especially the case when a non-totemistic people is brought into close connection with totem-worshipping tribes. Nothing is more common to-day in India than to give a child the nickname of an animal. Such a child grows up as Owl or Bear and founds a family, which, if the founder becomes distinguished, vaunts itself as children of the Owl or Bear. In a totemistic environment few generations are required to make the descendants believe that the owl or bear is their true ancestor. The distinction between a totem and a fetish must here be kept in mind. A totem is a sacred class-symbol or a class-god; a fetish is an individual, isolated symbol of divinity, or an individual god. This important difference is often overlooked. Even such a careful student as Crooke defines the Devak, or marriage-god of the Brahmanized wild tribes, as a totem in one place and as a fetish in another.[1]

But there are many animals which are gods in themselves to the later age of Brahmanism. The cow, elephant, tiger, monkey, eagle, flamingo, crocodile, etc., are divine, but they have no trace of totemism in their composition. Only in a few cases has there been evolved out of these divine animals an abstract class deity, such as Hanumat, the monkey-god, Bagh Deo, the tiger-god, or Ganeça, the elephant-god. The

[1] Crooke, The Popular Religion and Folk-Lore of Northern India, ii. pp. 155, 184.

boar was a tribal god in Rajputana not long ago; but, though sacred in many parts of the country, he is not generally regarded as a god. Ordinarily each divine animal is divine *per se*, on account of his wisdom, strength, or weirdness, as in the case of the elephant, tiger, and monkey. But some are divine merely because they are favorites of the great gods, as in the case of the peacock and the rat; though it may be that some have become favorites because they were originally totems of the wild tribes, and had to be received with respect by the Aryans.

When a fetish is made of part of an animal there is a transfer from one class of gods to another. The tiger is the embodiment of strong vitality and is revered as such: his claw, when he is dead, is also a mighty talismanic god. In the latter case the influence of the divinity is still felt in dead phenomena supposed to have volition, and the tiger-claw is nothing but a phenomenon-god of inanimate matter, revered just as anything is revered which has been intimately associated with divinity. The finger-nail of a saint is the European parallel, only in India the divine power has a will of its own, even in the paring.

Occasionally an animal-god is made by a fiat. Thus in the museum of Bangalore I found a stone with a long inscription, stating that the king's dog had distinguished himself and been killed in a fight, and was thereafter to be revered and worshipped as a god. A priest and a temple were appointed and the new divinity was to be worshipped daily by the priest, who was to have all the perquisites of the shrine so long as he kept up the cult. So, too, a Bengal tribe, as Crooke relates, has within recent years adopted the dog as its god, because it was "useful when alive and not very good to eat when dead," and the tribe "wished to have a tribal god."

The usual attitude of the Hindu peasant toward animals is that of kindly brotherhood. He recognizes no such barrier between beast and man as that created by the intrusion of a peculiar soul into human anatomy. To him beasts and men in this regard are on a par. Moreover, a beast may become a man after death, as a man may become a beast, since only the abnormally virtuous escape a reincarnation in animal form. It is, therefore, not at all strange that the Hindu should look upon certain animals as possessed by the souls of his ancestors and friends. In the earliest Vedic period, as has been shown, human souls were supposed to find refuge in plants and animals, and this belief has continued through all ages. Animals of extraordinary power are often regarded as reembodied men, or as animated by a god's vitality and superhuman intelligence. Thus in certain cases an individual animal may be Vishnu himself, or a class may be literally deified through favor of this god. But in other cases the simplest explanation is that the class possessing unusual intelligence, power, or utility, is all divine in itself. The same principle is here at work as in the deification of any powerful thing. The difference, however, is clear. In the case of the razor which the barber worships, the scissors which the tailor worships, it is not a spirit in the steel but the steel itself which is divine. A thing inanimate, senseless in itself, which yet can work good and ill, must be a god. But an animal is patently alive just as a man is alive, and his body is divine only as being in contact with a divine spirit. The difference comes out clearly in the treatment of these divinities when destroyed. A dead tiger may still prowl about as a fiend, and his claw still reflects divinity. But no one pays attention to a broken razor. So a triangle and a circle are not only divine, but, incredible as it may seem, they are to the Hindu, of course only to the uneducated, real divinities, to be worshipped as well as feared. But when the figure is broken there is no more divinity in its fragments.

As there are class deities, the abstractions of beasts, in the animal world, so there are purely mythical animals, such as the griffin, Garuda-bird, and the four elephants that uphold the world. These are, of course, neither ghosts nor phenomena nor animals; but, being derived from the last two, they are gods of the category of fancy, between whom and demons or sprites there is no appreciable difference.

At the present time, though the doctrine of pantheism is formally acknowledged, the native villager never thinks of his different gods as being other than separate entities. The All-god was by no means the last divinity to be created.[1] In each category that has been named new gods are even now constantly arising. India is in fact a kaleidoscope of deities; a turn of the hand makes ever new combinations out of the same elements. These elements, as they have been reviewed,[2] are quite distinct. Though we may admit that one god may change and pass into a class different to that in which he originated, yet it cannot be denied that there exist gods of essentially different origin, — gods of phenomena, gods of pure fancy, gods of ghosts, gods of animals. If one chooses, one may say that gods of ghosts are gods of fancy, but, so long as one believes in a soul, it is well to keep them separate, and in any case the historical difference is plain. In the case of gods of fancy, man creates a god without reference to human agency; in the case of ghosts, one simply assumes that men continue to live after death and act as in life.

These ghost-gods, animal-gods, man-gods, emotion-gods,[3] sky-gods, tree-gods, disease-gods, may all be grouped in subdivisions liable to be adjusted more nicely, but there remains intact the fundamental distinction between Dyaus, the sky-

[1] The (philosophic) nameless All-god was invented about the fifth century B. C. About the time of the Christian era the worship of the orthodox chief god, Brahman, was amalgamated with that of the two rival sects of Vishnu and Çiva, whence arose the conception of the triune god Brahman-Vishnu-Çiva, Creator-Preserver-Destroyer, as one.

[2] Though this sketch is necessarily brief, I believe that I have included in it every class of divinity known in India; not, of course, every individual deity, for, as the Hindus say, there are 333,000,003 gods, and only categories have been described.

[3] The shameful erotic rites of modern India are held in honor of Passion, represented mystically as a Çakti, or "female side" of the All-god. Such androgynous deities are as old as the Vedas at least, though the "left-hand" cult, as it is called, cannot be traced back much farther than two thousand years. Worship of the mysterious lies at the root of it, and obvious causes have tended, as in Greece, to make the worship of Passion more popular than that of Greed or other abstractions.

god, and the late Mr. Hardaur Lala, the cholera-god, a divinity as well as a ghost; between god "East-wind" and Bagh Deo, the tiger-god. This same distinction holds good not only among Aryans of the present day, but also among the Aryans of the remotest past, and among the un-Aryan wild tribes. It may be added that it obtained also among the American Indians, who, when first known, worshipped, as separate gods, phenomena, animals, spirits, and ghosts. It appears, therefore, to be an unsupported hypothesis that all gods have their origin in personified phenomena. But equally inadequate seems the hypothesis that all gods originated in ghosts or gnomes. Go as far abroad as we will and as far back as we can, we still find that, in any one human group, disease-gods, gnomes, ghost-gods, and gods of personified natural phenomena are independent creations, synchronous yet distinct. In each category the gods change as individuals, but the type remains; and it seems probable that the main categories have existed together, side by side, since man first began to worship.

There is, however, one limitation to this in the case of the gods of any one people, the economic conditions of the people themselves. For even the gods are subject to environment. The application of this limitation must remain for specialists to make in their several departments, and I will here merely point out one leading thought which, as it seems to me to solve the riddle of the quasi-monotheism of the Rig Veda, may prove serviceable elsewhere; namely, the influence of utility on the theopoetic tendency as shown in settled and unsettled communities, respectively.

There hung for many years in the Boston State-house, and perhaps it hangs there still, a monster codfish, a token of the regard felt by the legislators for the source of the chief local industry. It was placed there with respect, one might almost say with devotion, and it is not too much to hazard that, had our Puritan forefathers been less advanced theologically, they would have considered this effigy, or at least its original, to be not only regardable but worshipful.

This State-house cod is then a symbol of more than it was carved to figure. It is, in fact, emblematic of that utilitarianism which often underlies the adoration both of the benevolent and malevolent. This, of course, is by no means the only god-creative principle, but it is an important one and one generally recognized — recognized even as early as the Mahabharata in the words: "Men worship Çiva the destroyer because they fear him, Vishnu the preserver, because they hope from him, but who worships Brahman the creator? His work is done." Not a mere phrase, for in India to-day there are thousands of temples to Çiva and Vishnu, but only two to Brahman.

To linger, however, upon this principle of utilitarianism is not my purpose. If we glance at the rich collection of divinities in a settled tribe or nation, such as those of Greece or India, we shall see that in any given locality the greatest usefulness and potency is ascribed to the local god. In a low state of savagery or barbarism local gods are universally the most important, and even in a high state of civilization they still form the undercurrent of popular divinity. Again, a great city makes great its local deity even at the cost of some anterior great deity, originally worshipped by city and country alike. But a villager, too, worships at his village shrine alone, and his real god is the god of that shrine. When the village is influenced by a wider theosophy the temple may belong to some universal god, as is to-day the case with that of Çiva, but such a shrine does not faithfully represent the loftier conception to the lowly villager. He cannot see beyond his ken, and so he is continually reducing the great god to the size of his own small conception. Moreover, although a great god may be duly represented thus, if there is at the same time another shrine of a local deity, that local god will be or become paramount. Even more must this magnitude of the little have been operative before the higher conception become possible.

The environment which I have tacitly assumed is that of a settled people. Now let us change the economic conditions and ask ourselves what will, and must, have been the gods which obtained whenever a primitive people became migratory. It is evident that a migratory people can have no constant local gods. There is no perpetually familiar mountain or stream whose deity they dread. They may worship the sun, but they cannot worship him in a local form; they may worship the souls of the departed, but they cannot pay especial reverence to the man-god of one shrine.

What, then, are the gods that a wandering people can worship throughout their whole migratory state? Simply those gods which they have always with them. And what are these? Horace says *cœlum non animum*, but if we should interpret the *cœlum* very literally, the poet's Greek original were nearer the truth, *τόπον οὐ τρόπον*; man changes his abode, his mind remains the same, and the sky-god is not changed. The sky-god, not local but always with men, they will continue to worship wherever they go. This is not true of earth, for earth is not regarded by primitive people as one and the same, since a different locality implies a different divinity; there is a local mountain which is a separate god, etc.

Fire, on the other hand, though it often goes out, still remains the same magic fire, "the ever new god," as the Vedic poets call it; and it will continue to receive its antique worship, especially when, as may have been the case with the forefathers of the Romans, it is guarded and not allowed to become extinct.

But there is one more class of gods, the troop of spirits of the dead, that remains with migrating people. When people settle down they particularize in exact proportion as they localize the cult. This man's spirit, they say, resides here on the very spot where he lived. Here, then, we worship him, and he will protect us here. The result is the innumerable shrines which we find raised, for example, in India to-day, to the local Birs or man-gods of the places where these heroes used to live. But so long as the children's children roam about, they cannot localize nor particularize. Each family ghost soon becomes merged in one shadowy host of ghosts, travelling with the human tribe, worshipped by them in general. Only now and then the spirit of some special hero is worshipped by more than his own family; then he becomes a tribal god.

Now all other classes of gods are virtually enshrined in local material. Animal-gods depend on the environment for their very existence. Totems are possible only where the worshippers are fairly stationary. No one continues to revere a tiger or an eagle who has no idea what these animals look like, and no one claims descent, if he can help it, from a non-entity. Gods of the imagination — genii, devils of various sorts, and nymphs — lose their power in losing their habitation. As the dryads perish with the removal of their tree, so when the site is left, the special devil or fairy, potent in its local habitation, becomes vague and eventually perishes from the mind. The belief in such beings may be unimpaired, but the particular object of the cult is variable, so that no one individual demon, genius, or other supernatural being can permanently receive worship from the migratory people. The same is true of the disease-gods. No one worships the cholera or small-pox, as do millions in India to-day, who is no longer afraid of it. Diseases change with environment, and their malevolent gods are left behind by travellers.

Thus far I have considered the hypothetical case of any migratory nation. Before I take up a concrete instance let me point out one more fact. If such a people are once settled and afterwards wander for centuries, all traces of what used to be their local gods will have vanished. They, too, will hold as individual gods only those divinities which they have with them always, sky and fire; while they will believe in troops, not individualized, of fairies and ancestral ghosts. If they wander in the tropics they will doubtless, even at the start, have in addition to these the sun-god, and if they continue to wander there they may retain this god. But if they start in the north they are more likely to regard the sun as at most a kindly deity or as merely the eye of the sky-god. They will not worship him as a fiery, omnipotent, tyrant god till they reach the proper environment. So a storm-god may accompany one or more branches of a dividing people while they move in a circumscribed area; but just as soon as one branch settles down amid a different environment, this storm-god will yield his power and name to some new local product. Their regard for the moon will also be influenced by their environment and be affected by their enjoyment of the night as compared with the day, slight in a cold, great in a warm clime. In general, then, sky, with perhaps such celestial phenomena as sun, moon, and stars (but these latter are more dependent on circumstances), and fire, and the manes will be the most important, as they will be among the most venerable gods that a migratory people can remember; unless, indeed, they bear with them some effigy or memorial of another deity which tends to perpetuate artificially what would otherwise pass from memory.

Now let us take in illustration a concrete example. If these general statements, *a priori* as they are, yet seem probable, what gods should we expect to find as the oldest among the Indo-Europeans? — oldest, that is to say, from the point of view which we must perforce take, the view afforded by linguistic and literary evidence. This oldest evidence represents merely a phase of development, but it appears to me fully to support the interpretation I have made. What god is worshipped under the same name by more than two of the Indo-European nations? Only the sky-god, Dyauspitar, Zeuspater, Jupiter. Under another name the sky is worshipped as Varuna, Ouranos. Both in India and in Greece this god appears as the most venerable of all gods of phenomena. But what other gods are worshipped by several of these severed nations? The Fathers, Manes, *pitaras*, not under a particular name, but as a host, exactly as we should have anticipated. And lastly we have the fire-cult practised in India, Persia, Greece, and Italy as far back as records go.

But because the (later) twofold Indo-Iranians lived long together, we find also in India's oldest pantheon, as in Persia's, a *soma-haoma* cult and a Mitra-Mithra sun-cult not found among other nations. So too we find the same storm-god in Slavic and Vedic form, but not elsewhere.

Here we have, as I am convinced, the true explanation of an apparently mysterious fact, a fact that has led observers astray and is apt to do so still. I will not recall to criticise the older hypothesis of an original monotheism among the Indo-Europeans. Such theories were of their time, and represented a reasonable stage of scholarly accomplishment in the interpretation of religious phenomena. The great Sanskrit scholars of an earlier generation were profoundly impressed by the fact that the sky-god held the highest and apparently oldest place; that he was the most venerable deity of the Indo-Europeans; and that some of the Vedic hymns addressed to him show an almost monotheistic conception, certainly a much higher conception of godhead than attaches to any other god of the Vedic age. Hence they naturally argued a primeval monotheism. And it is true that the figure of the supreme Zeus and the majestic Varuna are such as to suggest this consequence.

These gods represent, however, as I have shown, not so much the most primitive belief as what was oldest in the migratory life of their worshippers. For all the Indo-Europeans were migrating for centuries; that is to say, they shifted from place to place, leaving behind what was local, carrying forward as great divinities only those which were really ubiquitous and were felt to be always identical.

The sky-god is physically lofty, and does not easily lend himself to the hocus-pocus of demonolatry. If we add to this the fact that to the Vedic Aryans he was, as has been explained, the highest object of their oldest remembered worship, we can easily understand why his figure stands out so large in the background of the pantheon. We can also understand why the figure fades and dwindles as the Aryan invaders exchange the tending of herds for agriculture, as they move more and more slowly from Kabul to Delhi (to use modern names), and become permanent settlers. For with the permanent home rise the local gods, Indra the war-god, true image of the monsoon-fury; Çiva, the combination of a Vedic storm-god and a local aboriginal disease-god. So with all the gods potent at a later date. Every one is local, not one is inherited. Even Agni, the fire-god, inwrought as he is into every sacrifice, and having thus a firmer hold than had most of his peers, becomes a mere godling, the servant of the great local gods who arise in settled communities. These latter appear even in the Veda itself, the first insignificant "god of the field," and such prototypes of the Bhairobas and Vitthalas (modern Vithobas, to give the exact form) of to-day, as at Pandharpur in the Deccan.

The Veda thus presents us with at least three strata of divinities: the newest local gods, already potent, and destined in the end to be most powerful; the intermediate gods, derived from the last protracted local settlements and not yet forgotten, Soma and Trita, and perhaps the storm-god Parjanya; and the still older gods which the Aryans revered even before their separation, which alone they could have preserved (as they had no images) through all changes of time and place, sky-god, fire, and ghosts. To these may be added the general host of undistinguished fairies and demons that, though revered, were regarded as spiritual underlings who never came into competition of worship with the great gods. The venerable position, then, of the sky-god depends on the economic position of the people who worshipped him as the one great god they always had with them. He naturally and inevitably superseded, in the grandeur of his history as well as in the loftiness of his physical attributes, all the merely local deities which the nation found on its route, adopted, and abandoned again, as they successively passed into, through, and out of their spheres of divine influence. It was only when the Aryans remained permanently stationary that they could adopt a permanent local god. As soon as they did so, this local god, as is always the case, began to gain ascendency over the sky-god and over Agni, and finally outstripped them both in the race for popularity, only to be in turn dethroned as the people passed again into a new environment. But in this and in all subsequent moves, the old gods were no longer obnoxious to the chances of fickle piety, for literature now had them comparatively safe. Even with this safeguard, however, Varuna becomes before very long a mere god of waters, and Dyaus is degraded.

On one aspect of the case I have scarcely touched. To become settled is to be agricultural. Now the settled condition of agriculturists raises a great crop of local earthly divinities. The peoples of the Rig Veda are in a transition state, represented now as tending and raping flocks, now as reaping fields; at one time as still in transit across the Punjab, but generally as permanently located. In this shifting of economic conditions there is reason to anticipate exactly what we find at this epoch. The figures of the ancient sky-god and fire-god are still held in greatest reverence, though already decadent in popularity. But what is most important is that the older gods are no longer unique in being historical gods. For the people are at least so thoroughly settled that they regard the local gods also as historical. In other words, the latter have already begun to become such inherited divinities as Dyaus and Agni, and in less degree Trita and Soma. But at the same time they are local, the reflex of the very conditions in which the worshipper lives, vivid personalities, near and real. When this happens, more important than the upper god becomes the god that holds life and death in his hands as the monsoon comes or, later, as the season of disease begins to slay. The god that answers to the environment, the local god, first Indra, then Çiva, becomes most important. And as Çiva rises, the sky-god falls, for the Aryans never again migrated beyond the reach of the local conditions into which they had now entered, descending as they did from healthy uplands to a land of monsoon and fever.

# CHRIST IN INDIA.

It must often have caused surprise in the mind of the candid student of religious history to note with how great regularity they that regard Christianity as better than Buddhism regard it also as quite uninfluenced by Buddhism, while they who believe that the nobler religion of the two is Buddhism, are they who believe also that Christianity is but a copy of Buddhism. That so marked a difference between the results obtained by the two parties of investigators is caused by a needless confusion of ethical and historical factors may perhaps be suspected. But there seems to be no reason why, in considering a question purely historical, other elements should be allowed to interfere with the full exercise of the critical powers. We may, or rather we must, if as historians we seek a definitive answer to the historical problem, which in itself is quite complex enough to require undivided attention, exclude all other aspects (such as the relative beauty of the two religions and the human or divine origin of one or the other), as introducing subsidiary questions. To prove that Buddha's ideal was higher than Christ's adds no weight to the contention that the latter was a copy of the former; nor does the argument that Christ was divine prove that features of his religion and of Christian legend were not borrowed from Buddhism.

But a second surprise awaits the historical student who ventures upon this field. At the time of Christ there were, among others, two great religions in India, Buddhism and Krishnaism. Now while one set of critics maintain that Christianity is borrowed from Buddhism and ignore Krishnaism altogether, another set claim that Krishnaism was the model, and that the Gospels are based on the teachings of this form of Hinduism rather than on those of Buddhism.

This division of the putative sources of Christianity leads further to the discovery that, whereas the life-events and miracles of Christ are supposed to be copied from those of Buddha, the sayings supposed to be copied are in the main those of Krishna; since the records of the events in Krishna's life, though comparable with those of Christ, are not looked upon as antecedent, and the sayings of Buddha comparable with those of Christ are but slightly similar. As Krishnaism is not represented in literature till a period subsequent to Buddha, it will be well to discuss the double problem in the chronological order of its parts, the inter-relation of Christianity first with Buddhism and then with Krishnaism.

Of what sort, then, is the evidence in the case of the former relation — direct or indirect, based on historical facts or on literary analogy; again, how much of it is valuable, how much worthless, has it, in fact, been properly sifted?

Now in answering these queries a not uncommon order of procedure is to begin by giving a mass of literary parallels and to end with a statement of the historical conditions. For example, the Buddhistic parable of the prodigal son is cited as a parallel to that in the New Testament, and afterwards it is stated that the medium of communication, by means of which in general Buddhistic parables were transplanted to Syrian soil, was probably a Buddhistic gospel current in Syria in Christ's time; for in the first century A. D. there was constant communication between India and Syria.

But it is perhaps more conducive to a clear understanding of the problem if we endeavor first of all to understand the conditions under which in general such communications may have taken place, and then to apply our knowledge to the special cases. The cogency of the argument in the case just adduced, for example, is somewhat affected by the two facts that, so far as we know, there was no such Buddhistic gospel in Syria, and that the Buddhist parable cannot be traced back of 200–300 A. D. It is, of course, possible that there was such a gospel, and it is possible also that a Buddhistic story appearing in literature in the third century after our era existed four centuries in secret without being mentioned in the voluminous accounts of Buddha's life, and was then transplanted to Syria and published for the first time in a Buddhistic gospel, belief in the existence of which depends wholly on its being regarded as the indispensable means of communicating this parable to Christ. But it is advisable rather to know first the facts than thus to begin by playing with fancies.

The historical facts, however, are not so complete as could be desired for the solution of so interesting a problem. But, though they too leave a large margin for the play of fancy, they are sufficient to answer one of the most important points in the taking of evidence. There is a large amount of early literature concerning the Christian religion, and in it there is no indication that Christianity was regarded as reflecting Buddhism, even at a time when Buddha's doctrines were certainly known. On the contrary, Buddha was regarded as such an arch-heretic that converts were required on renouncing Manichæism to anathematize both Zoroaster and Buddha.

But in this matter there will be found both undue depreciation and exaggeration of historical data in the evidence submitted. On the one hand they are made to prove less, on the other more, than may reasonably be extracted from them.

In the third century before Christ, the Indian king Açoka sent missionaries to the West, who, as he says, converted the Greeks, and among those to whom he sent was Ptolemy Philadelphus and Antiochus II., the latter ruling over the Bactrian Greeks, the former, who also sent an embassy to India, being king of Egypt. The Hindus were accustomed to give the name of Greeks to the Bactrian Greeks, and usually mentioned them as neighbors of the people living in Kandahar on the Northwest frontier.[1] Açoka claims, however, that he sent missionaries not only to Antiochus, who reigned

[1] See on this point the evidence collected in my Great Epic of India, p. 393 ff.

over these Greeks, but also to certain friends of Antiochus, the king of Epirus, and others. There is no outside evidence that such missionaries ever arrived, or, if they did, that they ever had any influence; and scholars like M. Senart, who have studied the subject most carefully, incline to the opinion that Açoka had simply heard of these kings through his friend Antiochus and had dispatched missionaries to them, when he boasted of the conversion of the Western world (within a year after the missionaries were sent). On the other hand, we know that in Bactria there were Buddhist missionaries as early as the second century B. C.

That the West was converted to Buddhism or even influenced by Buddhistic missionaries in the third century before our era, is not probable in the face of the fact that such influence is not to be traced in the literature, and that Buddha's name is quite unknown at that period; for Buddha himself was as central a figure in his religion as was that of Christ in his. The next tangible fact that presents itself is that in the reign of Augustus a king Porus of India sent an embassy to Rome, and the ambassador, who burned himself at Athens under a name that means "ascetic-teacher," may have been a Buddhist. At any rate, he was an Indian, and his presence in Rome in the first century shows that intercommunication of some sort between India and the West was not rare. The same conclusion must be drawn from the known general facts that there was political communication for centuries before the Christian era, and that a large number of traders passed between Egypt and India at this time.

Even before the Palmyrene trade with India, there were two routes which formed a means of communication, a trade-route by sea from Alexandria, and a land-route from Babylon to the Punjab. In the first century of our era, as we learn from Dio, Hindus had not only visited Alexandria, but were settled there as residents of the city. It is, however, easy to exaggerate the extent of the intellectual intercourse. The "Greek letter" borne by the embassy to Augustus about 20 B. C. purported to come from Hindus, but it may have been indited by Greek traders in Gujarat. The few Hindus in Alexandria must have been uneducated traders, or we should not have Strabo's testimony to the fact that it was very difficult for him to find any one to give reliable information about India. Strabo also tells us that only a few ignorant Greek traders had got to the Ganges, and states that only this one embassy to Augustus had ever been sent to the West. When, therefore, the advocates of Buddhistic influence claim that two hundred years before the Christian era Buddhist missionaries had been all through the West and had established churches there, we may well inquire on what they rely for a statement so extraordinary. Such tales must be discounted as fully as Philostratus' account of Apollonius' journey in the first century of our era, during which the latter is said to have found a Punjab king who, having been educated as a Greek, was on a certain occasion "reading the Heraclidæ;" while even the Punjab villagers spoke Greek. Up to the present, no trace of any early Buddhistic worship has been found in the West. The only known monument, a reputed Gnostic tomb in Syracuse, is only supposed to have been Buddhistic — two suppositions in regard to a monument of comparatively late date.

In short, while Eastern civilization had already impinged upon the West, and while there is therefore a possibility that the religions of the East were not unknown in Syria, such meagre reports as we have before the end of the first century make any special knowledge of Buddhism there at that time highly improbable. Within two centuries of this time, however, Hindu beliefs were studied, as we learn from Eusebius, who says that Pantænus taught in India before teaching in Egypt in the second century. There was, as we know, direct transfer of philosophy in the second century in the writings of Bardesanes, copied in the third century by Porphyry. That Neo-platonism at an earlier date may have been indirectly influenced by Hinduism as exploited by Pythagoras, is at least possible. That there were mystics in Syria at the time of the apostles, as well as other (immoral) doctrinaires hateful to the angel of the Lord, may also be granted in view of the Simonians and Nicolaitans mentioned in the Acts and Revelations.

But those who claim that these facts are sufficient to prove that Christ borrowed his religion exaggerate the importance of such slight acquaintance with the East as can be shown to have existed. There is, so far as objective historical data go, no warrant for the idea that Christ's religion was moulded on any other. To show that it was moulded on another, and that that other was Buddhism, requires some proof much more tangible than any facts furnished by external history.

We are then thrown back upon the literary evidence, where the proof is to a great extent subjective, though we have a right to demand that it should be of the strongest possible character. This evidence consists of parallels in the traditions of the two religions.

Of the fifty odd parallels established between Buddhism and Christianity, only five are considered to be cogent, that is, as necessarily implying a loan from Buddhism. This distinction of values in the quality of the evidence was not left to the adverse critic to demonstrate, but, to the credit of Professor Seydel, who first gave scientific form to the theory, it was conscientiously pointed out when the hypothesis was originally presented (in 1882 and 1884). Unhappily, however, later writers have often laid equal weight upon all cases reckoned as parallels, being content apparently to make their heap as large as possible. But it is scarcely necessary to prove that the fact that Tibetan Buddhism, which arose late in our era, recognized a virgin mother long after Catholic missionaries had been in Tibet (whereas the pre-Christian Buddhistic church denied that Buddha's mother was a virgin at all) is not to be put into the same category with the fact that long before Christianity Buddhists believed in the miraculous birth of Buddha.

The original segregation of material into parallels which (*a*) prove nothing, (*b*) seem to show that Christianity has borrowed, and (c) prove that Christianity has borrowed from Buddhism, makes it possible in a sketch of this kind to confine the attention chiefly to the third group, which, if it seems to offer good evidence, may be strengthened by the others.

Two of the five, which may for convenience be called the Cogent Parallels, are parallels between Buddhistic narrative and passages not found in the Synoptic Gospels, but in John. This point, however, may be overlooked at present, though I shall take up these cases first.

The first Cogent Parallel, then, is as follows: In the first chapter of John it is related that Christ saw Nathaniel under a fig-tree; in Buddhistic legend, Gotama Buddha becomes *buddha*, "enlightened," while sitting under the fig-tree which is now called the Bo-tree, or tree of enlightenment. The question here, as in the case of the other Cogent Parallels, is whether Nathaniel's fig-tree must necessarily have been borrowed from Buddha's fig-tree, under which the latter sat safely till he found enlightenment. It is added that both Buddha and Christ were calling their first disciples when the fig-tree is mentioned, but this statement is driven across the limit of accuracy.

If a fig-tree were a rarity in Hebrew tradition, it might be granted that there was something exotic about the scene itself. But, far from being unique in biblical allusion, the fig-tree is typical. It would be equally cogent to point to the fact that Buddha sat safely under the fig-tree and to the statement that "Judah and Israel dwelt safely every man under his fig-tree," and thence conclude that 1 Kings, iv. 25 was copied from Buddhism. But if we consider that the category of Cogent Parallels was established as a group of parallels which imply not only borrowing, but borrowing from Buddhism, on the ground that the Christian side is inconceivable without such borrowing, we must, I think, refuse to admit the fig-tree into this category, and can only wonder that it has been put there by any historian.

The next case is found in the ninth chapter of John.

Here the disciples ask Christ concerning a blind man: Who did sin, this man, or his parents, that he was born blind? If Christ had been under Buddhistic influence, he would surely have said, This man only; for the Karma doctrine of Buddhism teaches that a man's condition in this life is the result of his mental or physical acts in a former life. Jesus answered, Neither hath this man sinned, nor his parents. It is to be noticed, moreover, that this is not a parallel scene, for no parallel event is recorded in the life of Buddha, and it is not till two or three centuries after Christ that we find even an approximation to the biblical narrative, in the late Buddhistic account of a blind man cured by a physician, who gives the usual Hindu explanation that sin caused the blindness. The only parallel in the Gospel account is one of thought, for it is claimed that such an idea as is here presented in the disciples' question implies a doctrine that is specially Buddhistic (namely, sin working out in disease in a new birth), because it is foreign to Jewish ways of thinking. But the latter point may be admitted without any necessity of accepting the explanation, since an Egyptian source is quite as probable as a loan from India. Historically there is certainly nothing to compel the acceptance of a Buddhistic source, and therefore the parallel cannot be regarded as really cogent.[1]

The third Cogent Parallel is found in the fact that both Christ and Buddha existed in heaven before they were born on earth. But it is difficult to see how in Christ's case any other view could have obtained. Even if it were necessary to admit that the idea of the divinity having pre-existence

[1] The idea of sin in one life resulting in malformation or some other misfortune in the next is an addition to the underlying belief in metempsychosis. The latter belief appears to have obtained among Christ's contemporaries in Syria, judging from the matter-of-course way in which John is asked (John i.) whether he is Elijah, and Christ himself seems to have taught that John was Elijah (Matthew xi. and xvii.), at least "in spirit and power," as was declared by the angel, *καὶ αὐτὸς προσελεύσεται ἐνώπιον αὐτοῦ ἐν πνεύματι καὶ δυνάμει Ἠλίου* (Luke i. 17). Origen's objections to such an interpretation show that it was at least considered possible.

(before being born on earth) must necessarily have been borrowed, there would be no historical obligation to recognize the idea as Buddhistic, — which is, of course, the only reason for claiming that it is a Cogent Parallel, — since the same conception is not only found in Zoroastrianism, where also the prophet is believed to have had a pre-existence, but is in fact common, and necessarily so, to all the many religions holding that a divinity may be born as man.

The next Cogent Parallel is united with the following second-class (*b*) parallel. When Buddha was a babe, the old Yogin Asita flew down from his retreat in the Himalaya Mountains and prophesied concerning the child's future greatness, lamenting that he himself could not live to see the fulfilment of the prophecy. This is put as a parallel to Simeon's prophecy concerning Christ. It is not regarded as a Cogent Parallel, although it may be remarked that thus far it is the only striking one. The date of this legend is, however, probably anterior to our era, since it is well known in the first century A. D. It is necessary to mention it merely because unscientific writers ascribe it to a much earlier date and insist that it must have been the prototype of the Simeon story. But Max Müller very properly says that it is one of those parallels which are without any historical significance; and since even Seydel does not regard it as cogent, we may pass it by as unimportant.

But with this is linked a Cogent Parallel; namely, the presentation in the temple. The Buddhistic version is that when Buddha was carried to the temple of the gods, the idols fell down before him. First, however, it must be noticed that this linking of the two stories over-emphasizes the parallel in the former, for Asita is not represented as being in the temple at all; and, secondly, the Buddhistic presentation scene, far from being primitive, is not found till the second or third century after Christ, although it is just such a story as we should expect to find in the early tradition, where, however, it is entirely wanting. For the Asita story is found in the Buddha Carita of the first century, but the presentation story not till the time of the Lalita Vistara, which is at least a century or two later, and, as you will see, it may have been influenced by Christian tradition.

Four of the Cogent Parallels and one second-class parallel have now been examined, and thus far the examination has yielded the fig-tree and the pre-existence in heaven as the only Cogent Parallels dating from before our era, the blind man and the presentation in the temple as post-Christian legends, and the Asita story of middle date, though probably pre-Christian.

To the only remaining Cogent Parallel I add also another which has been much discussed, — the miraculous birth. This has been made more striking by ascribing virginity to Buddha's mother, although, as I have said, the early texts, far from ascribing virginity to her, expressly state that she was not a virgin. The introduction of this parallel under the caption Buddha's Immaculate Conception, Buddha's Virgin Mother, belongs, however, only to the popular and somewhat vulgar class of writers to whom allusion has already been made; and I cite it here merely as a typical example of the style in which grave historical subjects are treated by certain debaters, whose object does not seem to be to arrive at the truth, but only to convince others. But such advocates are not historians and may be ignored as unnecessary.

Freed from fictitious embellishments, there is still a certain parallel to the story of Christ's birth in the story of Buddha's birth. But it is not a very remarkable parallel when we consider that miraculous birth was a necessary concomitant of spiritual greatness, and that it is by no means necessary to seek the origin of the Christian account in India, when, if a source must be found for it, the Iranian parallel is much closer. According to early Buddhistic legend the mother was not a virgin, but a chaste wife, into whom miraculously entered in the shape of a white elephant the future Buddha, who subsequently came out of her right side. The Iranian legend, on the other hand, is as follows: "The Glory enters the house where the future Zaratûsht's (Zoroaster's) mother herself is about to be born. Uniting itself with her presence it abides in her until she reaches the age of fifteen, when she brings forth her own first-born, the prophet of Iran," etc.[1] With this parallel at hand can the Buddhistic elephant be regarded as an important parallel? The historian of the Orient knows that all religious teachers are regarded as divine and as such have miraculous births; in India, even from the time of Vasishtha, the Vedic saint. We need not cite the sculptured testimony to the antiquity of this legend in outline. Undoubtedly Buddha's miraculous birth was believed in as early as the third century B. C. and perhaps earlier. But is this enough to show that it was the model from which was copied the story of the virgin mother of Christ? I doubt whether any close student of Oriental history would be convinced by such evidence. It is at any rate not regarded as Cogent by Seydel himself; nor, so far as I know, by any one else whose opinion is of importance.

The last Cogent Parallel has perhaps been relied upon more than any other to show that Buddhistic legends are incorporated into Christian records. It is the fast preceding the temptation. In the New Testament we are told that Christ fasted forty days and was then tempted of the devil to turn stones into bread, to cast himself from the pinnacle of the temple, to take the glory of the kingdoms of earth in exchange for worshipping the devil; and when he had refused, angels came and ministered unto him. In the legend of Buddha, Death, who plays the devil's part, tempts Buddha (as the latter is on the point of becoming perfect and thus about to escape Death ever after) to yield to sensual pleasures. But, failing in this purpose, he attacks Buddha with a storm, which, however, does not disturb Buddha's serenity, and finally attacks him with an army. Buddha, however, still sits unmoved under the Bo-tree, and Death retires discomfited. Buddha continues to sit under the Bo-tree till he has become really enlightened, and then after

[1] Jackson, Zoroaster, pp. 24 ff. Ib. page 28, attention is called to a Zoroastrian parallel to Herod's slaughter of the innocents.

fasting for twenty-eight days, or, according to a later account, forty-nine days, begins his ministry.

It will be observed that, though this parallel contains a fast and temptation, the details are different. The inducements offered are dissimilar, and the order of temptation and fast are reversed. Nevertheless, it may be admitted that we have here rather a close parallel, though it may be added that the whole Buddhistic legend is not primitive. To cite the statement of Rhys Davids:[1] "When it is first incidentally referred to we find only the bare mention of a suggestion to the Blessed One that now . . . his work is done and that the time has arrived for him to pass away without attempting to proclaim to others the glad tidings of the Noble Way." But this is really of little importance for our purpose, since the story of Death making the suggestion (which is the germ of the temptation) is as early as the Book of the Great Decease, that is centuries older than Christ's birth. On the other hand, it must be remembered that this is one of the five Cogent Parallels which are represented as cogent because they contain elements which are unintelligible if they are Christian, while if they are originally Buddhistic they are perfectly natural. How far this trait is strained in the preceding examples has been shown. In this example we may well ask why a forty days' fast must be derived from Buddha's fast? Moses fasted forty days, and the type is familiar to the Jews, who also had the devil.

From these comparisons it becomes clear that the historical student's first duty is to make a sharp division between those parallels which can and those which cannot be referred to a time earlier than the birth of Christ. Thus in the Lotus, which cannot be referred to a date earlier than 200 A. D., is found the parable of the prodigal; and in the same work, the curing of a blind man by a physician, who says that the blindness is the result of his former sins. In the Lalita Vistara, which, as I have said, belongs to the second or third century of our era, occurs the temple-scene, and here also the

[1] Buddhism, p. 104.

scene where Buddha shows his precocity by exhibiting knowledge of all the kinds of alphabets, including the Chinese. Still more insecure are parallels based on Burmese, Tibetan, and Chinese traditions dating from the sixth to the thirteenth century, although they have all been used to support the structure of parallels. Some of the second-class parallels, those which may show borrowing, have already been given. A complete list may be seen in Seydel's Evangelium, p. 299 ff. Here the not very striking facts that Buddha and Christ both preached on mountains, and that verses occur in Buddhistic narration and in the prose of Luke's Gospel, are given as cases of probably Christian borrowing; while it is frankly admitted that "Die frappantesten Analogien aber gehören dem Lalita Vistara an" (p. 300), that work which cannot be traced back of 200 A. D., though Seydel opines, of course, that it implies older material.

Among the third-class (*a*) parallels, as explained above, are found the Herod story (which, however, has a still closer parallel in Zarathustrian legend than is found in the Buddhistic story of Bimbisara); the preference shown by Christ and Buddha for certain disciples; the fact that both Christ and Buddha are given genealogies. In this group, to the great credit of the author, is put the miraculous conception, which less scholarly writers regard as one of the most important parallels.

On the other hand, the following "parallel" is enrolled even by Seydel himself. Buddha sent out his disciples and ordered them not to go in pairs, "in strange contrast to Luke x. 1 (Christ sent them two and two), but this contrast is eliminated by"—what? the fact that "later" the Buddhistic missionaries went forth in pairs![1]

Parallels in the sayings of both teachers are illustrated by the following: Jesus said, He that findeth his life shall lose it. Buddha is not reported as having said this, but in Buddhistic literature is found, The King of Death does not see one who looks upon this world as (unstable like) a bubble or sunbeam. Another striking parallel: Jesus said, Be not anxious for

[1] Die Buddha-Legende, p. 66.

the morrow, sufficient unto the day; a Buddhistic verse says, The fool thinks, I will live here winter and summer, but does not think of the end of life. Still another: "Jesus' Judge not, and the Take the beam from thine own eye is paralleled by, Let one not have another's faults in his eye." It is almost incredible that such parallels should be cited, but the last case is more than usually venturesome, for on turning to the original it may be seen that what is translated "have in his eye" is so translated merely to make a parallel with "take the beam from thine own eye," whereas the original text, Dhammapada 50, *avekkheyya*, has merely "observe," or look at, of which *hab' man im Aug'* would be a correct enough translation, but for the fact that the author makes a special point of finding a parallel between phrases (Seydel's Evangelium, p. 212).[1] One more of these extraordinary parallels will suffice. Jesus said, Blessed are the poor, and, Sell all that thou hast, while in the Buddhist Dhammapada occurs a verse, "The greedy do not get to heaven, the generous wise man becomes happy above."

The fact that "parallels" are cited as historically connected on the strength of such resemblance as this shows how strained may become the whole argument. Yet many of the parallels are no closer or more convincing. The case might well be put on the other side: Why, if Christ copies Buddha, is there no real resemblance in his sayings to those of his presumed copy? In regard to parallel miracles we have, to sum up, two sorts, — those of universal origin, as we may call them, and those that are found only in Christianity and Buddhism. Now the only miracles certainly found in pre-Christian Buddhism are of the former sort, while the latter sort is found only in such dateless material as the Jatakas, or in material which, like the Lotus and Lalita, dates from after the Christian era. Two very striking Jataka parallels are given by Max Müller.[2] One of them is the story

[1] Another instance of this same method of making a fictitious resemblance is given in Max Müller's essay on Coincidences, reprinted in Last Essays, p. 282.

[2] *Loc. cit.*, p. 284 ff.

of a disciple walking upon the water; the other, that of Buddha making one loaf feed more than five hundred people. It is quite impossible to say on the historical evidence whether these stories were borrowed by or from Christianity. All we know is that they are Jataka stories, and there is no proof that these special Jatakas were pre-Christian; which, however, does not prove that they were not.[1]

As is clear from the last examples, one factor in all these parallels is of the greatest importance. We are accustomed in the West to deal with documents the date of which can usually be determined within a few years or decades, and it is not often that as with Homer we have to content ourselves with referring to literary works as probably belonging to any time within two or three centuries, — works of what we may call the period of nebulous history. Now the first thing that every student of Indian literature has to learn is that most of the works composed in India before the fourth century of our era have merely nebulous dates. There is not a single pre-Christian Sanskrit book concerning which we can say that the work as it has come down to us was certainly composed at any time within two hundred years. And, moreover, the Buddhistic records with which we are especially concerned are not only of very uncertain date, but they are also of very mixed origin, being for the most part works not composed by any one author, but collections of legends loosely connected and enlarged by late accretions of every sort, as is admitted even by those who exploit such works as historical material. We may think, and it is quite probable we are right in thinking, that such books as the Lotus of the True Law and the Lalita Vistara contain a substratum of legend much older than the date

[1] The Jakatas as a group are of quite uncertain date. The story of some has been found in stone wrought in pre-Christian times, but even the corresponding Jatakas as we have them (in literary form) may be much later, and as for the mass of these works, there is no proof at all that in their present form they antedate our era. A very few can be shown to be essentially (not necessarily in their present shape) older than this; but the striking parallels adduced above are not found in Jatakas (*jātakas*, Birth-tales) of this class.

to which we must in general assign the works themselves. It may even be shown that the Lalita Vistara, an epical history of Buddha without inner connection, reverts in origin to an older and simpler account; but this merely shows that the book has received accretions, and surely, on the basis of such an opinion or such a reconstruction, we are not entitled to operate with the presumed original as if it furnished the date of the completed conglomerate which now is called Lalita Vistara.

Of the Sanskrit works thus essential to the theory of a borrowed Christianity, the Lotus is referred vaguely to the third century, or at earliest to about 200 A. D., while there is no evidence whatever that the Lalita Vistara in its present shape antedates the third century. It is quite justifiable to suppose that the original of the Lotus may be some centuries earlier; but it is quite as unhistorical to refer legends of our present Lotus to a pre-Christian era as it would be to put the history of Herodotus into the eighth century because some of his stories may have had a more antique form. One of the oldest of these works is the Buddha Carita of Açvaghosha, which has the distinction of being assigned to a definite author, whose date at earliest is the close of the first century of our era; but even this date is a matter of conjecture, not of such certainty as to fix the time of the work definitively. For we are forced to depend upon statements in regard to it which are themselves made centuries after the assumed date. Now it is in relying absolutely upon such evidence that the advocates of the borrowing theory are constantly making historical blunders. If we remove from the parallels admitted to be close those which unquestionably belong to pre-Christian sources, we find very little left on which to base the argument that Christ drew his religion from Buddhistic sources.

More weight has been laid upon the Lalita Vistara and more ingenuity has been expended to prove that it contains ante-Christian tales than in the case of any other late

Buddhistic work, because it has so many interesting parallels. In allowing to this poetic hodge-podge of tales drawn from any source an antiquity as respectable as I have, I wish to show the greatest liberality consistent with historical possibilities. The actual latitude in age may be inferred from the following words of Rhys Davids, a writer who claims as great an antiquity as is possible, or even greater, for the simpler Pali tradition, but says: "The Lalita Vistara, a poem of unknown date and authorship, but probably composed in Nepal, and by some Buddhist poet who lived some time between six hundred and a thousand years — *i. e.* 500 A. D., — after the birth of the Buddha."[1]

This does not, of course, imply that outside influences cannot have helped in building up Christian tradition. It still leaves it, for example, an open question whether the story of the temptation or of the man born blind may not have been later additions (as already remarked, the latter is not in the Synoptic Gospels), and it is possible that the idea of Karma may have been received from India. That is neither here nor there. The point is that the evidence before us does not indicate that the chief features of the Gospel story were drawn from India, although India had the story of the temptation at least a century or two earlier than our era.

Strange to say, there is still another group of authorities which later writers especially have drawn upon without discrimination, this time from the literature on the other side. For not only is the borrowing theory based to a great extent on Sanskrit works composed long after the Christian era, but it is based in equal measure on Christian legends which are also late and quite as untrustworthy reflectors of

[1] Added to this are the words I here italicize:

"*As evidence of what early Buddhism actually was, it is of about the same value as some mediæval poem would be of the real facts of the Gospel history.*" Hibbert Lectures, p. 197. And again: "We have no external evidence which would justify the assignment of the Lalita Vistara to any date earlier than the uncertain one [the sixth century of the Christian era] of its Tibetan version," *loc. cit.* p. 200.

earlier belief; namely, the pseudepigrapha of the New Testament, many of which may have been composed under influences foreign to the New Testament itself.

And here the impartial historian has to observe that those who argue on the Christian side have also failed to be quite historical in regard to some of the Buddhistic monuments, the age of which they depreciate too much. For while, as already pointed out, the epical accounts of Buddha's life are of very uncertain date, there is a mass of documents which there is no reason to doubt are much older than our era, and some of the parallels are found among them. Especially important is the evidence of the sculptured gateways and other monuments, such as Açoka's edicts, whereon are carved, or actually referred to, the stories of the temptation and miraculous birth. The former are not, as Christian apologists have sometimes asserted, later than our era, but they belong pretty certainly to the second century; those at Sanchi are probably as old as 150 B. C. or older.

Nor can another item be passed over. The upholders of the view that Christianity has necessarily been borrowed from Buddhism have taken a position the weakness of which has not been exposed with the rigor that their opponents might have exercised. For, as has been shown, not a few of these parallels are referred as if necessarily to Buddhism simply because the theorist has ignored other possible originals. The base of the explanation is in many cases completely demolished by the simple fact that, even admitting a loan as probable, there are other sources which are quite as likely as Buddhism to have given rise to the parallel case. But the Christian apologist has at times neglected to point out the truth that his own traditions are often not unique, and thus by ignoring the possibility of any borrowing whatever he has played directly into the hands of his opponent, whose strongest point is the tacit assumption that if there was any borrowing it must have come from Buddhism.

There is one great likeness in the work of Christ and Buddha. Both gave a new definition to the word "religion."

It was assumed by each teacher that men wished to be religious. But each teacher made it his life-work to inculcate the new idea that religion was not an outward observance but an inner state. In teaching that religion was not sacrifice and ceremonial, but purity and charity, Buddha and Christ in turn had to inveigh against the priests that taught a religion devoid of both essential elements. The same conditions gave rise to the same result. Granting that a stereotyped formality had formed itself independently in Judea, it was inevitable that the reaction against it should emphasize the true nature of religion. There is then in this reaction as personified in Christ merely a logical parallel to the reaction as personified in Buddha. If the relations were one of historical connection, we should expect to find that Christ utilized the teachings of his predecessor. But both the teaching of Christ and the history of missionary effort in the East are stumbling-blocks that the borrowing theory with all its ingenuity has been unable to cross successfully. We must look at each of these points in turn.

Is it probable that Christ copied his religion from one that in every metaphysical particular was opposed to what he himself taught? Buddha believed neither in God nor soul, but he believed, and every form of his church believed, in the transmigration of character, as an entity, into a new body, — a theory which has nothing to do with heredity, with which it has recently been compared. This was an ingenious but wholly unscientific compromise between the popular belief of the day in metempsychosis and Buddha's own denial of a psyche. If, then, Buddha's doctrine in these fundamentals, atheism, apsychism, character-transfer, affected Christ's teaching, why is there no trace of any one of these essentials in Christ's teaching? It has always seemed to me that the theory of a plagiarized Christianity finds itself here in a dilemma from which it is impossible to escape. For if Christ simply copied, why is there no trace of the copy? If, on the other hand, he was imbued with a Buddhism current and well known in his day, — as think the pleaders for plagiarism, —

but was antagonistic to it, his attitude in regard to these points must have been as decided as it was in regard to other views held by the many and denounced by him, and we should hear at least something said in regard to the moot points of soul and God. But not even the disputatious apostles show any sign of their religion having been a reaction against an atheistic and soulless faith, although it is one of the cardinal tenets of the borrowing theory that Christ must have imbibed Buddhistic ideas current in Syria in his day. The only escape from this dilemma is in assuming that Christ copied a modified form of Buddhism, and this escape is essayed. But here there is difficulty in pointing to any faith which reflects Buddhism. As the Essenes were mystics, they have been selected, however, and another development of the theory is that the medium of communication was not a Buddhistic gospel current in Syria, but the Essenes. The double claim is here made that Christ was an Essene and that the Essenes were Buddhists.

This explanation of Christ's religion is unsatisfactory from an historical point of view because it involves two unknown factors. Even if it were certain that the Essenes were Buddhists, there would still be as much doubt in regard to Christ being an Essene as there would be in regard to his being a Pythagorean or Neo-platonist or Zoroastrian. To this uncertain factor is added the mere conjecture, which is without proof of any kind, that the Essenes were Buddhists. The evidence, such as it is, is decidedly against either of the two suggested relationships. First, as regards Christ's connection with the Essenes, the fact that Christ does not inveigh against this body as he does against the other two sects of his day, the Pharisees and Sadducees, is counterbalanced by the antithesis between his doctrines and that of the Essenes, who were "superlative Pharisees," the strictest Sabbatarians, and sun-worshippers. Celibacy, community of goods, and a very strict moral law were characteristic of both religions. But Christ's attitude toward the outer world and all Pharisaical tendencies does not accord at all with an Essene's views on these points. On the other hand, the Essenes were so strictly Jewish that they condemned to death not only him who blasphemed against God, but also him who blasphemed against Moses, while the element of sun-worship, which is not Buddhistic, but is Persian, would seem to show that they were affected by a religion nearer home than any in India. Finally, all that they taught in regard to a previous existence and the soul's recovery is easily accounted for on the supposition that they were more or less Hellenized Jews; while their stern insistence on the two points of soul and personal God are in direct antagonism to the chief tenets of Buddhism. They appear to have been a set of religious mongrels, Jewish in origin, but crossed with various foreign strains, among which, however, there is no certain trace of a Buddhistic element. The double hypothesis of Christ being an Essene, and the Essenes being Buddhists, thus resolves itself into a desperate guess to explain in Christ's religion factors which another guess suggests against all probability may be Buddhistic.

The history of the early Christian church in India is a side of this whole question that is often ignored by the upholders of the hypothesis of borrowing. But what we know in this regard is so important that to slur the facts or to omit them from consideration is to belie history. These facts are briefly as follows, though it must be said also that the acceptance of foreign ideas has from the very earliest phases of their religions been characteristic of the Hindus. Far from being unchanging, as is often asserted, all the Hindus, both Brahmans and Buddhists, were mentally most progressive and receptive. They have always taken new gods from outside their own pale, and have always been prone to assimilate the thoughts and traditions of those with whom they have come in contact, especially in religious matters, as is shown by their absorption of un-Aryan elements in early times and in what I shall have to say immediately in regard to Krishnaism.

As to the missionaries sent to India: The legend that

Thomas went to India and labored in the realm of Gundoferus could be regarded as a legend only so long as Gondaphares, to give his real name, was a myth. But in the last century we have learned that exactly at the time when Thomas is reported to have been in India, and on the route which he would most naturally take, a king by the name of Gondaphares ruled over all the Parthian and western Punjab region. We know also that a great colony of Jews emigrated from Palestine — ten thousand in all — and settled on the Malabar coast in A. D. 68; that Pantænus was expressly sent to teach the Brahmans in India, and found a Christian church already established there in 190 A. D.; that in the sixth century there was in South India a Christian church, which according to its own tradition had been founded in the first century; that Christian influence was perhaps strong enough in the Northwest to leave Christian scenes depicted in the Peshawar and Kandahar sculptures of the fifth century;[1] that in the seventh century missionaries were in middle India; and that about the same century they were sent to China, where, indeed, as in Tibet, it is probable that they had already been located for some time.

In short, from the first to the seventh century of our era there was strong Christian influence at work in India, and the time of missionary activity in India is coincident with the time of the most striking parallels, not of the universal sort but of the minute and particular kind, which is really the only kind that has significance, parallels which reach their perfection in the modern Llamaistic church of Tibet, — a form of Buddhism which has about all the paraphernalia of

[1] This is the opinion of scholars whose judgment in regard to these sculptures is respected. Such works as I have seen show Buddhistic and Hindu scenes treated under Græco-Persian influence, which I think will be the eventual verdict in regard to all Buddhistic sculpture, none of which is free of Greek influence (as all of it post-dates historically the presence of Greeks in India). Some writers lay a good deal of stress on the Christian origin of the Kandahar sculptures, for which reason I include the item with a "perhaps," though I think the influence is not quite without doubt. The other factors are unquestioned.

the Roman Catholic sect, a pontiff, sacred pictures, a virgin madonna, and many other remarkable parallels, carefully to be distinguished, however, from those religious factors which this church shares with other forms of Buddhism, such as nuns, monasteries, the rosary, confession, and other primitive elements. These have been referred to so often that the detailed list may be omitted here, as it can be found in every popular presentation of the subject. But it must be said that in giving the whole list there has not always been a careful distinction between what is antique and new in the Llamaistic service. When we eliminate the antique, which we can do by grouping the elements found in primitive Buddhism, we find a certain number of minute resemblances which are found only in that church of Buddha which arose in the seventh century A. D.; that is, after the Nestorian missionaries were in full activity in Northern India. As these were the historical conditions, it is, to say the least, extraordinary that any one should imagine that the Roman Church got its ritual from the Llama form of Buddhism; yet the unhistorical parallelist (he really deserves a special name in distinction from historian) unhesitatingly jumps to this conclusion. When dissected carefully, his amalgam of parallels of all ages shows only one Catholic feature that may reasonably be supposed to have been borrowed from the Buddhistic paraphernalia; namely, the rosary. This seems to have been a loan because its name is unintelligible; whereas the Hindu form is a compound word that means prayer-wreath, but at the same time, owing to the word "prayer," *japa*, being almost or quite identical with the word for rose, it may be translated rose-wreath. This prayer-wreath under an older name was borrowed by Buddhism itself from Çivaism, and is certainly older than our era.

We may say then with every regard for historical accuracy that the presence of parallels to Christian tradition in such Buddhistic works as cannot be referred back of the first century A. D., is not necessarily explained by borrowing on the part of Christianity. For this would be almost as much of an anachronism as to see in the parallel passages of Vergil and Theocritus a proof that Theocritus copied Vergil. Where the parallels make borrowing seem probable, as in the case of the miracles and legends not found in other religions and striking enough to suggest a loan, the historical evidence is strongly in favor of Christianity having been not the copyist but the originator.

The possibility that the Buddhists have borrowed from Christian tradition has been recognized by the more scholarly advocates of the opposed theory, and Seydel, for example, meets it with this rejoinder: The Lalita Vistara and other works of this class are, indeed, so late that they may have been exposed to Christian influence; but that these works did not borrow from a Christian source at all, is proved by the fact that they did not borrow more Christian legends. It is interesting to observe that this is the best argument that can be brought up. Reverting to our classical illustration, we might just as well say: It is clear that Vergil did not take phrases from Theocritus, for Theocritus has many phrases which are not found in Vergil at all.

To conclude this half of our study, we may, I think, as open-minded historical students, safely assert that the Christian religion, according to all the evidence, was not plagiarized but original. At the same time we must admit that there is historical possibility in the view that the Christian narrative may have been affected by Buddhistic tales, but we must just as decidedly maintain that no cogent proof of this view has yet been furnished.

It seems to me that this is the only scientific opinion possible, and I urge it particularly as against Max Müller's demand (*loc. cit.* p. 290) that we should not "shilly-shally" with a *not proven*, for "what is wanted is a straightforward English verdict, Yes or No," that is, to the question as a whole. Müller himself, who was quite as well able as any one else to give an opinion on the subject, was very careful to avoid saying what he thought. He left the verdict to others and refusing to say what he believed denounced as un-English any hesitation in saying yes or no. But a categorical reply to many scientific and historical questions is the most unscientific answer that can be given; for when the fact asserted is not proven, Not Proven is the only honest answer. Personally I incline to believe that the early tradition of the Christian Church may have received additions from outside sources, and I think it is quite possible that Buddhistic stories and ideas may have had some influence, such as was shown later in taking Buddha into the Christian list of saints. But no such influence on the earliest form of Christianity has been made very probable, and what is more important (and Müller reiterates this very properly) there is nothing in any of these parallels that fundamentally affects Christianity. At this point every student finds himself as to the New Testament in much the same position as he occupies when he compares geology and Genesis. If he has so little faith in the Bible as to fear every new discovery of science or to think that Christianity's truth trembles in the balance of Buddhistic legend, he should close his books and in solitude demand of himself whether he really understands the difference between the essential and the adventitious in his belief, and whether he ought to weight the wings of Faith with unnecessary burdens.

But let us, on the other hand, remember this also, that whereas it used to require courage to be liberal it now requires courage to be conservative, to brave the undeserved reproach of narrow-mindedness, to lag on the path of presumptive progress and walk with slow-paced Doubt rather than run ahead with nimble Imagination. All of you, I know, wish to be fair, and some of you may think that it is narrow-minded not to "accept results" and admit all that is claimed against the historical Christianity taught in the Sunday-school. Well and good; I too try to be as liberal as facts permit. But let us not mistake assertions for facts. And as to liberality, you need not worry or be disturbed at the liberal spirit of those whose contention is that Buddhism has been the model of Christianity. As I have said on another occasion, it is not what a man believes that makes him liberal, but the attitude he assumes toward that which he does not believe. You may believe in nothing and be most illiberal. And so you may accept all new ideas and fancy you are thereby broad-minded, yet be as wanting in wisdom as if you rejected all that was new. In a word, both in one's general attitude and in one's acceptance or rejection of ideas and statements, to be loose-minded is not to be liberal-minded.

But not to preach to preachers (and I ought to ask pardon anyway for leaving history for other matters), though I give this general warning as one useful in considering many historical problems, I cannot admit that it has any especial application here except for those who feel that the Not Proven leaves a margin of doubt which troubles them. I say feel, because the subjective element undoubtedly plays a part in the decision, try as hard as we may to make it objective only. For them I repeat that the vital truth of Christianity is not affected by anything discovered in Buddhism. For others, who, like myself, would not be disturbed by any real discoveries in history, it is enough to repeat that the historical evidence in this particular case makes it at least probable that Christian missionaries were not idle all the time they were in India from the first to the seventh century, and that Buddhism has borrowed somewhat from Christianity; while it is doubtful whether Christianity has borrowed anything from Buddhism. Of the Cogent Parallels, one only seems to me indicative of a possible loan, that of the temptation, but this is only possible, and perhaps not very probable. Even if it were shown to have been borrowed, however, the fact would certainly detract nothing from Christian truth.

The reception and adaptation of Christian legends by the rival religion which dominated India as Buddhism began to decline form a very instructive parallel (though one carefully shunned by the parallelist) to the way in which Christianity was (or at least may have been) utilized in exploiting Buddhism. This rival religion is Krishnaism, a form of Vishnuism. The influence of Christianity upon it is shown clearly in its later stages and may with good reason be suspected in its earlier form. In discussing now this form of Hindu religion as it resembles Christianity, I shall first have to give some historical data in regard to it.

The worship of Krishna as a popular divinity, corresponding to Herakles in the Greek account of Megasthenes, is probably as old as the fourth century B. C. In the second century it appears to have still been no more than the cult of a hero-god, who may have been regarded as an *avatar* of Vishnu by his special adorers, the inhabitants of the district about Delhi and Muttra. But he was still a hero rather than a god, as Megasthenes says in identifying the valley-god with Herakles and the mountain-god Çiva with Dionysos. This is Krishna's character in many parts of the epic, always divine, though this means little in India; but often he is clearly only a hero-divinity, and he is once, when assuming to be Supreme God, sharply rebuked for his pretensions, though of course he triumphs over his revilers. Elsewhere, however, in the same epic, Krishna is unquestioned God. But whatever he is, godling, man-god, or God, he reveals himself at first only in human form.

The great epic of India is a huge compilation which, while its story has doubtless swallowed up material that was centuries older, belongs in its present condition to the century or two immediately preceding and following our era. Some of it may be several centuries later than our era, but by the fifth century A. D. it was about its present size and presumably had about its present content.

Now this epic has had inserted into it a little poem which in origin is evidently a late Upanishad. It is nevertheless one of the earliest of the poems set in the frame of the epic. But it is by no means a poem in its original form. Both the beginning and the end are later additions and the poem has been retouched, as were most other parts of the epic.

The epic itself as a whole lies across our era, part of it being older, part of it later than the time of Christ, and as it is difficult to be accurate in regard to the date of the whole, it is still more difficult, although we may recognize early and late parts of interpolations, to decide whether these parts belong to a pre-Christian era or not. For example, the theory of the special Grace of God, which saves the sinner, and is the correlate to the latter's "loving faith," is a comparatively late doctrine of the Upanishads, appearing first in those of the third chronological order. Only here is to be found the technical word for this idea, *prasāda*, but rarely withal and still interchanging with the earlier notion of graciousness, or literally calmness, not of God toward a sinner but of a man's own mind.[1] So the epic poem to which I have referred uses this word at first only in the old sense, "one attains calmness," or graciousness of mind; but in the last chapter, which is clearly an addition, we find it in the later meaning of Grace of God (just as it is used in the sectarian Upanishads), not once but half a dozen times in this one chapter, as, for example, in the following:

He that is faithful to me, whatsoever be the acts he does, obtains immortality through my grace.
Having thy thoughts fastened on me, through my grace thou shalt pass over all difficulties.
The Lord of all beings abides in one's own heart. Go to him as thy refuge; through his grace thou shalt obtain immortality.

[1] The general idea of the grace of a god as a special favor is of course as old as the gods who could show favors. In the Rig Veda the divinity Speech, Vac (*vāc*), says that she elects whom she loves, and makes him mighty. In this has been seen the germ of the Logos doctrine, and as this study takes up so many sides of possible relations between Christian and Oriental doctrines, I may add here a word on this point. Without denying that Gnosticism may have influenced the Logos doctrine, I yet think that the part played by speech ("Word," as it is often freely rendered) in Indian theosophy has been greatly exaggerated throughout. Vac, Speech, at no time represents Logos. She is simply a deified abstraction, like Sarasvati, Eloquence. In the Vedic hymn just alluded to, moreover, Vac is nothing more than the personified power of the priest's utterance; and when the priest sings, "I, Speech, make powerful whom I love," he expresses simply the oft-repeated idea that the prayer of the priest, his eloquence with the gods, makes the gods

He who speaks is the divine man Krishna, who in this poem, called the Lord's Recitation, Bhagavad Gita (*gītā*) is imparting to his disciple the truths of a religion which in the epic is recognized as essentially new. For the old religion was the worship of the Herakles-like popular divinity, but in the epic Krishna is represented as having but recently made claim to be the *avatar* of the Supreme God, a claim not yet wholly recognized by other epic characters and one which Krishna himself naïvely says is admitted only by a few persons. It is therefore of peculiar interest to find that there is a close parallel between the words of this Krishna and those of Christ's disciples. The question naturally arises whether the Gita, which contains these parallels, has been affected by Christian influences or has itself affected the New Testament.

When this question was first broached, it was answered with some lack of critical discrimination. Those who held that the Gita was original referred the New Testament parallels to this "ancient Upanishad;" while their opponents neglected the data of history. I will speak first of the latter, who exaggerated the modernity of Krishnaism.

For both the antecedents of the religion were overlooked and that which is universal in the parallelism was ignored. Thus it was said that Krishnaism in this form presented the first instance in Hindu religion of *bhakti*, loving-devotion or faith like ἀγάπη, and consequently this idea was thought to be drawn from Christianity. Now it is true that the word *bhakti* scarcely occurs before the epic and does not occur at all in the Krishnaite sense before the epic, for though it is found in one late Upanishad, yet there it is not love but devotion to a fearful God before whom "one comes in fear," just as in the older Upanishads. But, on the other hand, although other Hindu religions had nothing corresponding to ἀγάπη, yet this notion had long

well-disposed to the priest's employer (the king), and the moral is the usual one that the king must treat well a priest whose speech is so productive of good (or bad, according as the priest will).

been a feature of Buddhism, and the loving devotion to the great master who was a real personality was simply transferred to the sectarian god, whose rise in dignity was contemporary with the first political rebuff experienced by Buddhism. As in other cases, the attributes of Buddha, the teaching of Buddha, notably in a stricter "non-injury" doctrine, and perhaps the events of Buddha's life, were transferred to the popular divinity, though formal Buddhism is argumentatively rejected in the epic itself. Further, there was a lack of perspective in these parallels. Thus, such a phrase as "I am the letter A" as compared with "I am Alpha and Omega" was cited as illustrating a loan from Christianity, although in one of the oldest Upanishads, centuries before Christ, we read,[1] "Brahma is the A" and "A is the whole of speech (or the word), and the word is truth, and truth is the spirit."

Then, again, many of the parallels belong rather to the class of universal similitudes such as we find in Buddhism and Christianity; while some are too slight to deserve notice, such as, "Thou, God, alone knowest thyself," as compared with "No man hath seen God at any time;" or "Save from the sea of death," as compared with "Who shall save from the body of death?"

On these vague resemblances, however interesting they may be, too much historical weight has often been laid even in modern essays, as when the idea of adultery in the heart, Matt. v. 28, is compared with G. 3, 6: He is called a hypocrite who, while subduing the organs of sense, sits remembering in his mind the objects of sense; or when the command to abjure sin and lust, and the statement that the mind of the flesh is enmity against God, Rom. vi. 12 and viii. 7, are grouped together to make a parallel to G. 3, 34: Let one not become subject to lust and hate, for they are enemies of the soul. Some of these "parallels" have not even a remote connection. For example, What shall I do to inherit eternal life, Luke x. 25 (this do and thou shalt live), has actually been "paralleled"

[1] The references are given in my Religions of India, p. 226.

with G. 4, 16 (I will tell thee the act by knowing which thou shalt be freed from evil), although the answer of the former passage is not even suggested in the latter. Such a "parallel" is in truth merely an historical impertinence.

Moreover, we must not forget how remarkably similar may be by mere chance the phraseology of different religions. This point too may be illustrated here, lest it be overlooked in making an estimate of the parallels between Krishnaism and Christianity. For this purpose I choose a few verses of the Rig Veda and compare with them Old Testament verses that cannot be suspected of having been either their source or their copy:

*R. V.* His own works witness to his might and wisdom,
Who fashioned firm supports for earth and heaven,
Who set on high the firmament uplifted,
And fixed the stars, and spread out earth's expanses.— vii. 86, 1.

*O. T.* He that made the earth by his power, he hath established the world by his wisdom and hath stretched out the heavens by his discretion.—Is. xliv. 24.

*R. V.* He mingled with the clouds his cooling breezes,
He gave the cow her milk, the horse his vigor,
He in the heart put wisdom, in clouds the lightning.— v. 85, 2.

*O. T.* Hast thou given the horse strength . . . given understanding to the heart.—Job xxxix. 19; xxxviii. 36.

*R. V.* Do not punish us according to our sin, whether we sinned consciously like gamblers, or unconsciously. . . . Whatsoever evil we have committed . . . forgive us.—v. 85, 5-7; vii. 88, 6.

*O. T.* Remember not against us former iniquities. . . . Cleanse thou me from secret faults.—Ps. lxxix. 8; xix. 13.

*R. V.* He knows the track of the birds flying in the air, he knows the ships upon the sea.—i. 25, 7.

*O. T.* The way of an eagle in the air . . . of a ship in the midst of the sea.—Prov. xxx. 18.

Here, then, we find Isaiah, Job, David, and Solomon using almost the same language with that of the Vedic poets; an object lesson on the danger of drawing rash conclusions from parallel phrases. So in story, both in the Old Testament and the Rig Veda, the divinity is lauded as having made the sun stand still in the heavens, changing night to day, and as having overwhelmed his enemies in a flood and given passage through the flood to his worshippers; as may be seen by consulting the parallels cited in Kaegi's Rig Veda, pp. 63 ff., where also are collected not only the citations just given, but many more like them.[1] ' The Gita itself has a few parallels with the Old Testament: As a man puts off old garments and takes others that are new, so leaving the old bodies the (unchanging) spirit enters others that are new, G. 2, 22; All of them shall wax old like a garment; as a vesture shalt thou change them, Ps. cii. 26; Lay aside all works upon me, G. 3, 30; Cast thy burden upon the Lord, Ps. lv. 22.

But even granting the force of the warning I have just given, we may yet doubt whether chance can be made responsible for all the parallels between the Gita and the New Testament, especially when the important fact is noticed that these parallels are not drawn, as in the case of the Rig Veda and Old Testament, or in that of the whole Buddhistic literature as compared with all the early Christian literature, from a voluminous body of writings, but that they are crowded together into one short Hindu poem, and, for the more part, into one gospel.

For, in exploiting all possible Gita parallels with the New Testament, Lorinser, who wrote on this subject thirty years ago, cited every verse and phrase containing the remotest resemblance. But if we exclude such unconvincing examples as make a large part of Lorinser's collection, as when Love your enemies is paralleled by a recommendation to be "indiffer-

[1] On the other hand, Solomon's Judgment in the Tibetan version, instanced by Müller in his Coincidences, is more probably a loan, as it is unknown in Buddhist literature till centuries after the country was entered by Christian missionaries.

ent to friend and foe," Matt. v. 44, G. 6, 9; or as when Pray in the closet is paralleled by a recommendation that one should stand in a deserted place when practising Yoga concentration, Matt. vi. 6, G. 6, 10; or as when the mere word "rain" in the expression, Rain on the just and unjust, is made the base of a comparison with the words of the Supreme Being, who says: I glow (as the sun), I hold back and let out the rain, Matt. v. 45, G. 9, 19; if we exclude these, and take up the really striking parallels, we shall find that with the exception of Be of good cheer, thy sins are forgiven, as compared with Come to me as thy refuge, I will release thee from all thy sins; grieve not (in Matt. ix. 2, and G. 18, 66, respectively), which are rather similar, almost all the close parallels to the Gita are found not in the Synoptic Gospels but in John. Those from the Synoptic Gospels are all of the class just referred to, or are made by combination, as when All ye that labor and are heavy laden, Matt. xi. 28, is joined to xi. 5, The poor have the gospel preached to them, and then again to John xviii. 37, Every one that is of the truth heareth my voice, to make as a whole a parallel to "four kinds of men" who in the Gita 7, 16, are said to worship Krishna; namely, the oppressed, the one desiring wisdom, the needy, and the wise. I give a list of these passages, however, without further remark on their appositeness, that it may be seen just how the theory stands in its exaggerated as well as real strength, though even in such a list I cannot bring myself to admit absurdities and so must refuse to include, Let one elevate himself through himself, Gita 6, 5, as paralleled in any way with Let one deny himself, Matt. xvi. 24.[1] As "parallels" in the Synoptic Gospels are cited:

Matt. vii. 14, Narrow is the gate, and few there be that find it; G. 7, 3, Among thousands of men (scarcely) one strives for perfection; even of those striving to be perfect (scarcely) one knows me truly; and G. 9, 11, They know me not.

[1] The Sanskrit word is *uddharet*, and Lorinser suggests that it may mean "withdraw;" but it means simply "raise," as is clear from the antithetic context, "let one not lower himself," *avasādayet*.

Closer is John, i. 10, The world knew him not. Matt. xxiv. 35, Heaven and earth pass away, but my words shall not pass away; G. 8, 20, He who is not destroyed when all beings are destroyed; ib. 9, 2 (in the secret purifying knowledge), *imperishable*, and *easy* to perform (with which is also compared, My burden is light, Matt. xi. 30). Matt. xxii. 37, With all thy heart and all thy mind; G. 9, 13, Knowing me as the imperishable source of beings, they love me without having the mind on anything else. Matt. xvi. 16, Peter's confession of faith, is compared with that of Krishna's friend, who in G. 10, 12, says that Krishna is Brahman, the highest goal, and unborn primeval God and Lord. Matt. xvii. 2, and Mark ix. 3, the transfiguration, are compared with G. 11, 12, where Krishna reveals himself in the glory of a thousand suns. After the apocalypse Jesus said, Be not afraid (xvii. 7), and Krishna "reassured him frightened" (12, 50). The description in Matt. xi. 19, and Luke v. 33, (came eating and drinking) is compared with the definition of a true Yogin as one who neither eats too much nor not at all, G. 6, 16 (Buddhistic). The Beatitudes, Matt. v. 3–10, are compared with G. 12, 13–19, which has the refrain, He who loves me (or is devoted to me) is dear to me, with a list of descriptive adjectives applied to the word "he" and implying condition: If without hate, kindly, merciful, unselfish, without egoism, alike in weal and woe, patient, contented, always restrained, of subdued nature, firm in resolution, and having thought and mind fixed on me, — he who is devoted to me is dear to me; he (refrain) whom the world fears not, who is not disturbed by joy, anger, or fear, who is unconcerned, pure, assiduous, indifferent, who desires not the fruit of his action, who neither joys nor hates nor sorrows nor desires, who is unaffected by pleasure or pain (refrain); he who is equal-minded toward foe and friend, honor and dishonor, cold, heat, pleasure, and pain, devoid of affections, the same in blame or praise, silent, content with anything, homeless, firm-minded, — such an one devoted to me is dear to me. In Matt. xvi. 26, Lose his soul (as a phrase) is compared with

G. 13, 28, He that recognizes the Lord (in truth) does not destroy his soul, but he attains the highest course. With Mark xvi. 16, He that disbelieveth shall be condemned, is compared G. 4, 40, He that is ignorant, he that has no faith, he of doubting soul, is destroyed. The widow's mite, Mark xii. 42, Luke xxi. 2, is compared with G. 9, 26, I accept what is offered to me with loving devotion, be it but a leaf, a flower, a fruit, or water. Christ had *compassion* on the multitude, Mark viii. 2; Krishna, G. 10, 11, through *compassion* destroys the darkness of ignorance with the light of the lamp of knowledge; where the parallel is closer with 2 Cor. iv. 6, God said light shall shine out of darkness, who shined in our hearts to give the light of the knowledge of the glory of God in the face of Jesus Christ, as in the next verse of the Gita (or again in 4, 38), the knowledge is a purification, *pavitram*, as it is said in Titus ii. 14, That he might purify unto himself a people. In Luke xiv. 33, Whosoever renounceth not all his belongings cannot be my disciple, πᾶσι τοῖς ἑαυτοῦ ὑπάρχουσιν is represented as the exact equivalent of the phrase in G. 4, 21, He sins not who, having renounced all his belongings, is of restrained mind and senses (*tyaktasarvaparigrahah*).[1] In Luke xiv. 26, If any man hateth not, etc.; in G. 13, 9, Attachment to son, wife, home and such objects (must be abandoned).

In Rev. xxi. 23–24, And (the celestial city) has no need of the sun, neither of the moon to shine upon it; for the glory of God did lighten it; in G. 15, 6, 12 (In my imperishable home), there shines no sun, nor moon, nor fire. . . . It is my glory that is in the sun, that illumines the world, the moon, and fire. But this notion, however parallel, is older than the Gita and is found in the Upanishads. So also with the phrase in Rom. xii. 1, Present your bodies a living sacrifice, and G. 4, 26, Sacrifice the senses in the fire of self-control, for this is an ancient Upanishad image.

From the Epistles the closest parallel is found in 1 Cor.

[1] Lorinser and others compare also *atyartham* in G. 7, 17, translating "more than goods," but the word means "exceedingly."

x. 31, Whether ye eat or drink or whatsoever ye do, do all to the glory of God, as compared with G. 9, 27, Whatsoever thou doest, whatsoever thou eatest, whatsoever thou offerest in sacrifice, whatsoever thou givest, do all as if it were to me. The expression in James ii. 8, Fulfil the royal law, has also been compared with G. 9, 2, where Krishna's "secret wisdom" is called the royal secret and royal wisdom, *rāja-vidyā*. So Eph. iv. 18, Darkened in their understanding . . . because of ignorance, and G. 5, 15, Their understanding is covered by reason of ignorance; which is antithetic to G. 5, 16, The understanding which like a sun illuminates the highest (compare The light of the knowledge of the glory of God, 2 Cor. iv. 6).

There is certainly enough parallelism in these passages to suggest the notion that the phrases are not similar by accident, yet if it were for these alone the theory of borrowing could be answered by the objections already made to a too facile explanation of such cases. But when we turn to John we find in brief compass so large a number of parallels, some of which are surprisingly close, that, taken in connection with the more general cases in the other gospels, they present a body of evidence that is, I think, almost conclusive in favor of one of the religions having borrowed from the other. Thus:

All things were made by him, John i. 3; All things have their source in me. It is by me that the universe is created and destroyed, G. 7, 6–8. There was the true light, John i. 10; I am the light of moon and sun, G. *loc. cit.* Without him was not anything made, John i. 3; I am the seed, without me is nothing made, G. 10, 39. The world was made by him, and the world knew him not. He came unto his own, and they that were his own received him not, John i. 10–11; Men distraught know me not in my godly nature; I take a human form and they honor me not, G. 9, 11. Whosoever believeth in him shall not perish, John iii. 15; He that believeth in me doth not perish, G. 9, 31. My father worketh even until now, and I work, John v. 17; There is nothing for me to attain and yet I remain at work, G. 3, 22. (The scriptures) are they that bear witness of me, John v. 39; By all the Vedas I am to be known, G. 15, 15. Every one that . . . hath learned cometh unto me, John vi. 45; They that worship me come unto me, G. 9, 25. I know whence I came, . . . but ye know not, John viii. 14; I have come through many births and thou also; I know them all, thou knowest them not, G. 4, 5. If a man keep my word he shall never see death; whosoever liveth and believeth on me shall never die, John viii. 51; xi. 26; They that trust in me come to escape age and death, G. 7, 29; also, He that truly knows my divine birth and work, on casting off this body is not born again but comes to me, G. 4, 9. The Jews therefore said unto him, Thou art not yet fifty years old and hast thou seen Abraham? John viii. 57; (He said to Krishna) Thy birth is later, earlier was the birth of Vivasvat; how then may I understand that thou hast declared this in the beginning? G. 4, 4. I am the way, and the truth, and the life, John xiv. 6; I am the way . . . the refuge, the friend, life and death, the support, the treasure, the eternal seed, G. 9, 18.

Compare also Rev. i. 17–19, I am the first and the last and the living one. I hold the keys of life and death; ib. xxii. 13, Alpha and Omega; with G. 10, 32–34, I am the beginning, the middle, and the end, the wisdom of all wisdom, the speech of them that speak, the letter A among the letters, time imperishable, the Creator, death and life. Also the phraseology, Ye in me and I in you, John xiv. 20 (so vi. 56 and xvii. 20–23); In him we live and move and have our being, Acts xvii. 28 (Phainomena); In him are all creatures, all is pervaded by him, G. 8, 22; If any worship me in loving devotion, they are in me and I in them,[1] G. 9, 29. Also John xiv. 21, He that loveth me . . . I shall love him, and G. 4, 11, I love them that are devoted to me, even

[1] In the imitation of the Gita found in the fifth book of the epic it is said by the Supreme: "I am the father and the son; ye abide in me, but ye are not of me nor am I of you," v. 46, 29 (C. v. 1.)

as they to me, so I to them (also 7, 17, He is dear to me). In the same chapter, with the thought already illustrated above, we find, The world beholdeth him not, neither knoweth him, John xiv. 17, compared with, I am not beheld of all . . . the world knows me not, G. 7, 25. To this end have I been born and to this end have I come into the world, that I should bear witness unto the truth. . . . That the world might be saved, John xviii. 37 and iii. 17; I am born age after age for the saving of the good, the destruction of evil-doers, and for the sake of establishing virtue, G. 4, 8. Compare also John xvii. 3, This is life eternal that they should know thee, the only true God, and him whom thou didst send, with G. 10, 3, He who knows me, the Lord of the world, is freed from all sins (*i. e.* gets life eternal).

It seems to me that the parallels here given are almost too close in thought as in diction to have sprung from two independent sources. But, as has been said, in attempting to answer the question which work has borrowed there has not been entire unanimity. Some scholars point to the fact that the Gita is in Upanishad form, and contains old Upanishad material, that it is an antique part of the epic, and that the epic existed before our era. The fact that the most striking parallels, as in the case of the Buddhistic parallels, are found in John, naturally suggests also that this gospel has been the borrower. On the other hand, there are several considerations tending to modify these statements, which are true enough in a general way, but they do not allow for several ignored facts. In the first place, Upanishads may be of any age from 600 B.C. onward, and sectarian Upanishads are uniformly late. Then the metre and language of the Gita are such as to make it impossible to connect it closely in time with the ancient Upanishads even in its oldest parts, and it has besides two different parts, one of which is later than the other, so that it is pretty clear that it has been rewritten. But above all, not only is the religion as inculcated, with its devotion not to a stern master, but to a sin-forgiving, love-demanding savior-god in human form, something absolutely unique up to the time it appears, but it is acknowledged also both by friend and foe in the epic narrative itself that Krishna is a new form of God (not a new god, for Krishna had long been a popular god), and that the new religion has as yet few adherents. When these facts are weighed together with the fact that the epic as we have it is at most not more than two hundred years older than the Christian era, and that it is almost certain that parts of it are as late as two or perhaps more centuries after our era, it seems possible that the original Gita, which was without doubt composed at least 200 B. C., and appears to have been at first a Yogin tract simply, was affected by the introduction of a new religious spirit[1] and that it absorbed some of the ideas presented in the form most Oriental and nearest to Hindu conceptions; namely, in the fourth Gospel.

The most reasonable explanation of the data as a whole appears to me to be that the fourth gospel, perhaps not uninfluenced by the Gnosticism of the time, but not necessarily influenced by Buddhistic tradition or by any Sanskrit texts, was of a mystical tone that made it peculiarly suitable to influence the Hindu divines, who transferred from it such phrases and sentiments as best fitted in with the conception of Krishna as a god of love. For it must be remembered constantly that before Krishna's advent in his new *rôle*, those characteristics of Krishna that bring him into closest likeness with Christ are entirely lacking in the conception of any previous Hindu divinity. Buddha never pretended to forgive sin, and no old Upanishad suggests that the grace of the divinity does more than elect a servitor. But suddenly there appears this benign man-god, who proclaims that all sins are forgiven to him who believes in Krishna; and that, though those who believe in him are very few in number, yet this new religion of love and faith is better than the old Brah-

[1] A fact of some importance, to be set beside Megasthenes' distinction between a great god Dionysos (Çiva) and a demi-god Herakles (Krishna), is that Krishna is unknown in the older Buddhistic literature, which could scarcely have ignored him (in favor of Brahman) if he was already a great god.

manic religion of works and ceremonial purity. I admit freely that on a first superficial glance at the relations between John and the Synoptic Gospels on the one hand and John and the Hindu texts on the other, the easiest solution seems to be that John has borrowed from the East; but I think a closer acquaintance with the position of the Gita in relation to other Hindu texts and a due recognition not only of the very important admissions made by this "new religion" itself, but also of the two factors to which I have already called your attention, namely, the early influence of Christian missions and the very doubtful age of all old Hindu texts, will tend to make careful scholars still more careful not to join the ranks of those who announce, apparently without taking any of these points into consideration, that the Gospel came from India.

In other respects also, the language and tales of the later epic suggest the possibility of Christian influence quite as much as Christian tales suggest Indian influence. I lay no great weight on them, but they should be known, if only as a companion-piece to what is found in the West and referred to the East. Krishna is a by-name of Vyasa, the author of the epic (in so far as the arranger of the mass may be called author), who, though not identified with Krishna as Supreme God, is himself divine, and is described as "the unborn (that is, the eternal) and ancient one, the only son of God, born of a virgin, very part, *ança*, of God."[1] He is a figure unknown till the end of the epic, and even his name Vyasas, *vyāsas*, has a certain similarity with *ièsos*. Then of the god Krishna it is said: "He, the guardian of his flock, the sinless God, the Lord of the world, consented to the death of (himself and) his race that he might fulfil the word of the seers," where, if we had shepherd and prophets, the comparison would be very striking.[2] Another passage not connected with the Gita, but close to biblical phraseology, may be found in the description of the avenging spirits:

[1] Mbh., xii. 350, 4, 5, 51.

[2] Mbh., xvi. 6, 15–16.

"If thou goest into the depths of the earth, or if thou shouldst fly above, or if thou fleest to the further side of the sea, still thou shalt find no escape from them"; as compared with the Psalmist's words, "Whither shall I fly . . . into heaven . . . Sheol . . . the uttermost parts of the sea?"[1] Compare also "I am not crying in the wilderness," followed by, "Thou seest the faults of others, though they be no larger than mustard, but thine own faults thou canst not see, though they be as large as a *bilva* (tree)."[2] As these comparisons have not, I think, been noticed before, I give them for what they are worth. Even the crucifixion has its analogy in the story of the Stake-saint (impaling being the equivalent of crucifixion), who was unjustly impaled with thieves, but he did not die like the thieves and so awakened the wonder of the royal guard. They went and told the king, who was frightened when he heard of it and came to the Saint on the Stake and besought his forgiveness, which was granted, as the king had acted ignorantly. He is besung in all the worlds as the Impaled One.[3] But all the rest of the story is grotesque. It is perhaps not impossible that there is here the echo of Christian story.

A curious historical sketch in the epic relates that the cult of Krishna as one God was introduced after the notion of Unitarianism had been gained by three pilgrims, who went to an Albion in the Northwest and there found this religion practised by White Men. Professor Weber, despite the repeated statement that the White Island was located in the extreme North or Northwest, referred this to Alexandria, and all sorts of suppositions have been made in regard to the locality, the three sages being identified with the Three Wise Men of the East, and the Northwest being referred to every Western land from Parthia to Rome. The legend is late and an obvious intrusion into the epic. It lays stress on the Unity of God, rather than on the All-god idea, though the latter is, of course, not given up, and

[1] Mbh., iv. 14, 60 (also late in the epic); Ps. cxxxix. 7 ff.

[2] Mbh., i. 74, 35, 82.

[3] Mbh., i. 107 and 108.

the devotees of Krishna who insist on this idea call themselves *ekāntinas*, or Unitarians. For myself, I am more inclined to believe that the Çivaite faith of Kashmere (a philosophical deism) is here recast into Vishnuite form; for the sea to which the pilgrims come is merely the mythical milk-sea of the Himalayas, and Kashmere men are almost white as compared with Hindus. The doctrine taught shows no trace of Christianity, but only of a belief in One God. Yet it is possible that, as the section is very likely not earlier than the fourth or fifth century of our era, a pilgrimage may have been made to Herat or Merv, where there were already at that time Christian bishops.[1]

But it will be asked, Is there any warrant for supposing that Krishnaism is a religion which would absorb Christian ideas?

As I have said already, the Hindus have always been exceedingly liberal in religious opinion. Sub-sects quarrelled about minute differences, but between the great bodies, Buddhists, Vishnuites, Çivaites, there was an easy tolerance. Side by side in amity dwelt the most diverse faiths, and Hindu emperors have often professed two religions at once. It was recognized that creed was an intellectual matter, and a difference of religion was like a difference in philosophy. Thus, amicably consorting, the Hindus borrowed from each other both rites and ideas. A new religion was a matter of interest rather than of hatred, and what was deemed good in it was quietly accepted. So we find that Buddhism borrowed from Hinduism, Hinduism in turn from Buddhism, and both probably from Christianity, just as the Aryans, ever since they settled in India, have borrowed all sorts of religious notions from un-Aryan peoples.

We are by no means obliged, however, to rely on generalizations in support of the statement that Krishnaism would

[1] As Krishna in the Gita says that there are very few who acknowledge him to be the Supreme God, so it is expressly stated that these Unitarians are few in number, xii. 349, 62. Such repeated admissions only bear out the belief, otherwise well supported, that Krishnaism in the Gita and *ekāntin* forms are two late developments, though the latter is the later.

naturally be influenced by Christianity. In the first place, it was of all Hindu religions the one which contained elements most likely to expose it to Christian influence. Buddhism was a godless, soulless religion; Çivaism was a religion of rites and austerities. But Krishnaism in its popular form was a religion of joy. It discountenanced bloody sacrifice and inculcated love. It needed only the safeguard of moral cleanliness to turn this love, which in a native form tended to voluptuousness, into a refining influence, and fit the devotee of Krishna to appreciate the tenets of Christianity.

Yet to show not only that Krishnaism was a religion likely to be affected by Christianity, but that it actually was so affected, and that it did borrow from the latter religion, we must advance from the ever dubious dates of epic episode to a later period in the history of both cults.[1]

After the great epic come the Puranas, *purāṇās*, some of which may be in part as old as the later sections of the epic. Most of the Puranas, however, follow in the wake of the epic, and, although some of them inculcate the worship of Çiva, are especially devoted to the praise of Krishna.

But in these works as they appear in their later form a sudden transformation takes place in the character of the god Krishna. Not only is he now always recognized as identical with the Supreme God, but in certain of the later Puranas, as has been shown in detail in the master-study made on this subject by Professor Weber,[2] he is worshipped less as an adult, a man-god, than as a sort of Christ-child. His birthday, like Christmas, becomes the holy day of his worshippers, and it is to the Madonna with the Child that the offering is

[1] Before leaving the older man-god Krishna, a word may be said in regard to his name. The crude notion that Krishna is a corruption of the name Christ was easily dispelled by showing that Krishna is an ancient Vedic poet and later saint. So also his attribute of Jishnu, "victorious," is as old as the Rig Veda, and hence the form Jishnu Krishna is only a chance collocation and of chance likeness with the name Jesus Christ, though possibly the similar sound may have led more easily to the identification of Krishna with Christ, which is found at a later time.

[2] Krishna's Janmashṭami, Abh. Berl. Ak. 1867, pp. 217 ff.

given, as the whole rite and ceremony are in their honor. The scene too of Krishna's nativity is not only like that of Christ's, but in becoming so, it has altered all the old inherited features of the Krishna tradition, which has been renounced in favor of this new presentation. Krishna is no longer heroic in birth as in life. The place of his nativity has become a stable, *gokula*, and his birth, which in the older tradition occurred in prison at a time of fear and danger, is now of peaceful character. His mother Devaki, scarcely mentioned in the older tradition, is now represented as a Madonna Lactans, holding the infant Krishna in her arms to her breast. This Krishna performs too the miracles of Christ, and the events of his life are those of Christ. Some of these traits are indeed antique. Thus Krishna's killing of Kansa, the local Herod, is an old heroic legend of the god. But they are now embellished with features as utterly dissimilar to the old presentation of Krishna's personality as the new legends are unlike the old tradition. Never before this time did Krishna appear in the *rôle* of a god whose glance destroys sin, whose pity for his believing followers leads him to cure them of sickness by performing miracles in their behalf. Thus, beside the massacre of the innocents, there is the restoration to life of a woman's son, the healing of a cripple, and the pouring of a box of ointment over Krishna, — stories which agree with Christian tradition far more closely than does Christian tradition with that of Buddhism. All these stories are in the later continuation of epic narrative, either in the Jaimini Bharata or equally late Puranas, and their modification of the old legend is much too sweeping to be brushed aside as accidental. The especial weight laid upon the Child-cult in this worship of Krishna, so utterly opposed to that of the older Krishna-worship, makes it impossible to doubt that at least this form of Krishnaism derives from a Christian source.

Those points in the connection of Krishna and Christ which scholars have at times urged, but which seem to be without special significance, I have not mentioned, because such details, if not utilized, do not affect the argument, and I need say only as regards them what I have said before, that exaggerations will be found on both sides. On the other hand, it would not be fair to leave the Child-cult as here presented without an additional remark in respect of a discussion of the subject by one eminent critic who, while "constrained to admit a body of common relations" and recognizing that the representation of the Madonna Lactans "has really been copied from similar representations in Christian iconography," may nevertheless be thought to depreciate the force of the *bouleversement* which has taken place in the whole Krishna legend, and which Professor Weber in the essay cited above has very justly emphasized. M. Barth, from whose work on India's religions, p. 223, have been taken the phrases just quoted, says that "traces of Christian influence do not appear with any clearness till much later (than the Krishnaism of the epic) in certain peculiarities of worship;" that is, as he has previously explained, he does not think that all the pastoral effect in Krishna-worship is modern. He instances as antique the Kansa legend, and says that Devaki does not occupy a prominent place in the worship of her son. A casual reading of the page, however, is likely to give a false impression. Part of M. Barth's criticism is quite justified. As remarked above, the Kansa legend is old. But we must disentangle the critique of the early connection of Christianity with the epic Krishna and that of the Christ-Child and Krishna-Child. Now, as it happens, M. Barth is speaking of both together, and his discussion of the borrowing is concerned mainly with the more dubious or older part. But, as was perhaps inevitable in this grouping, he has so knit older and later together in his critique as to combine both in one verdict, where it would have been safer to judge each separately.

Thus, M. Barth gives no reason at all for refusing to recognize the peculiar force of the stable-birth (in connection with the Madonna Lactans) except a statement which unites with this factor another with which this has nothing to do, namely, the pastoral scenes of Krishna as a grown man. Taking both together in one clause, he says that "the pastoral scenes, and the idea of assigning to Krishna a stable as his cradle, are connected with the most ancient representations of the Veda." Even as regards the pastoral scenes, this is questionable, and as regards the *gokula* it is a mistake, if the somewhat ambiguous phrase "are connected," etc., means that the *gokula* is part of Krishna-worship in the Vedic age. But if this last phrase means only that the Vedic age had cows, such a general asseveration has no bearing on the fact that in all the old worship of Krishna, as given in the epic, and in detail in the older Puranas, there is no child-worship and no stable-birth. Surely there is here a new feature, and one that cannot be shunted with the remark that cows and stables, without any bearing on Krishna, are Vedic. Then as regards the Madonna, the remark of M. Barth cited above is true of the normal attitude taken toward the Mother in the older accounts; but this is the very point of the proof, for in the texts devoted to the Child-cult, the mother, on the other hand, does "occupy a very prominent place." It will be seen, therefore, that the objection to the derivation of the Child-cult from a Christian source is in part due to uniting this side of the Krishna-cult with an older and more dubious phase of historical relationship, and that the argument against one of the most important points either has no bearing or is contradicted by the facts. Even then M. Barth recognizes that the special Madonna Lactans representation itself is drawn from Christian sources, and I know of no one else who has since cast any doubt on the truth of a theory which, as affects this later phase of Krishnaism, seems to me scarcely a theory, but as well established a case of borrowing as is recorded in the annals of religious history.

The epic itself refers but once, and that is in a passage generally admitted to be late, to Krishna's exploits in childhood. Even then the feat ascribed to him is merely killing a hawk. The later stories have been drawn not only from the gospels, but from the pseudepigrapha; for we find, besides the statements that Krishna's look heals from sin, and that at the time of his birth his reputed father was journeying with his mother to Muttra "to pay his taxes," the later notion that the water in which the child is washed is curative (found also in a late apocryphal Evangelium); just as we find too in the history of Krishna the late Christophoros legend.

But it is especially in the alteration of the character of Krishna as thus drawn that the proof of outside influence is given, and we may notice here how this differentiates these parallels and those between Buddhism and Christianity. For whereas the latter concern characters not dissimilar in their manhood, their compassion, and their gentle graciousness, the former transform completely the old Indian divinity and present it in a light exactly like that of the Christian parallel, as this character was delineated at just the time when the Indian divinity also was thus radically changed. For the cult of the Madonna with the Child and the peculiar worship of the Child as a suckling in his mother's arms is not a feature of primitive Christianity. It arose probably in the second century, but it did not become a common feature before the third or fourth century,[1] and before this time there is no sign of the cult of the Krishna-Child in India. In the fourth century, too, arose the practice of observing Christmas Day, which was celebrated not at first on December 25, but on various dates, for in the third century Christ's birthday was variously held to be on January 5 or 6, March 28, April 19 or 20, May 20, and November 19; just as the Puranas that describe the Birthday Festival of Krishna give the time variously on different dates (between June and September), though they all agree that the hour is midnight.

We cannot think, as was taught when Krishna's name was first explained as the *nomen ipsum corruptum Christi*, that Krishna-worship is all a corruption of the Christian religion. For with more light on the background we can see more clearly what lies behind the Child-god Krishna. But in seeing this we are also brought to recognize how great is the

[1] Compare Weber, *loc. cit.*, p. 336.

change in the character of the Hindu divinity. So decided is the alteration and so direct is the connection between this later phase of Krishnaism and the Christianity of the early centuries of our era, that it is no expression of extravagant fancy but a sober historical statement to say that in all probability the Hindus in this cult of the Madonna and Child have in reality, though unwittingly, been worshipping the Christ-Child for fully a thousand years.[1] And when we see, as we can see in this case, how ready were the Hindus to adopt Christian forms of worship, we shall perhaps not hesitate to admit that that earlier phase of Krishnaism, which is found in the epic, may also have reached its present form not without some influence from that religion which, in so many ways, has been potent in inspiring the pious imagination of the Hindu.

For not in Akbar's time alone did Christians expound their doctrines in India; and not only among the lowly were they received. Kings as well as peasants welcomed them, and though we have no direct evidence of this before the time of Çiladitya, yet, as this Hindu monarch received Christian Syrian missionaries at his court in the seventh century, so we may well believe that the liberal-minded Rajas of antiquity did not shut their doors to any creed. Even in the epic, the court of a great king is picturesquely described as filled with learned teachers of religion, "who argued this and that" and taught freely every form of religious philosophy, idealism, "may-be-ism," and nihilism; while the epic itself declares that "All names of God are synonymous," and in the Gita Krishna says in substance: "My way is the easy path of salvation; but if any one prefers the hard path of asceticism and philosophy, he too may be saved." Until the Mohammedans taught it, it is doubtful whether such a thing as religious persecution was known in India. Such a soil as this was already prepared for the seed when the sowers first came from the West.

[1] The worship of the Krishna-Child and Madonna in India is probably not older than the sixth or seventh century A. D.

What has been of still later planting may be surmised only, for monotheistic growth cannot be referred with certainty to Christianity after the Mohammedans entered India. But, on the other hand, who can tell how great has been the influence exerted by the teaching of the first centuries? We do not know. We may exaggerate its importance and we may unduly depreciate it. For my own part, though I do not know that it was an influence which materially affected the thought of the people, I must confess that the ingrowth of Christian ideas may have been deeper than we can state with certainty, and that, for example, the little band of early Christians in South India may have been instrumental in fashioning the lofty ideals of some of the noble religions which we know existed in after time and the influence of which in their turn may still be potent among the sects of to-day.

That there was a late counter-growth from seeds of the Orient, which, starting in India, blossomed in the Occident in tales of saints and in moral legends, found first in Persia, then in the Talmud, and finally, perhaps, in the vision of Dante, may be admitted. The West owes much to India, and though most of this was brought westward centuries after the Christian era, it is still within the bounds of possibility that even the New Testament was not completed without a graft from such a foreign growth. But this is as far as the historical data permit us to go, and such a possibility, affecting at most only what is secondary in the account, furnishes no base for the belief that the original narrative of Christ's birth and teaching derives from Hindu sources.

## ANCIENT AND MODERN HINDU GUILDS.

### GUILDS IN ANTIQUITY.

THE guilds of India can be traced back to about 600 B. C. But it is probable that they are still older, for when they are first mentioned it is as a factor of considerable importance in the state. They may be as old as the Vedic period, and it has even been claimed by Professor Geldner that they are referred to in the Rig Veda, but this is quite doubtful. Nevertheless, although the earliest law-books recognize the authority of the guilds, they do not assign to them so conspicuous a position as does the later law and we may therefore regard the first six centuries before our era as a period of development, when these associations still had much to gain. But what they still lacked they had gained completely by the third or fourth century A. D.; and it is not likely that they ever possessed more power than they did at that time, although they have maintained a very autocratic position down to our own century, and in certain districts they are still the rulers of the business world about them. Even in the third century B. C. they were very powerful.

Unfortunately, the oldest texts make no clear statement in respect of the powers of the guilds or of their organization. But their growth in influence may be inferred from two typical rules of the law-books. Gautama, about 500 B. C., says: "Laws of districts, castes, and families, when not opposed to sacred texts, are an authority,"[1] and then adds

[1] As I cannot quote the original texts (here and in the following passages from the ancient literature), I will comprise in one note most of the references made to my authorities in the order given. G. xi. 20–21 (Vas. i. 17; xix. 7); xv. 18; Y. i. 360; M. viii. 41 (B. i. 1, 2, 3–7), 46; Vas. xvi. 15; M. viii. 219,

to this the words: "Ploughmen, merchants, herdsmen, money-lenders, and artisans (are also authority) for their respective classes." Here local usage and the laws of castes still stand pre-eminent. But in Manu's law-book, completed somewhat earlier than the Christian era, we read: "A king should enforce his own law only after a careful examination of the laws of castes and districts, *guild-laws*, and family-laws," where the laws of the guilds are already reckoned as on a par with those of castes and families. In the late epic, the people at a court are grouped as "ordinary people, priests, and Naigamas," xvi. 7, 8. These last are undoubtedly the Sheths of the Buddhists and of modern times.

If the king was bound to respect the laws of the guilds, he was none the less expected to see that the members of the guild followed their own laws. These laws were in fact as authoritative as royal decrees. This is a point often touched upon in the early law-books, where (in the words of Yajnavalkya, whose code belongs to the beginning of our era) "the king must discipline and establish again on the path (of duty) all such as have erred from their own laws, whether families, castes, guilds, associations, or (people of certain) districts."

Till the time of Vishnu's law-book, third century A. D. no one of these guilds appears as pre-eminent, but in this work "metal-workers and smiths of silver and gold" are mentioned particularly, though this pre-eminence may be due to accident. But the circumstance is interesting, because exactly these guilds became the chief guilds of ordinary towns, and because they were very likely the first to band together in self-defence, all the guilds originating in this way, but the goldsmiths per-

221; Brihas. viii. 9. On the possibility of guilds in the Brahmanic period, compare the use of other words for corporations and the early use of the later, technical word in TS. iii. 4, 5, 1; AV. i. 9, 3; Ait. Br. iii. 30, 3; Kaushit. Up. ii. 20; and compare the *pūja* and *grāmayājaka*, G. xv. 16; Mbh. iii. 200, 7; M. iv. 205; iii. 151, 164; Yāj. i. 161, 360; ii. 192; M. iii. 154; V. x. 4. In Buddhistic literature, the following passages: Cullav. v. 8; vi. 1, 4; Mahāv. i. 7, 1; viii. 1, 16 ff.; Ep. Ind. ii. p. 98. From the epic, further, Mbh. v. 34, 49; xii. 88, 29–30; 59, 49; 140, 64; xv. 7, 8; iii. 249, 16; xii. 107, 10–32; ii. 5, 80; xii. 36, 19; xii. 321, 143; Nar. i. 40, 155; x. 1; Brihas. xvii. 5 ff.

haps first of all, since the old law in regard to smiths was so extremely severe as to call for some union on their part.[1]

All compacts made by guilds as corporate bodies come under the general law of compacts, and both the older and later law-books content themselves with saying on this point that "the king should see to it that guild-compacts are enforced;" while in regard to compacts made by the guild-members for their own observance, the older law enjoined that the king should banish the member who violated any agreement made by the association to which the offender belonged.

The reason why the guilds came into prominence just when they did is doubtless because it was at that period that the Buddhists arose, who reached the acme of their power in the third century B. C. and were important for a thousand years afterwards. In accordance with this fact stands, too, the special prominence of guild-life in the eastern part of India, the home of Buddhism. As the Buddhists placed the warrior-caste before the priest-caste and gave unrestricted freedom to the third estate, it is not wonderful that guild-life is characteristic of a Buddhistic environment. The same, however, is true in regard to the Jains, a rival heretical sect, which also arose in the sixth century B. C. Hence it is that, on the one hand, early Buddhistic literature, from 350 B. C. onwards, teems with references to the guilds and speaks of the Heads of Guilds as of the highest social position, while, on the other hand, the seat of guild-power to-day is still found among the Jains (the Buddhists having left India), and especially among the descendants of those who claim to have come originally from the eastern seat of Buddhistic and Jain

[1] The old law in regard to a goldsmith found guilty of defrauding was based on the principle that a goldsmith can most easily deceive, and that when he does so he is "the vilest of sinners." The king is therefore directed to see to it that a goldsmith found guilty of cheating shall be chopped up into very small pieces with sharp knives, whereas ordinary thieves or cheats are merely beheaded. By uniting together and ostracizing a guilty member, the guild could inflict a punishment which, if it was not so severe, probably had a still more deterrent effect.

culture. Even in the earliest Buddhistic sculptures we find reference to guilds and guild-masters. From the literature we see that the Heads of Guilds were great householders, who were not only high state officials, but on occasion became kings, at all times being represented as in the social set of kings and princes, friends and intimates of the various Rajas of Oudh [1] and Benares. They bore, too, the same name conferred to-day on the Heads of Guilds; namely, Sheth, meaning *optimus*, the Heads being in name as in fact a literal aristocracy. The Sheth in old times was often addressed simply as householder, but with the connotation of land-owner, landed-proprietor. From the law it appears that there were guilds of various sorts, but the only prominent one in Buddhist literature is that of the merchants, those members of the "third caste" so oppressed by Brahmanism, so liberated by Buddhism. The Sheth who is a Householder (a higher title) is sometimes the king's treasurer, as if the word (literally "house-lord") meant ruler of the king's house, for he is the chief official of the kingdom. The Sheth's office, either as treasurer or simple Sheth, was, however, hereditary. Such, in Buddha's day, were the great Sheth families of Benares and the neighboring towns. They represent a cross-cut through the ancient system of castes, a plutocracy perpetuating itself as an aristocracy. This view was adopted by the Brahmans themselves, who soon after this period began to make a sharp distinction between the very wealthy and the ordinary members of the third estate, who still remained a despicable caste "created for the king to devour;" till the new democratic tendency finds expression in the words of the epic sage, who says: "That which is called *the wealthy* is a very important member of the state; for verily a man with money is the top of all creation." The great epic is full of allusions to the guilds. Their power is reckoned as equal to

[1] This word is with us regularly but erroneously pronounced as if *ou* had the "continental" sound; but it is the English form of the native name (pronounce *Owdh*). Raj and Punjab, too, have the English j-sound and the vowel *a* is here long (pronounce *Rawj*, *Punjawb*).

that of the army; their Heads must be "talked over" by spies when the king would subdue another kingdom; they are "supported by union," and the king is especially charged not to tax them too heavily, lest they become disaffected, which is represented as a very great calamity. As the epic was probably completed soon after our era, it is interesting to notice that perhaps the modern Panchayat was already known at that date. For in one of the didactic portions, mention is made of the "five, valliant and wise" who in each town "preserve order." They are expressly stated to be a united body "among the people," that is, in the country. There is also one passage where the later Mahajans may be referred to in the epic. For many centuries this word (*mahājana*, literally "big people") has designated the masters of the more important guilds as well as the guilds themselves. Nowadays it is usually applied in the eastern part of India to wealthy bankers and gold-merchants. The passage in the epic, however, does not certainly use the word in its modern sense, and it is several centuries before the word occurs again in its modern meaning.

In the law-books of Narada and Brihaspati, assigned to the fifth and sixth centuries of our era, some new legal material is found in regard to guilds. We learn that the guild is governed by a board of from two to five persons. The villages are directed to "take the advice" of such a Panchayat, which oversees the affairs of smaller associations as well as its own. Banishment is the punishment of any one who injures the joint-stock of a guild or disobeys its laws. Banishment and confiscation of his entire property is the penalty for a man's failure to perform an agreement entered into by all the guild. The power of the guilds at this epoch is shown by the fact that *the king must approve of whatever the guilds do to other people*, and that there may be no mistake is added, *whether what they do is cruel or kind*. This is a plain advance on the earlier law in this regard. The question as to what is to be done if a dispute arises between the Sheths and their guilds is also opened here, and it is ruled that the king shall act as umpire between them. On the other hand, if the king learns that a whole guild, *actuated by hatred*, is boycotting one of its own members, he is directed to "restrain them." All funds donated (by the king) to a single member of a guild shall belong to all and be divided among the guild, or be bestowed on needy persons. All royal gifts and all expenditures of the society are common to all.

The guilds at this time (the fifth or sixth century A.D.) tried their own law-suits, but a right of appeal to the king as final court is permitted. If, however, a case is appealed and is again lost, the appellant must pay double what he was fined by the first court. A very decided stand is taken by Narada in regard to the old question whether scriptural law or local custom is authoritative. "Custom," he says, "decides everything and overrules scriptural law."

It is Narada who gives us the first rules in regard to apprentices. From these it appears that a young man desirous of learning a trade was free to do so (in other words, "caste" was not so strict an index of occupation as it is supposed to have been). The young man left his father's house and lived with a master. This master taught him and fed him and made him work, but might not make him do any other than the trade-work which he was learning. The youth was "bound out," for there is a special law which permits the master to compel the apprentice's return should the latter run away. The apprentice might be whipped or shut up if he was disobedient. In fact, he was to be "treated like a son." That he was bound out for a given length of time and that the advantage from his work was wholly his master's, follows from another law, which specifies that in case the apprentice has learned the trade more quickly than the contract calls for, the time left over shall be his master's, and all the profit derived from the apprentice during that period shall accrue to his master. If agreed upon in advance, however, the apprentice might be rewarded with a fee when he became proficient, but he should continue to work for his master till the stated time was up. The pupil is expressly commanded to be humble before his master. The reason given is quaint enough to quote: "For science is like a river, ever advancing downward to a humbler level; therefore as one's knowledge grows broader and deeper one should become ever more humble toward the source of one's knowledge."

Very important evidence is given in regard to the guilds by the inscriptions on rocks and copper-plates, found over Northern India. At one time we read of guilds presenting moneys as religious bodies, at another a man registers himself as "merchant Head of (such) a guild." In one inscription of the fifth century there is a very instructive account of a sun-temple built and endowed by a prosperous guild of weavers, who had emigrated from their native district and after various hardships prospered sufficiently to build a temple. Here is brought out prominently the fact that a change of occupation is not unusual. Some of these weavers, it is recorded, took to other trades.

Another inscription shows that the guilds acted as banks. They received as a body moneys in perpetuity, a trust-fund, the principal of which they kept, but for the use of this they paid, to the beneficiary named in the grants, five per cent interest (a month). Here the *sabhā*, "guild hall," is spoken of.[1]

A Nepalese legend of the third or fourth century records that Thana, which is minutely described, was ruled by a strong merchant guild.[2] Later literature down to our own time contains frequent references to such bodies, but no thorough treatment of them is to be found, though the allusions to the conspicuous position held by the guilds and their Heads fully attest the correctness of the law-books in laying so much stress upon their power.

The check on this power was held by the king, in his prerogative of taxing at will whenever he could claim that "hard times" induced hard taxes. Ordinarily, a small tax is put on every marketable article, the tax to be paid in kind or in

[1] Corpus Ins. Ind. vol. iii. No. 18; Nāsik Ins. Arch. Surv. vol. iv. p. 102.

[2] Oppert in the Madras Journal, 1878, p. 194; Bombay Gazetteer, vol. xiii. p. 406.

money. But when occasion arose, the king might tax as he pleased, or even take what he pleased from all subjects save the priests. When land-grants became common, it was customary to have stated in them just what tax each trader or inhabitant of the town deeded in the grant was to pay to the grantee. Most of these imposts were decided by the king (or officer) "in consultation with the Heads of guilds."[1]

## MODERN GUILDS.

In the autumn of 1896, thanks to the courtesy of the distinguished Sheth of Ahmedabad, Mr. Lalbhai Dalpatbhai, I was granted the privilege of an interview with the leading Sheths and Patels (heads of artisan guilds) in that city, who very kindly consented, at Mr. Lalbhai Dalpatbhai's request, to meet at an informal conference and answer the various questions which I should put to them in regard to the rules and practices of their local guilds. The value of the information received lies partly in the fact that Ahmedabad is the centre of guild-life in India; but particularly in this, that the guilds have no written laws and in many cases no clear plan of procedure in unusual circumstances; and that the power of the guilds is declining and their practices will soon be modified through the ever-increasing number of merchants and manufacturers who do not belong to any guild, and whose methods are more modern, so that their influence is destructive of old conditions. Some of the statements made at this conference by the guildmen agree with those embodied in various reports of guilds published in a more or less fragmentary manner in different numbers of the Bombay Gazetteer. Others are in direct contradiction to such reports. In the former case, I have given precedence to what has already been published; in the latter, I have generally presented the corrected statement first, for in instances of this sort I inquired particularly of different members, in regard both to their personal knowledge and to what they knew by hearsay,

[1] Compare the first Sûrya grant in the Bhaunagar collection, pp. 67–69.

and when all agreed as against a printed record made by some official, I judged that they knew best. But in regard to historical data I was unable to learn anything of value. In answer to what had happened in the past, the members of the conference always referred to two or three aged Sheths who "remembered" this or that. Sometimes they remembered in unison, sometimes they remembered variously. When this happened they accepted it as a proof that there was "no use in asking about things too far back." I came to the same conclusion and omit all cases of divergent recollections.

To the information obtained at Ahmedabad, I have here added what I could gather elsewhere in Gujarat and in Rajputana, collecting also what I could in other towns to the east and north. But I soon found that, though the name remained, and some guild-activity was to be found as far away as Lahore and Benares, yet it was always a lessening ripple as compared with the centre of guild-interest in Gujarat, where, indeed, after the earlier Buddhistic period, the guilds seem to have always had their firmest stronghold.

To those unacquainted with modern conditions it may be necessary to say that, apart from Rajas and scholars or saints, the modern merchants, Vanias, or Bunias, are practically the most important caste; after them come common priests. There is no warrior-caste. The Rajputs regard themselves as distinct. Small traders, such as the Lohanas and Bhatias of Kathiawar, usually claim Rajput descent, as do most artisans. But goldsmiths claim that they are pure Vanias. The merchants of the North, when not Parsees or Mohammedans, are usually either Shravaks,[1] that is Jains, or Vishnuite Vanias, or Smartas, — that is, Brahmans of the Çiva faith; more rarely they are Meshris, that is, Brahmans of the Vishnu faith. Thus it will be seen that all the old castes have become more or

[1] The word is always spelled in this way, and I keep this and other forms, such as Rajput, *rājaputra*, now almost Anglo-Indian. Shravak is, of course, *çrāvaka;* as Smarta, Mahajan, etc., are properly *smārta*, *mahājan*, etc. Towns in *-ābād* are also usually written without circumflex.

less mercantile. It may be observed, further, that guild-men are usually Hindus, who claim Aryan descent. But in the North, Mohammedans occasionally form guilds, as they form castes, in weak imitation of Hindu models.

## THE GUILD AND SHETH OR PATEL.

No perfect uniformity exists in regard to the names and titles of guilds and their chiefs. But there is a general distinction between artisan and merchant guilds. There is, again, a distinction between the village-guild and the guild of a large town.

In a village there is sometimes but one guild, and the head of the guild is then the head of the village itself, the Patel. In many cases there is but one guild-occupation, all other villagers being "outsiders," who do not belong to the "village-guild" at all. These outsiders are people of the lowest class, public servants and the like. In some cases they are recognized as "intruders;" that is, as people who have come into the village and settled there, but do not belong to it, "outsiders" with a touch of their profane birth still adhering to them. But all trades usually form one guild in a village, and the members form one corporate body against encroachments on the part of the government or the entrance of new families with like trades into the village.

Distinct guilds are formed by the scission of separate guilds as the village grows into a town. But there always remains a loose trade-union between all the guilds even of a large city. The guilds thus separate are often identical with caste. This, however, is not the case in very large towns, where, owing to outside influence and other causes, trade (guilds) and caste are more apt to be diverse.

The complete guild-system of a city makes a clear distinction between the Panch or artisans' guild with the Patel as its head-man, and the Mahajan or guild of merchants, bankers, and large dealers, the leader of which is called a Sheth.

This title of Sheth is used in two ways, the one I have just described, and another, according to which Sheth is a title of honor given to the head-man of the city, hence called Nagar-Sheth, or City-Chief. As a merely complimentary title this name Nagar-Sheth may be applied to wealthy traders, but properly it is bestowed upon a prominent civilian who may or may not be a merchant. Not very long ago, at the time when Mr. Lely wrote for the Bombay Gazetteer, the Nagar-Sheth of Ahmedabad was still a very influential person, but he has already lost much of his power, which has been taken by a leading manufacturer, a man who does not belong to any guild, but by public gifts and wealth he has won in the business world a position of commanding influence, — a fact indicative of the rapid passing away of the old order. The Nagar-Sheth of Ahmedabad is the head of a great Jain family, and his title has been inherited for several generations. He is practically the leader of the religious community of the Jains, and a few years ago he and the chief of the cloth-makers' guild, who happened to be the head of the Vishnu sect, could, in Mr. Lely's words, "carry public opinion on a religious or semi-religious question." In other towns this title has become a mere name, and even in Ahmedabad the Nagar-Sheth has now only a religious and social importance. As Sheth of the bankers' guild he is, apart from his civil office, influential socially, but his pre-eminence as City Chief was due originally to the standing of his family rather than to the importance of his guild.[1] It would appear, therefore, that we have in the Nagar-Sheth the survival of an office which corresponds very nearly to that of an old-fashioned mayor, though the incumbent of the office is neither appointed by the ruling power nor elected by the people, but chosen on account of his social superiority from among the guild-Sheths to represent the dignity and power of all the commercial classes of the city.

[1] Compare Lely, Bombay Gazetteer, vol. ii. p. 821.

The usual Sheth, however, is the head of a guild of "big men," Mahajan, and a union of all trades in a small town is sometimes called a Mahajan, as in Broach, where the "city Mahajan" includes bankers, money-changers, agents, brokers, cotton-dealers, and so forth, being in fact a sort of board of trade, or chamber of commerce, though it is also a protective club against artisan-guilds. For where there are guilds of artisans it soon becomes necessary to have some sort of union against them. Otherwise, on the slightest occasion of discontent a man of superior social rank would become obnoxious to great misfortune, since all the artisan guilds would boycott him. The only defence, therefore, is to be able to boycott the artisan and his guild. This is sometimes done, but generally, since a mutual boycott is a mutual disadvantage, the mere presence of the union on the part of the victims of the artisans leads to a more conciliatory tone, and unpleasantness is averted by mediation.

The word "Panchayat" is applied in large towns to trades that are coterminous with castes. In Ahmedabad this would appear to be always the case. Mr. Lely's statement to the contrary, in the Gazetteer, vol. iv. p. 106, was contradicted by all the members of the conference, who said that the word "Panchayat" was used only when guild coincided with caste. But in other places, as in Surat, a Panchayat may include different castes. The same is true of the Panch Mahal district, only here, where the population is small, the general trade-regulating merchants' guild is more apt to be dignified with the name Mahajan. As all the small guilds are called Panchs in Ahmedabad, there would seem to have been evolved here a nicer terminology, by virtue of which the original application of Panchayat was more carefully preserved. In respect of the wider use of Mahajan, which obtains in some parts of Kathiawar as a designation of artisan guilds (according to the statement made in his report by Mr. R. Proctor-Sims), the conference was unanimous in saying that only when all guilds were united could they be called, as a collective body, Mahajan; and that no single artisan guild was ever so dignified. Nor have I personally found anywhere in Kathiawar corroboration of Mr. Sims' remark that tailors, blacksmiths, potters, and other lowly people "have each a Mahajan."[1] The Patel of the blacksmith guild at the conference said he did not believe that the title Mahajan was applied "to any single artisan-guild in the country," and I am inclined to think he was right. Another slight error in Mr. Lely's account is found in his statement that in Ahmedabad "there are four castes of carpenters and therefore four assemblies for caste purposes, but only one carpenters' Mahajan." The chief of the carpenters told me personally that he was Patel of a Panch, not of a Mahajan, and that the castes were not true castes, for they intermarry.

On the other hand, the same caste may have subdivided guilds. This I found to be the case among the silversmiths. They all belonged to one caste, but not to one guild. But it sometimes happens that one guild comprises different castes. Thus the chief of the confectioners stated that there were three castes in his guild. These were real castes; that is, the members of the guild were divided into groups which would not eat together nor intermarry. The chief explained this by saying that the castes were geographical. This is probably so. In old days, one caste was more apt to imply one occupation; but now strangers, with different habits and of different origin, unite in one occupation as they drift locally together.

There is an intermediate stage in large towns between the great merchants' Mahajan and the humbler artisans' Panch. This is represented by the "pure Vania caste" goldsmith. The smiths of gold (and silver) are the highest Panch or the lowest Mahajan, depending on whether the goldsmith is at the same time a banker. If there are several goldsmith-bankers,

[1] Compare the Bombay Gazetteer, vol. ii. p. 321; vol. iii. p. 251; and vol. viii. p. 265.

they are called a Mahajan. But the mere artisans belong to a Panch, as do all lower smiths, carpenters, masons, tile-makers, dyers, and so forth. Of these humbler organizations the most powerful is usually the tile-makers' guild, on the goodwill of which every one is dependent, and which controls absolutely the still humbler but important guild of potters.

The number of guilds in a town differs greatly, most large towns having from thirty to one hundred and fifty. In the fifth century of our era, one of the late law-makers says there were eighteen guilds; but they have evidently been increasing in number, as even to-day they show a marked tendency to multiply rather than decrease. The less important they are in any large city, the more there are of them. Thus the guilds of Jeypur have not nearly the power of those of Ahmedabad, which is a smaller city, but there are forty guilds in the latter place, while there are thrice that number in Jeypur. This is due rather to the splitting up of the guilds themselves than to the formation of new corporations. Where the guilds are influential, they remain undivided. But when they lose the significance they once had, they tend to become mere clubs, which an irreconcilable quarrel will frequently cause to divide; so that the same profession will be represented by two opposed factions. Even in Ahmedabad there are ten more guilds to-day than there were twenty years ago.

In the country, when an outsider is opposed to the guild, the Panchayat will deliberate on the case and invariably settle it in favor of the guild, unless the outsider be rich enough to corrupt the Panchayat or strong enough practically to overawe it. In ordinary cases the Panchayat of a village-guild practically forbids all competition.

The Panch may contain different castes, but the Mahajan may comprise different races. Ordinarily, however, two guilds to a trade is the limit of expansion, as in the case of cloth-merchants of Ahmedabad, where workers in silk and in gold form two distinct guilds in the brocade trade.

## APPRENTICESHIP.

The old law, to which I have referred above, seems to have fallen into desuetude. No articles are made out, no premium is paid, and in fact there is no real apprenticeship. Artisan boys learn their trade at home or receive small wages while they learn it under a master, but in no case are they bound out, being free to leave their own work if they (or their parents) think it best to do so. The old idea of an inherited trade is generally kept, but it is violated frequently and with apparent impunity. Sometimes the boy's keep is considered a sufficient return for his work till he has mastered his trade. What may appear at first sight to be apprenticeship is in reality a private arrangement between a father and a master-workman, who is asked to take charge of the boy's education, but he does not take the boy with legal formalities. Twenty-five rupees a year after the first year of training is considered sufficient recompense for the value of the boy's labor, and thereafter three rupees (one dollar) a month, till the trade is learned. In Jeypur, I was informed that there used to be a fine inflicted on any man whose son learned a new trade; but no other means to prevent a change of family occupation was ever taken, and nowadays the old rule is not enforced.

## THE HEAD-MAN AND ELDERS.

The Sheth, or Head-man of a guild, holds his position by hereditary right, which may, however, be set aside. But the right is that conferred by custom and is therefore very strong. Only unusual circumstances would prevent a son's succession to his father's position as head of the guild. The dignity of the guild is represented by its Sheth, so that the usual rule is for the son to succeed, provided he is fitted to uphold the moral and financial standing of the family and guild. Otherwise he is set aside. In this case the new Sheth is elected from a new family, not usually from the same family, as Mr. Lely asserts; who also remarks that the unworthy son "still retains the title," a statement denied by the conference. They said that a new family would in all probability be selected, but they admitted that the second son of an old Sheth might possibly get the office.

The election is made by the whole guild and is settled by a majority vote. The case where a new candidate has to be selected appears to be rare, for the members of the conference were unable to say what would happen if there were more than one candidate, or whether there would be more than one. They seemed to think that only one name would ever be submitted to the guild to vote upon, and I fancy that this is a fact, since the personal influence of the rich is very great, and they would rather settle the matter first among themselves and then submit the name to the whole guild *pro formâ.* No one in the conference had ever heard of two candidates being put forward. They said that "of course the best and biggest man" would be made Sheth. But indeed to have any real candidate is extraordinary. Ordinarily the eldest son of the deceased Sheth becomes Sheth with only the form of an election. The procedure, however, as imagined by members of the conference, would be as follows, in case there was need of a new Sheth from a new family (I cite verbatim from notes made on the spot): "There would be but one candidate, for there can be but one best and biggest man. The most influential men, quietly coming together, on making in their minds the sad discovery that the son of the Sheth was not fitted to inherit the dignity of his fathers, would agree upon that person who would best represent the guild, and having amicably agreed upon this man they would go before the guild and say, 'Vote for this man.'" Question: "Suppose the guild refused to vote for him?" Answer: "The guild is sometimes opinionated in other matters, but we have never known a guild refuse to vote as its influential leaders directed it to do when the question was one of election." Question: "Do the venerable Sheths remember no such case?" Answer: "It is not remembered." In short, the guilds elect as the leaders select.

These "influential leaders" are the elders or Council of the guild, and they too bear the name of Sheth, but only as a decoration. There may, however, be two real Sheths, in which case each Sheth is originally the Sheth of his own caste (guild) or sect. Thus the local silk-cloth guild of Ahmedabad has two heads, one to represent the Shravaks and one to represent the Vishnuites, and in nearly all the great city-guilds in Gujarat the two prevailing sects are thus represented. The sons of councillors inherit the title as a matter of courtesy and are often in reality the councillors of the next Sheth, so that the Sheth in council seem to represent an hereditary body. The proverb cited by Mr. Lely, *loc. cit.*, p. 108, "Energy makes the Sheth, no one asks what family he is," represents a theoretical possibility, and doubtless an historical fact, but not the present condition of affairs.

In small country towns in Gujarat every leading merchant is politely called Sheth, as in Benares he is called Mahajan, or as in New England a country lawyer is called 'Squire.

As a great part of the charity performed by the guild is of a religious character, when the Sheth is of a different sect to that of most members of the guild, and the latter have no sectarian Sheth of their own, the guild will often give over its charity-moneys to the Sheth of another guild of identical sect. Thus Shravaks with a Vishnuite Sheth will entrust their moneys to the Shravak Sheth of another guild, lest their own Vishnuite Sheth expend them for a temple rather than for the Shravak Pinjra Pol (asylum for decrepit animals). As for this, it shows how religious is the community, but it may be observed that the people are as conservative as they are religious, and though in a Shravak environment it sometimes happens that a Vishnuite Sheth finds his guild slowly becoming Shravak, yet he never thinks of relinquishing his position on this account, nor does the Shravak majority think of ousting him. [1]

[1] The city Mahajans are usually made up of Lohanas and Bhatias, as well as Vanias, though, properly speaking, the last should include the first two. But Vanias in common parlance are bankers and cloth-merchants of the Shravaks, that is, laymen of the Jain faith, or trading Brahmans, such as Meshris, who are found in some localities; while Lohanas are Vishnuite grain-dealers (the poorer sort being husbandmen), as are the Bhatias.

## AUTHORITY OF THE SHETH IN COUNCIL.

The guilds have been growing steadily more democratic, and in matters other than the election of a Sheth not infrequently stand out against the decision of the Sheth and Council. Half a dozen leading members of the trade make the council (though the number is not fixed), and these with the Sheth are recognized as guild-men apt to work for the interest of the whole body, so that there is no natural antagonism between guild and leaders. The Sheth and Council are, as it were, the president and cabinet of the guild. The interest of one is that of all, and in ordinary circumstances there is a ready acquiescence on the part of the whole guild in any measure brought forward by the Sheth and supported by the Council. But occasions do arise when the whole body stand in conflict with their officers. The venerable men who "remembered" for me assured me that in the good old days a guild never objected to any measure proposed by the Sheth and Council. But in these days many wish to adopt "perilous modern methods," others think that they ought to be consulted, and still others "take every opportunity to object to authority." Only twenty years ago, as may be seen in Mr. Lely's report already referred to, it was possible to state truly that the Sheth and Council have virtually the whole authority. The rather unwilling admission of my informants (it must be remembered that they were all Sheths and Patels) tends to show that this is no longer the case. I was in fact rather mournfully assured by various members of the conference that "a majority of ordinary members of the guild always can, and often do, carry a measure over the heads of Sheths and Council." In less guild-ridden towns and cities I was told that Sheths were now without much power, and even the Sheth and Council combined had only an advisory function. But it was everywhere recognized that this was a changed condition, and that formerly the advice of the Sheth was practically law to the guild.

## OFFICIALS AND MEETINGS.

The only officer besides the Sheth is the Gumasta or clerk, who in the case of the great Mahajans calls the meetings and acts as secretary. The title really means an agent, and the Gumasta acts in this capacity in so far as he is authorized to drum up recreant members and urge them to attend the meetings. The Gumasta, if one exists (for there is often no such officer), receives a salary; but no Sheth or councillor receives a salary or accepts any money in his official capacity, unless it be the Sheth of a Mahajan in a small country town, who may receive a fixed sum for collecting fees imposed by the government on his own and other local guilds.

The duties of the clerk consist also in collecting moneys and keeping accounts, but he must discover and report transgressions on the part of members and "execute any order that may be given on the part of the corporation." To this description of the clerk's functions (furnished by Mr. Lely, *loc. cit.*, p. 107) I am unable to add anything of importance.

The meetings of the guild are held in the local Vadi or guild-hall; the clerk calls the meeting at the request of the Sheth or of any other influential member of the guild or on the demand of ordinary members. There does not seem to be any regular practice in this respect. The conference said simply that when a meeting was wanted by any important person or demanded by several members there was a meeting. Meetings are not held at stated intervals, but as occasion presents itself. If there is no clerk, the Sheth calls the meeting (when requested to do so), sending a written or verbal message to the different members. If there is no guild-hall, any convenient room, as in the house or shop of one of the members, is selected for the meeting. So far as I could learn, there is an utter absence of formality at these meetings, and no parliamentary rules are followed.

## MEMBERS AND FEES.

As occupation usually goes by caste, any member of a caste engaged in a certain occupation is, *ipso facto*, a member of the guild. In small towns there is often no entrance fee in artisan guilds, but the Mahajans exact one from new members. All sons, however, of a deceased member, without paying an entrance fee, become members of the guild on his decease, and are received into the guild without formality. Membership is a family right which, once acquired, is inherited. But from other new members an entrance fee is demanded, which varies from one hundred to three hundred and fifty rupees. A fair average of the fees of the more important guilds is three hundred rupees, or about one hundred dollars. But the borders-guild of Ahmedabad has a fee of only two hundred rupees. Three hundred are demanded by the cloth-guild; several guilds demand three hundred and fifty; and even five hundred was quoted as a possible fee, but no guild represented at the conference admitted that its fee was so high as this. Some of the artisan-guilds ask a fee of one rupee as matter of form, but their fee is generally a dinner-party. The fee, though usually the same for all, may be partly remitted in the case of a desirable member who is too poor to pay the large sum demanded by some guilds.

A discredited member may not return to the guild when once cast out (by vote of the guild). If his offence is a caste-offence his children are debarred from admission. The practice varies in different localities. In Jeypur, for example, a member is not dismissed, but he is allowed to drop out of the guild. Here too the sons may enter, though the father has been informally ostracized. When the father has dropped out on account of poverty, the son that has prospered and desires to enter the guild may do so, "not usually at once, but after some years." There is no rule on the subject. It is largely a social question. If a member changes his business, he of course leaves the guild, but he may be reinstated if he resumes it. A change of trade or business is not unusual, nor was it so in ancient times, though our notions of caste based on the law-books lead us to think so. As to a new entrance fee from reinstated members, in Ahmedabad the general opinion was that it was not customary to demand it. But in case a discredited or dropped member dies, while it is permitted to his sons, it is not permitted to his grandsons to enter without a fee. If a member fails he is not dropped on this account. The guild investigate his business, and if it is found that he has failed dishonorably, he is dropped; if honorably, "the creditors in the guild accept a part of the debt and help him to tide over his difficulties when he repays all. But the funds of the guild are never used for this purpose." In this particular there is a difference between the guilds of ancient times (when it is expressly stated that they help their needy members) and of to-day, when all the funds are devoted to religious charity. No Sheth of the conference would admit that any guild-money was ever spent on a member of the guild, however much he might need it. Nor does the guild care for the needy families of deceased members.

The dinner-party fee of artisan guilds is not always the rule. In Broach, for instance, the bricklayers demand a small fee of each new member. But generally the family (or it may be the caste Panchayat) raises money enough to give a dinner to the rest of the guild. The rite constitutes the entrance fee, and is the only formality observed. This applies only to those who have learned a new trade different from their father's, and are hence obliged to enter a new guild.

In many cases there is no fee at all. Thus in Bhaunagar and in Jeypur, one in Gujarat and one in Rajputana, there is no fee. It is customary only where the guilds are most stringent in their rule and most conservative. There is no annual subscription (though Mr. Lely says there is), and consequently there are no arrears to be paid.

## FINES, REVENUES, EXPENDITURES.

Fines are imposed for non-observance of the rules of the guild. This is found to apply chiefly to the matter of holidays. Every caste and guild has its stated holidays, and any member that keeps open shop or works on such a day is liable to a fine, unless he has bought the privilege. A prime source of revenue in the case of most guilds is the proceeds of the auction sale of this privilege. The fine is heavy for violation of this right on the part of others; and if the offence is repeated, the delinquent is sometimes expelled rather summarily. This custom of auctioning off the right of not keeping a holiday is one more common in the smaller towns.

Large guilds get revenue also from purchases of the members, on which a tax is levied. One quarter of one per cent. is the annual impost, but when paid in kind, as is often done, an approximate amount, reckoned roughly according to this ratio, is taken by the guild. Thus from every cart bringing in a load of grain, a few handfuls are taken out and cast in a heap at the city-gate. There is no precision; often the cart does not stop at all; the toll-man puts in his hand and takes out a little, not enough to make any appreciable difference in the load, but it adds to the slowly accumulating heap at the gate. The law is strict, but its observance is kept more in the spirit than in the letter of the per cent. It must be remembered that it is all for religious charity (the funds of the guild are devoted to this object solely), and the exact amount is of small importance. I fancy, however, that the very precise rules in regard to king's toll in the old law-books were probably interpreted much in the same loose way.

When the article taxed is not payable in kind, the tax assumes a more formidable appearance. In Bhaunagar there is such a tax (about ten cents on every bale of cotton) levied by the manufacturers' guild. So in Broach, the Mahajan's chief revenue is said to be from a similar tax on every bale. This is sometimes as high as a quarter of a dollar. All bills of exchange negotiated by a banker are taxed in the same way, the tax in this case being about ten cents.

None of the guilds is a provident institution. Regular banks have done away with their old function of trust companies, and they usually spend their moneys at once, in the case of small guilds on dinner-parties, in the case of Mahajans on Pinjra Pols (asylums for animals) and temples. But if there is anything on hand, the moneys are credited to the corporation at the local bank. The large guilds sometimes possess considerable real estate, which has come to them in the shape of gifts, and they are often the beneficiaries of rich members, who give to them in the knowledge that they will expend principal or interest (as desired) for their pet charities. Where there is a loose organization, as in Jeypur, without fees or assessments, money for charity is collected by subscription. In Surat, on the other hand, where the organization is perfect, fees and taxes come in so regularly that the members seldom give directly for any charity.[1]

I was told that on an average over fifty per cent. of the whole income of a guild went regularly to charity. The old rule was that the local Pinjra Pol of Ahmedabad, for instance, should receive one quarter of one per cent. on all goods purchased by any member of the guild. This rule is not now so strictly observed, but some guilds, as, for example, the gold-thread guild, still holds to this rule. Other guilds spread their charity over more general ground, giving part to one object, part to another. In some cases, again, there is no such tax at all. It is a matter which is decided by each guild for itself annually. Thus the chief confectioner said that in his business a tax was levied on all purchases of sugar and condensed milk, but the amount of the tax and the disposition of the moneys when collected were matters settled by the guild once a year. He asserted too that for the last year the rate had been eight annas on one hundred rupees, but this would be half of one per cent., and some of the other mem-

[1] Compare also the Bombay Gazetteer, vol. ii. pp. 321, 442.

bers of the conference looked so astonished at the statement that I came to the conclusion he was exaggerating, to give a good opinion of the charitable work of his guild. In the case of the cloth-merchants I was told that one quarter of one per cent. was a fixed amount (not settled annually) deducted for charitable and religious purposes, and that the rest of the money on hand was spent for the guild "at the discretion of the Council." The funds are sometimes spent for semi-religious purposes, such as are urged as worthy charities in the ancient texts, — tanks, shade-trees, fountains, rest-houses, etc. Thus at Junagadh the goldsmiths' guild has built a *dharmaçāla*; that is, a house where pilgrims can be put up over night. There is a fine *dharmaçāla* at Jeypur, built in the same way. In small places in Gujarat all spare funds are usually given to Pinjra Pols by the Shravak guilds and to temples by the Vishnuite guilds. I was curious to know what happened with the funds of a mixed guild, and was told that "the amount for each sect is decided upon amicably by the council." When nothing special is required and the Pinjra Pol and temples are in a flourishing condition, there is always the outlet of a dinner-party, so that funds never accumulate. The artisan-guilds do not appear to give much in charity, preferring to spend their small income on an annual guild-picnic. I was told that in Surat the difference is most marked. Here all the Mahajans spend their money on charity and all the artisan-guilds spend theirs on picnics. Where, as is often the case in Kathiawar, the caste and guild are identical, these picnics are merely family reunions. Besides the food, new pots and kettles and dishes are bought for each picnic. It is seldom, however, that artisan-guilds have any money to spend.[1]

[1] Mr. Proctor-Sims, in the Bombay Gazetteer, vol. viii. p. 265, mentions as objects of charity, feeding the poor, Pinjra Pols, *dharmasçālas*, cattle-troughs, and water-sheds or *parabs*. He says that artisan-guilds usually spend all they get for dinners and cooking utensils. This I found to be true everywhere in Gujarat, but not elsewhere. But, as I have already stated, the Sheths at the conference said that they never gave guild-money to the poor for food or for anything else, save as the poor benefited by the erection of fountains, etc.

## JURISDICTION OF THE GUILDS.

To fix trade-holidays, to enforce their observance, and to collect and administer the funds of the guilds, are functions to which I have already referred. The right to arbitrate is assumed by all guilds. When a trade quarrel is referred to a Mahajan, or when the Mahajan, without being requested, decides a quarrel, this is the final arbitrament. Refusal to abide by it or indeed to carry out any decision arrived at (as in the case of payments thus adjudicated) results in ostracism. When a member is thus cut off from the guild he may be ostracized by the caste. In the latter case he becomes a social pariah, more wretched than a village dog. But even if one is only cast out of the guild, one is often, *ipso facto*, outcasted. In the country, such an outlaw is debarred from all social recognition. No man will work with him or for him, nor will any one employ him. In the cities, no dealer will serve him, no broker will act for him, no servant will remain in his house. The carpenter, the baker, the confectioner, the blacksmith, the tile-maker, the very potter, lowest of the lowly, refuse to take his orders, deliver goods to him, or perform any service for him at any price. Caste here has yielded entirely to the guild. The rule established by a low-caste corporation may involve such ostracism in the case of the highest caste, but it is enforced regardless of caste. A typical instance is cited by Mr. Proctor-Sims. In 1878, in a small town in Kathiawar, the Vania Mahajan levied a religious tax which the traders of the Brahman caste refused to pay. The Vania guild, therefore, boycotted the Brahman traders and forbade all dealings with them, till the high-caste traders yielded and paid the tax.

In small places, the Mahajan is thus absolute master of the town. No individual can stand against his local guild; nor where there are several small guilds which form a Mahajan can a whole guild resist the union. Owing to the number of traders and workmen in large towns who do not belong to guilds, the power there is not so great, but it is generally coercive. Thus in Ahmedabad, as I was told, a banker who had half his house tiled got into a quarrel with a confectioner and could not get the other half of his house tiled till the sweetmeat-guild had told the tile-guild that it might resume work for the representative of the bankers' guild.

The artisan-guilds are practically more powerful in this way than are the more aristocratic Mahajans of large cities. For there are a dozen cases where the artisans are able to mar the serenity of a banker's life against one where the banker would be apt to exercise power over the artisan. The whole Ahmedabad conference stated publicly (and different members of the conference assured me privately after the meeting was over) that despite the annoyance, this was "all for the public good." Even the victims regard themselves as martyrs in a good cause, and think themselves protected where they are tyrannized over.

I submitted the following questions to the conference in regard to other matters of jurisdiction: In the case of disbursement of funds, if the guild objects to expenditures proposed by the Sheth and Council, what action is taken? Does the guild alter prices and the rates of wages? Does it decide what shall be the number of working-hours? Does it prohibit or give formal sanction to improvements?

In answer to the first question, I was told that "there would probably be no such objection; but if there were, the Sheth would talk with the members of the guild and induce them to change their opinion, or there would be an amicable compromise." The chief question would be whether Shravak funds should all go for Shravak charities. In Ahmedabad itself a normal proportion is observed between Shravak and Vishnuite expenditures, but the exclusive use of sectarian funds for sectarian purposes is not countenanced. In other towns, particularly smaller towns, the latter is the rule.

In regard to prices, I was informed that in Mahajans they were regulated only in the grain-guild. In cloth-guilds, for instance, two men of the same guild may sit side by side in the bazaar and sell the same kind of cloth at different prices. But wages are fixed by the guild, though in places where modern manufactories are found, wages are regulated to a great extent by the action of the factory-owners, who are usually not members of a guild. Both in Gujarat and in Rajputana, the mill-owners operate against the guilds as a general thing, though they are sometimes guild-men.

The method of fixing the rate of wages and keeping it there without protest is very simple. It is the practice to advance a certain sum to every workman at the beginning of his term of service. As his wages give him just enough to live on, he can never save enough to repay the loan, or if he could he is usually so improvident that he does not do so. If he asks for more wages, his employer refuses the request. If he says he will leave unless he gets more, the employer replies, "Very well; but first pay me what you owe." The result is that the man remains at the old wage. When an employer wants to pay extra wages to induce a special workman to enter his employ, the employer "must ask the guild about it and abide by their decision."

In a Panch, price and wages are ordinarily fixed by the guild and also the number of working-hours. On these points the guilds act in combination and especially combine against outside competition. "The lowest rate allowed by the local guild" may not be altered. If outsiders come in and work for less than this, it is the duty of the members of guilds on which the workmen are dependent to refuse either to work for them or to supply them with the means of their trade. Thus if a confectioner should sell sugar-cakes at less than the permitted rate, the guild that supplied him with sugar would cease to do so; if a tile-maker should work for less wage, the guild supplying his material would boycott him, etc. So in regard to working over-hours; though here there is this license, that if a man wishes to work over-time the guild will not ordinarily object, provided there is enough work for all to do. But otherwise the rule is very strict. When work is scarce, a fine is imposed by the guild on any one that works more than the permitted time.

Incidentally I inquired at this point whether the guilds took cognizance of disputes between employer and employed when the former alleged unsatisfactory work as a reason for dismissing the workmen employed. I was told that the guild "took action in regard to every grievance and had jurisdiction over everything." A case "remembered" was as follows: "Some years ago I (a merchant Sheth) discharged a carpenter who did unsatisfactory work. The carpenter-guild refused to let any workman work on the house till the incompetent carpenter was taken back." I then asked the Sheth whether he considered guilds in general to be advantageous or disadvantageous to the common weal. "They are very advantageous," he replied, "though their action is sometimes open to criticism. In this case I was the sufferer, but the carpenters acted for their own best interests, and they cannot be severely blamed."

The conference denied that the guilds ever exerted themselves actively against modern improvements. A case cited from the beginning of the century (1820, Dunlap, *apud* Lely, p. 111) indicates the spirit of opposition that used to obtain; but though a certain unfriendliness to modern methods was perhaps to be suspected from casual remarks of some of the older members of the conference, I was unable to elicit more than a general statement to the effect that "guilds never object to improvements, but are the first to sanction them," which is doubtless true when the word "improvements" is defined as it was meant, and may perhaps be a correct statement in any circumstances.

As the guild controls the output of energy in the workman, so it controls the output of the merchant's wares. Whether goods might be sold out of town was a question which the guilds of Jeypur refused to answer (in view of the famine), but in Ahmedabad the grain-dealers decided it the day before the conference, determining that no grain might be sold out of town. At the same time they raised the price of the chief staple by ordering that only sixteen pounds instead of twenty-four pounds should be sold for a rupee. I may add that, though the general government refuses to regulate trade, it does not prohibit such regulation on the part of the guilds or on the part of local governments. In extra-British territory it is customary. Thus the Nizam of Hyderabad regulated the output of grain during the famine.

Rates of exchange and insurance (in the case of Mahajans), and rates of sale and amount of marketable material which may be made by each artisan, are always settled in advance by the respective guilds.

Despite the fact that the jurisdiction of a guild generally extends over members of other guilds, by virtue of the mutual support given by all such organizations, it not infrequently happens that the guilds quarrel among themselves. There is then no power to adjust the difference, and a battle of guilds is fought out, usually by manœuvres rather than by force. A case on record in one of the small towns of Kathiawar is as follows: A sweeper, having been insulted by a merchant, got his guild to refuse to sweep for the member of the local Mahajan. The Mahajan promptly got the grain-dealers to refuse to sell grain to the sweepers. When starved out, the sweepers swept again. In another town, the Mahajan objected to the action of the potters, who had raised the price of pots. The potters stood firm and seemed likely to win, till the Mahajan bought the right to dig clay in the village lands. They then had the potters at their mercy, and the price of pots resumed its old level.

When the Mahajan is not identical with the village Panchayat, elders of the village, the power is divided, and in this case it is doubtful which party will win the war of tricks. But in most villages the Panchayat consists of members of the Mahajan, when its power is quite absolute. Thus in one town in the north of Kathiawar, the Panchayat, thinking that cholera, which had broken out, was caused by witchcraft, determined to burn all the houses where the magic influence had shown itself. The owners of the houses never thought of resisting the order, and the whole plague-district was burned up, without compensation to the owners, at the command of the Panchayat.

## SATTAS.

Sattas are time-bargains in the grain-market, corresponding to our "futures." The grain guild takes cognizance of these bargains and arbitrates in all disputes arising from them between members. The price of grain is regulated daily by the guild, and the assumed value of grain on a given day is fixed in the interest of time-bargains or stock-gambling.

There is another mode of gambling, very popular in northern India, known as Kabalas, or rain-bargains, but these are not recognized by any guild. They are simply a method of betting on the time when rain will fall, "real rain" being estimated by a continuous flow from a certain house-gutter, which a watchman is stationed to watch. These bets are regularly entered, but they are regarded as private affairs like any gambling bets, and failure to pay such a bet is not officially recognized.[1]

## GUILDS AS COURTS OF LAW.

It will have been observed that the jurisdiction of the guilds relieves the local courts of a good deal of business. Disputes which in the Occident would be settled by a legal appeal are in the land of guilds settled by the societies of the disputants. In small towns, the Mahajan is usually the accepted referee in all petty disputes. In cities, on the other hand, trade disputes are often brought into court only to be referred back by the court to the Mahajan for settlement. This, I was told, is frequently the case in Jeypur and in other cities under native rule.

Small guilds, again, are in the habit of appealing to the great guilds, Mahajans, when the former quarrel among themselves. This is particularly true in small places, where

[1] The Kabalas stand to the Hindu in the place of card-debts or racing-debts, and are so important a vice that in 1897 the government sought to stop them by law. To this the Hindus of Calcutta retorted that so long as the British were allowed to bet on horses, they would claim the right to bet on rain, and I believe the matter was not pressed. There is a description of this fascinating excitement in the Bombay Gazetteer, vol. viii. p. 209.

the grain-dealers, grocery-dealers, and tobacco-dealers (*i. e.*, the usual Mahajan) stand in social antithesis to the guilds of the petty dealers and common workmen, representing an educated intelligence to which the lowly guilds of the uneducated can and do appeal for arbitration. As far as I could learn, the matters thus brought before the Mahajans are settled fairly and satisfactorily, and there is seldom any complaint of injustice. Custom gives force to this arbitrament, and appeal is rarely taken from a decision of the Mahajan. Occasionally, but not often, disputants engage their respective guilds in a dispute without interesting the guilds in it. In such a case, instead of referring to the Mahajan the nominally opposed guilds will appoint a council or committee to settle the dispute. In a small village where there is no Mahajan, the Patel is the referee in disputes among members of any artisan guild.[1]

## POWER OF THE GUILDS.

The power of the guilds is rapidly declining. At present their ancient control, which it is evident was exercised not only two thousand years ago, but until very recently, is preserved only in a few places. In Gujarat the guilds are at their strongest, and are best represented in the city of Ahmedabad; in Rajputana the power of the guilds is much less than in Gujarat, and in some of the cities of this district is almost nominal. Jeypur is an example of the intermediate position of the guilds, where they still exist, but do not exercise the powers they have in Gujarat; while Oodeypur, another city of Rajputana, shows a still weaker organization, for there is here no attempt to regulate trade or wages, and the nomenclature is changing to the purely conventional use of Mahajan (as the title of an individual), such as is found in the eastern districts. In Ajmere, which is not a native state, there is practically no guild-power, and the terms Sheth and Mahajan have only a social meaning.

[1] Compare Mr. Little's account of the Panch Mahals in the third volume of the Bombay Gazetteer, p. 251. His remarks in regard to the referee may be generalized.

Southwards, the guilds have a sort of loose existence among artisans and the lowest workmen of Bombay, but the modern emporia, Bombay and Calcutta, have grown up under influences foreign to the cultivation of guilds, and the latter have in these cities the appearance of weak exotics. During the plague some of these Bombay workmen's guilds made a stand against certain sanitary regulations, but they could not maintain it. In Poona there are no Mahajans, and even the Nagar Sheth, who used to be a power there, exists no longer. There is here a sort of Panch or committee of all trades. This now takes the place of the council of chiefs, which used to be influential. In case of need of conference or mutual support the different trades confer informally and may unite in combined action, but there is no real organization of guilds. This seems to be about the southern boundary of the guild-system, as Benares, where Mahajan simply means "banker" and the guilds are only loose associations, is the eastern limit.

In the Punjab the country villages are almost guildless. There is, to be sure, on extraordinary occasions, a sort of union of people interested in business, such as a mutual agreement to close shops as a sign of popular discontent, or some such concert of action for a definite cause, but there is no constant union. The only approach to the dignity of Sheth and Mahajan[1] is an agreement on the part of grain-dealers in regard to prices. Similar agreements are sometimes made by other business men acting as a temporary body, but not as a legal corporation. The only officer in the lower grades of work is the semi-governmental Chaudhari or Head-man. But this Head-man's office is merely to act as spokesman for men of his class and be their agent in dealing with the government, especially in arranging service which they have to perform,

[1] The word "Mahajan" is here synonymous with (any) Vania. It is interesting to see that the name of the third caste is still retained in the Punjab, where Vania interchanges not only with Mahajan, but also with Wesh, *i. e.* Vaiçya, the old name for merchant (and farmer). — Census Report, 1891, i. p. 291.

settling the terms of a contract, etc. As an agent, he may retain a percentage out of the pay of the men who do the work for the government. Thus the *shuturban* or camel-drivers, cartmen, dhooly-bearers, and such workmen, all have a Chaudhari, who in some respects seems like the Patel of a guild, but he is really only a Muccadum, head-man or boss-workman. There is of course a Panchayat, but that is concerned only with caste-matters, and the term is not used of guilds as it is in Gujarat.

Eastwards, in the Delhi district (now called Punjab), there is more guild-organization, but without solidarity. A sort of caste of rich merchants is all that the Mahajans amount to in the Northwest Provinces generally, but only from Delhi to Lucknow has the word its western meaning. Still further east in the Northwest Provinces, and along the eastern Ganges, the name has only its literal signification. The artisan-guilds of the Northwest Provinces either have not developed fully or are a weak imitation of Gujarat models. A third possibility may be, however, that they have lost power which they used to possess. In Oudh they were formerly powerful, but now they are often nothing but castes. In some cases the guilds have actually become castes, just as castes have become guilds. For occupation has produced caste, not, as is sometimes claimed, as the only root of the institution, but as one factor in the upbuilding of that conglomerate structure. The word Nyât or caste (*jāti*) is in fact sometimes applied to those lower artisan guilds, which as a collective group stand opposed to the union of Vanias and Brahmans (Mahajans). This is true of all districts. Thus in the Kadi division, North Baroda, there is often no distinction between guild and caste in the case of Nyâts, which are practically dependent on the Mahajan. The latter directs and commands the Nyâts and admits to its consultation only the latter's Patels. Here the real guild has shown its power over the pseudo-guild of the caste.[1]

[1] On these points compare further the Gazetteer of the N.W. Provinces, vol. v. pp. 47, 582; and the Bombay Gazetteer, vol. vii. p. 160; vol. xviii. p. 178. In some cases the Mahajan even fixes the wages of the Nyât workmen.

## STRIKES.

The guilds often go on a strike. One of the latest cases was in the spring of 1897, when the *holalkhores*, or cleaners, of Bombay refused to work and "went out" in a body. Wages and working-hours are not often the cause of strikes, but religious differences and fancied injuries to feelings. Refusal of government to give redress when a guild considers itself wronged in respect of taxation sometimes precipitates a strike. A few years ago the hand-loom weavers of Ahmedabad struck on a mixed complaint and were largely replaced by boys. In general, lads are employed to a much greater extent than with us, partly on account of the smaller wage given to boys, and partly because they are less apt to give trouble. One of the largest carpet-manufactories in Ahmedabad employs boys altogether with the exception of two grown men.

Religious differences have caused strikes in Kathiawar within the last few years, as has been recorded by Mr. Proctor-Sims. Thus in 1845, the Vanias of Gondal could get no redress for the insult offered to their Hindu feelings by the Mohammedan butchers, who sold meat openly, and they were driven to shut up shop; which compelled the government to pass a rule that all butchers should kill secretly and sell behind a screen, — a provision now usually observed everywhere. On the other hand, twelve years later the Vanias of Dhoraji wounded the religious feelings of the Mohammedans. The latter killed a few Vanias, and the state in turn punished the Mohammedan ringleaders. The malcontents struck work in a body and some of them left the town; but their strike failed, as the government, taking the side of the Vanias, ordered all Mohammedans to leave the place. This was too much for the latter, and a reconciliation took place. In 1881 a sacred cow was wounded by some Voharas, and as nothing was done about it, the Hindu Vanias, whose feelings had been outraged, struck for three days and thus forced the offender to be imprisoned. The year before this, the barbers of Wadhwan struck — a rare event — for higher wages. But this strike failed because the general public (*i. e.*, all the other guilds) opposed the demand. To prevent a fall of wages a strike has sometimes been ordered by the councils of guilds (acting together). A case of this kind is reported by Mr. Little in the Panch Mahals,[1] but such a motive appears to be very unusual. In such instances the guilds form a true trade-union. Strikes of a semi-religious nature, as, for instance, against the execution of sanitary measures regarded as religiously offensive, are not uncommon. But, as sanitary measures are instituted only by the British, when the officials are not deterred by threats such strikes usually fail.

## THE GUILD AND THE STATE.

It is clear from the passage on guilds, cited above from the Sanskrit epic, that in ancient times there was a mutual support of state and guild. The strict advice to the king not to provoke, but to conciliate the guilds, the steady increase of power which is portrayed in the later as compared with the earlier law-books and is based on the yielding of the state to the demand of the guilds for self-government, — all these items of growth are shown to us in the extant literature, but the connection between state officials and the guilds is left to the imagination or to *a posteriori* reasoning. Judging, however, from what has continually happened during this century, that relation cannot be very doubtful. Reciprocal protection has doubtless always figured largely as a factor in the maintenance of the power of the guilds. In plain English I mean a "deal," but the opprobrium attaching to this word is wanting when the synonym is employed, and there is in fact no Oriental prejudice which would suggest immorality. A state official does what he can to strengthen the hands of a rich city corporation. The corporation, on the other hand, would not be so ungrateful as to neglect the official's interest. The guild may intrigue for him. Or it may be a trifle; he wants some

[1] Bombay Gazetteer, vol. iii. p. 251.

cloth dyed. The guild sees that it is done and charges nothing. Mr. Lely, *loc. cit.*, p. 107, cites cases of this sort which occurred not many years ago. Of course, no such practices are known to-day. The conference, when asked in regard to reciprocal protection, said that it was all a thing of the past. In the old days "a favor for a favor" was usual; nowadays favors were neither asked nor given. The only relation existing between state and guild is to-day a union of guilds (into a sort of trades-union) to protest against taxes regarded as too heavy. The local authorities sometimes help out the guilds in this matter, but there is "no bribery." The first part of this statement agrees with what Mr. Proctor-Sims says in the report already cited; the last part may be accepted on the evidence of the honorable Sheths who give it. The only state support at present consists in fees to a local Sheth for collecting trade taxes.

In manufacturing centres where modern mills are in operation, there is often but a faint reflection of old conditions, even in Gujarat. In Ahmedabad the mills have influenced the guilds, but the latter are still vigorous. In Bhaunagar, however, a model city of Gujarat, in the heart of the old guild district, there are mills owned by a Hindu whose workmen are mainly Mohammedans, and there is no guild in the old sense, though the term "Mahajan" is employed. But the intercourse between master and men is one of a personal rather than of a corporate nature. There is a Sheth, but the office is not hereditary.

This breaking up of old conditions is seen in many aspects of contemporary life, notably in the effacement of the lines of sect and caste. I met a gentleman in Oodeypur who told me that he was a Kshatriya and a Vaiçya, a Vishnuite and a Jain. He was of Rajput descent, but a Vania merchant, a Vishnuite by sect, but a Shravak by descent, as his father had been converted to Jainism. He regarded himself as a member of both religious bodies and of both castes. Odd as is this combination, I am not sure that it would not have been possible, even in the ancient world. We know that there were many who were practically adherents of two religious sects at once, and we need go no further than the great epic to find distressed Kshatriyas, or members of the warrior-caste, who were at the same time goldsmiths by profession. The latter have always regarded themselves as Vaiçyas, or members of the third caste. In epic phraseology, these distressed Rajputs were Kshatriyas by their social order, *varṇa*, but goldsmiths by their *jāti*, the word for caste profession.[1]

It is probable that the time when the guilds can be looked upon as economically useful has passed by. But if we review their history we must, I think, see in them an important factor in the development of mercantile interests at a time when such a combination as they represented was indispensable to the advancement of the middle classes in their struggle for recognition at the hands both of despotic kings and of an organized priesthood that was bent on suppressing the elevation of the third estate. With the growth of the guilds the new axiom of later law was evolved, whereby the king was advised not to oppress the guilds and not to tax too heavily. So commerce in the modern sense became possible.

In conclusion, I wish to record my best thanks to Sheth Lalbhai Dalpatbhai, the enlightened Sheth of the Shravaks of Ahmedabad, for the very kind efforts made by him in my behalf. It is owing largely to him that I have been able to gather at first hand the material which has made this study seem worthy of publication. As the record from living witnesses of the workings of an institution more than two thousand years old, it may, perhaps, be of interest.

[1] Mbh., xii. 49, 84: *ete kṣatriyadāyādāḥ . . . hemakārādijātiṁ nityaṁ samāçritāḥ*. The *jāti* here is the modern Nyât. Nowadays, as stated above, p. 177, goldsmiths claim only Vania descent.

## LAND-TENURE IN INDIA.

SINCE the days of Sir Henry Maine the glory of the Hindu village-community has wellnigh departed. Till a decade ago it was still taught that the "primitive Aryan," an individual with whom we are less familiar now than formerly, held only a partner's right of possession in his native soil. Communal ownership of land was at that time believed by most scholars to have been an Aryan institution, common to the primitive German and Hindu alike.

It was, therefore, with the feeling of being very heretical that I ventured, on the basis of a merely literary acquaintance with the social conditions of ancient India, to state in 1888 that "practically the ownership of land is vested in each hereditary occupant; his right is secured by title;"[1] and to say that there was need of a fresh investigation of Indian village-communities and Hindu land-tenure.[2] At that time I did not know that Mr. Baden-Powell's wide researches into present conditions had concentrated themselves upon this very problem and were leading him to the same general conclusion, which he afterwards established more firmly in the recasting of his material. In The Indian Village Community (1896) the perfected theories of the author of Land Systems (1892) are explained at length. These are the more valuable as they were propounded solely from the point of view of the practical observer of things as they are. That from these two quite different points of view has been drawn substantially the same result is surely an argument in favor of its probable correctness.

In his last work, Village Communities in India, published in 1899, just before his death, Mr. Baden-Powell gave a popu-

[1] Journal of the American Oriental Society vol. xiii. p. 88.
[2] *Ibid.*, p. 57.

lar exposition of his theory (which may now be called the accepted theory) of the origin of the different systems of land-tenure in India. Some points were here slightly modified, as compared with earlier statements respecting historical conditions, but in the main this work repeated what had been said in the previous volumes.

Sir Henry Maine died in the same year that my article was published; and, strangely enough, no follower of his ever undertook to see whether his views were corroborated by the monuments of antiquity. The outline here drawn attempts to give the growth and change of land-tenure as these are shown in the literature of Aryan India, from the earliest Vedic period to about 500 A.D. It may be regarded as a sort of historical introduction to the vast array of facts collected by Mr. Baden-Powell, whose unrivalled presentation of modern conditions still lacks the perspective given by the literary evidence of the past.[1] In regard to some points I shall be obliged to differ from the views expressed in Mr. Baden-Powell's monographs, but these do not affect the general propositions he upholds. On the contrary, to my thinking, the chief contention, that the early Vedic Aryans were not grouped in village communities (using this word in its strict sense), is irrefragable.

I would say one word more before beginning this sketch. Writers on economic conditions in India are still prone to cite from the "early law" of the Hindus; and unfortunately, to many who know other things well but Sanskrit only by reputation, "early law" is synonymous with the law-book of Manu. Now, Manu may be cited with discretion, but not at haphazard as an authority on early law; for he stands to early law much in the relative position of Justinian, where the old may be found, but where not all that is found is old. Before Manu there are a number of earlier law-writers known as authors of law-manuals, Sutras (*sūtras*, threads of discourse,

[1] For the legal data may be consulted Professor Jolly's excellent little book Recht und Sitte, the compass of which, however, prevents detailed analysis of theories of land-tenure.

concise treatises). Behind these, again, lie all the (informal) legal provisions of the Brahmana age, and back even of these, the Vedic hymns. It will readily be seen, therefore, that Manu is not synonymous with primitive or even very early Aryan. What is found in Manu may be as old as the Vedas or older, but on the other hand it may be as late as 200 B. C.

No very definite statements in regard to land-tenure can be gathered from the earliest literature. The Vedic hymns, the oldest literary monument, show that different tribes at different periods are involved in any data that may be collected. At one time a poet speaks of his people as advancing "from a far land," searching for "pasturage and water;" at another, a singer is interested mainly in agriculture, and prays for rain and a good harvest. The people were in part nomadic: all together they sought fresh lands; "give us wide pastures" was their cry. But only an occasional prayer for meadow-land to be bestowed on one worshipper would lead us to lay stress on this poetic phraseology. The contrast is there, — on the one hand, between the sole petitioner and the cry of land for all; on the other, between the grazing and agricultural population, — but only the latter antithesis is pronounced. Taken as a whole, the stage represented is that of a people devoted to cattle rather than to the plough, and before the time when agricultural life prevailed there was probably little question as to land-ownership. This stage was reached, however, in the Rig Veda, though in the whole of this work there are less than a dozen references to ploughing, while those to grazing are innumerable. Landed property is gained by conquest, and the "winning of fields" or "conquest of fields" is recognized as the usual aim of battle — as much so as "the conquest of cattle." The booty of such conquests, as is expressly hinted, was distributed by shares. At a coronation the prayer is: "Grant him, the king, a share in village, horses, and cattle." But the king distributes, as is said in another hymn: "From the height of sovereignty do thou, terrible one, give us a share in goods." Private ownership in land is plainly expressed, not so much by the image of the gods measuring time with [their] staff "like a field" (which Mr. Baden-Powell translated incorrectly, through the medium of a German version, as "a man measures a field with a staff of reed"), as by other passages where ownership is really implied. Thus, a young woman prays that something may grow on her father's head and on [his] plough-land; and a gambler cries that a god has warned him to go and plough the plough-land for a living instead of playing with dice, which leads only to regret as he looks on the happy homes of others. The implication seems to be, in the very few pertinent passages, that the plougher owns his field as he does his plough; but there is really nothing in these hymns, which are mainly part of a divine service, to establish this with certainty.

The "heads of families," casually mentioned as grouped around the "active lord of the host," may possibly imply joint families; but the evidence for this is also very vague. On the other hand, there is direct evidence, as I shall show below, that a joint family in the legal sense was not recognized; but that the indications of separate ownership of fields in the Rig Veda are substantiated by a passage in the Atharva Veda, where a man prays the god to bless "his men, his cattle, his horses, and his field." Separate houses are of course to be assumed, but they are also implicitly established. The kings give to their priests great gifts of thousands of cattle, not as part of a common possession, but as their individual property to be driven off to their own home. But the great owner of property, the "wealth's wealth-lord and people's people-lord," as the Atharva Veda calls him, is the king. This wealth he wins "from foe and friend;" but there is nothing at this period to indicate indubitably in whom is vested the ultimate ownership of land. The people are taxed, — that is, they give requisite offerings, — but long before the close of the Vedic period the tax is obligatory.

The domestic priest of the king was the first, as far as the records show, to be the recipient of a gift of land from the king. In one of the earliest Brahmanas, the first prose literature, the king is directed to give this priest "a field;"

but we shall look in vain through the still earlier literature of the hymns for any such donation. In the Vedic hymns, cattle, horses, slaves, clothes, and jewels are given in profusion, but nowhere is there any mention of a gift of land. When thus given, however, in the second period, the land may not be alienated. Even if the king at another time should give all his land to another priest, that piece which he has formerly given to the first priest is not included in the later donation. The prototype of those extraordinary gifts (so frequently mentioned in later literature), whereby a king gives all his land to a priest, is found in the Brahmanas. As Mr. Baden-Powell seems to have thought that all such stories are late, — and, in fact, he seems to have known only of the latest, — it is well to remember that, so far as such stories affect the question of land-tenure, they are really a product, not of a late age, but of the Vedic period in its second stage. Such gifts in that age are, however, rare as compared with the succeeding period. Gifts of whole villages are recorded in the earliest Upanishad and legal literature.

A general view of the intermediate age, represented by the later Vedas and the Brahmanas, shows that, when a king with the help of an ally conquers a third king, he "goes shares" in the booty with his ally; that the country is governed by the sovereign through local officers; that the *grāmaṇī* or "leader of a host" of the earlier period has now become a "village head-man;" and that the king bestows land for a place of sacrifice only when he has been "begged" for it by the priests.

A question arises at this point; and it is perhaps the one that Mr. Baden-Powell, from an historical point of view, answered most unsatisfactorily, when he claimed that the Aryan Vaiçya was an agriculturist only incidentally and chiefly by proxy, being really a trader. He based this view on the fact that in Manu's (late) law-book the Vaiçya seems to be principally occupied with trade. In the course of his argument he was here led to make one or two statements of fact, the truth of which cannot be determined upon the slender evidence adduced, and which a closer acquaintance with Sanskrit literature would probably have modified.

The subject is really of prime importance, owing to the use to which Mr. Baden-Powell put his results. He drew from it the conclusion "that the upper classes of Aryan origin had little feeling for agriculture, and that India does not owe to them either the introduction of settled cultivation or (directly) any particular policy or principle of land ownership."[1] Mr. Baden-Powell was of the opinion that agriculture was performed only by the humblest classes of Aryans, scarcely differentiated from the original inhabitants, and was much surprised that he could not find, in accordance with his theory, any mention of the Çudra (slave, *çūdra*) as an agriculturist.

This is rather a startling statement, in view of the fact that, as I have already mentioned, agricultural labor is alluded to in the very earliest Aryan literature. In the Brahmana literature also, although one does not expect to find many allusions to agriculture in books devoted to the exposition of a sacrificial liturgy, ploughing is very often mentioned and the processes of the year's work in the plough-land are all described. Then turning to the Sutras, or earliest manuals of law, some of them much older than Manu, we find, not only constant allusion to agriculture, but plain evidence of the fact that Vaiçyas were particularly agriculturists, and that members of the warrior caste and of the priest caste were very apt to adopt the same occupation. It was therefore a grave slip to say, as did Mr. Baden-Powell: "Whatever be the true date of the *Laws of Manu*, we have no earlier literary mention of agriculture, after the Vedic Hymns,"[2] and I am glad to see that in his latest volume he accepted the corrections which I made as regards this point,[3] and so modified it

[1] The Indian Village Community, p. 192. [2] *Ibid.*, p. 190.

[3] In an article in the Political Science Quarterly, December, 1898. The present essay has, of course, been modified accordingly.

as to extract from it all its force. "I meant only" (he says) "that non-Aryan races had established villages for agricultural life before the Aryans, and that the latter furnished the element of over-lordship and manorial growth" (Ind. Vill. Comm. p. 54). In this new statement Mr. Baden-Powell is doubtless right, as he adds unequivocally, "The lower ranks of Aryans practised agriculture." But, as a matter of fact, we can trace almost step by step through the Sutras the gradual change from cowboy and agriculturist to trader in the case of the Vaiçya. Long before Manu's law-book was known, had arisen the famous *ahinsā* doctrine of non-injury to living creatures; and the objection to agriculture on the part of the priest is based expressly on this ground in the law-books. But, as to-day and in the last century in Rajputana, so in ancient times, recourse to agriculture was the first thought on the part of the upper castes, and agriculture was the usual occupation of the third estate. It is true that the upper castes had no "feeling" for agriculture, but noblemen and priests, as a general thing, have feeling neither for agriculture nor for trade. In India the Vaiçya was first a tender of cattle; then from the Vedic period onwards an agriculturist or cattle-man; and, lastly, by preference a trader. But, on the other hand, traders existed in the Vedic age, so that the very gradual change of occupation of the caste as a whole is the more remarkable if Mr. Baden-Powell's view was correct. There is, again, another factor ignored in Mr. Baden-Powell's work. "Vaiçya" was the old inherited caste (or, better class) name and could not be dispensed with. It had to cover various new livelihoods in the law-books, as in the older literature it covered all occupations not knightly, priestly, or menial. But in the epic, trader and Vaiçya are sundered outright, grouped as two classes; and here Vaiçya, in sharp distinction from trader, means agriculturist. The epic, moreover, in numerous passages intimates that, when a Vaiçya is spoken of, it is *par excellence* an agriculturist who is intended. Thus, in the words of the Goddess of Bliss: "I dwell in the home of the Vaiçya" (that is) "the one devoted to agriculture"; and again: "This is the expiation of a Vaiçya, to give part of his crops to a priest." The same work contains a list of priests who lead irregular lives: "Some [priests] practise agriculture and tend cattle; some rely on begging," etc. Sometimes the word connotes simply a cowherd; sometimes it includes the trader; but it never indicates the trader alone. But not to quote more, though it would be easy, I will conclude this paragraph by saying that the town Vaiçyas were usually guild-men, and became naturally much more important economically than their stupider brothers who stayed on the farm.[1] To draw from such evidence the sweeping conclusion that India owes agriculture to the Dravidians would be a surprising bit of logic. There is in reality no evidence whatever to show that the Aryans learned agriculture from the Dravidians. All that we can say is that there is no proof that the Vaiçyas were a large special caste who introduced agriculture into India. As Mr. Baden-Powell in this respect also modified his original statements to this form (*loc. cit. supra*, p. 53), it is perhaps unnecessary to argue this point further.

The appointment of officers over various parts of the kingdom as subalterns very likely dates back to the Vedic period; and as Mr. Baden-Powell says of the officers in Manu's law-book: "These were in all probability 'over-lords' simply, who drew revenues from the landed proprietors." In one of the Upanishads it is said in a simile: [The vital breath commands the other breaths] "just as a *samraj* or universal king commissions his officers, saying: Be thou over these villages or those villages." But in many cases these villages do not seem to have had much tenacity as regards land. When, as is related in a Buddhist text, one village is annoyed by dacoits, it is regarded as the most natural thing in the world that the village should be moved, — that it should even divide

[1] But even trading (town) Vaiçyas kept up agricultural pursuits, as is shown in many Buddhistic stories. See the preceding article on Ancient and Modern Hindu Guilds.

into two bodies, one part going to one place and the other to another.

Now this instability of the village is characteristic of the eastern part of India. From the east comes the account of the division first mentioned; and similarly it is in the later epic, which is probably an eastern addition to the western poem, that the king is warned continually to be kind to the agriculturists, as they are liable, if displeased, to leave their villages at any time and to seek homes elsewhere, even in the realm of his enemy. This, too, is corroborated by the proverb-wisdom of the period: "A wife and a home, — these are secondary matters; one can find them everywhere."

The gift of whole villages on the part of a king is a noteworthy feature of Buddhist literature (*c.* 300 B.C.), as it is of the epic. It is foreshadowed, as we have seen, in the tales of the Brahmanas, and there is a case or two mentioned in the early Upanishads. By what tenure these lands were held is perhaps not quite so certain as Mr. Baden-Powell thinks. But before describing the terms of these grants I must touch on another topic.

The joint-family is the ideal of the later age, but it is not an ideal which is favored by the jurists. In the later law it is held to be more meritorious not to keep the family united, the principle being that of the so-called "increase of religion." That is to say: the more householders, the more sacrifices; the more sacrifices, the more spiritual merit (and the more gifts to priests). But the joint-family stands in a poetic ideal light in the eyes of the epic poets. This tends to show on the one hand that it was old, and on the other that it was no longer customary. An example or two will illustrate this. An elder brother, who has all to gain and nothing to lose by keeping up the joint-family, reproves his younger brother, who demands partition of the family estate: "Many through folly desire partition, but such divided heirs are weakened before their foes." Again, in plaintive retrospect of the good old days it is said: "In that age sons did not divide with their father." The strange thing about this is that, according to all the legends and traditions of antiquity, the joint-family is unknown: the divided family is the rule. There is, to my knowledge, not a single instance in the mythical accounts of the past, where a father is represented as leaving his property to the family in general or as possessing it in common with them. The historical or legendary evidence, on the contrary, all points the other way.

If, for instance, we turn back to the oldest period of which we have any knowledge, we find in the Rig Veda a distinct allusion to the fact that, when the father grew old and feeble, he was ousted from his property and his sons divided it among themselves. In the Brahmanas, again, there are two mythical accounts of Father Manu (not as the lawgiver here, but as the Adam of the race) and of the division of his inheritance. These differ only in details. One of them, either really the older or at least contained in an older work, describes the fact thus: "Manu divided his property for his sons; one of them, living elsewhere as a student, he excluded from a share." The other account says: "The brothers excluded from a share one of Manu's sons." In both accounts the property is divided during the father's life. The position of the one son who assumes his father's place is described in the later literature of the Upanishads, where it is said that when a father, thinking he is about to die, bestows everything on his son and that son accepts it, then the father, if he recovers, must live under the son's authority or "wander about, a beggar." But this is a later case of only one son, and affects solely the status of the father when he has disposed of his authority; whereas the earlier tale recognizes each son as special owner of a special share. So, too, in the Yajur Veda is found another indication to the same effect, when it is said: "For this reason they fit out the eldest son with [an extra share of] property," as the sentence must be interpreted according to the context and according to the oldest commentator, who is himself a jurist.[1]

[1] Apastamba's Law-Book, ii. 6, 14, 12. The accounts of partition are from the Black Yajur Veda and Aitareya Brahmana, references in Jolly, *loc. cit.*

Again, in mythology we find constant references in the Brahmana period to the "division of inheritance" of the Father-god, whose children, the gods and the devils, "both being children of the Father-god," fight for their respective shares and "enter into their inheritance" by dividing it. In terms of real life this would show that the divided family was the ordinary family through the Brahmana period. So when a man has no son, he divides his property between his two wives, according to another well-known story of the same period.

But the marriage hymn of the Rig Veda indicates that the man takes his bride home and expects her to be mistress of the household, which expressly includes her father-in-law and brothers-in-law. Now this hymn represents, in all probability, a period much older than the mass of Vedic hymns; and it would really be consonant with all the facts in the case, if we saw in this unique passage (for "hymns of concord" do not prove anything) a reference to the joint-family, though no longer in the "patriarchal" stage. In what way, however, can this be harmonized with the apparently contradictory evidence already adduced? Clearly by the otherwise not improbable assumption that the joint-family was already on the wane in the earliest (literary) period. It is for this reason, as it seems to me, that the two forms go theoretically hand in hand at a much later date, as in the law-book of Manu and the epic. In the latter, for instance, the same paragraph gives directions for maintaining a family in either way after the father's death. Here the joint-family is formally disapproved of, while theoretically it is allowed; but the only case where a really joint-family is represented is that of the chief epic heroes. These, however, are ideal types; and even in their case the separate ownership of a younger brother is distinctly recognized. Thus, in order to give away property belonging to his junior, the head of the family asks the latter's permission; and when this is refused, the younger retains his possessions undisturbed.

When it is remembered, however, that the Aryans of the

Punjab are looked upon by the writers of this epic as outside the Brahmanic pale, and that many customs lingered among the former which the more advanced Aryans of the "middle district" (around the present Delhi) had long since renounced, it is clear that another element than that of time may be involved. It is a mistake to think that the Punjab was as un-Aryan two or three thousand years ago as it is to-day. In the epic, the inhabitants of what is now the Delhi district revile in no measured terms the western Punjab allies they unwillingly associate with, but it is not even suggested that they are not Aryans: it is merely said that their customs are strange, remote, not in keeping with the more eastern usage of the "middle land." It is therefore possible that the older joint-family was retained among those Aryans who, instead of striking southeast with the later Vedic poets, lingered behind in the Punjab.

But the kind of property "divided" in the ancient tales I have referred to is never land but always flocks. Even the early law-books are very reticent in regard to the kind of property to be divided. When partition is expressly spoken of, however, it is in terms of cattle. "Impartible property" is described at length, the list increasing with the lateness of the author. Thus Manu's list includes "a dress, a vehicle, ornaments, prepared food, water [that is, a well], females [slaves], religious property, and a path [or pasture]," while Gautama, who states that land is not lost by adverse possession, mentions only water, religious property, prepared food and females [slaves]. Uçanas says that land is impartible, and this may be implied by Gâutama, but the late jurists of the fourth and fifth centuries of our era specify houses and lands as partible. Fields owned by individuals are mentioned, not only in the case of a man who clears a piece of jungle and is therefore admitted to be the possessor, but also in the laws concerning the establishment of disputed boundaries. It is therefore the more remarkable that in the laws of inheritance real estate is so often ignored. The later jurists are, in fact, as careful to give minute rules of inheritance in regard to house and land as are the early jurists to avoid express mention of such forms of inheritance. Professor Jolly finds in the implication of impartible real estate (as opposed to express rules for partible property) Spuren einer ehemaligen Feldgemeinschaft ganzer Dörfer, and is perhaps inclined to retain the village community, though he is not explicit on this point (§§ 23, 27, of Recht und Sitte), perhaps owing to lack of space to discuss the subject. This would at any rate be the natural inference if one believed that village ownership necessarily implied a village community. But, as will be seen, there is no necessity for accepting this conclusion.

On the other hand, I think there can be no doubt that the general Hindu theory of impartible real estate is a distinct blow to the sweeping generalization made by Mr. Baden-Powell when he stated that the early Aryans in India recognized only private ownership in land. If the theory he advanced depended on the truth of this generalization, it would have to be abandoned as no less unsatisfactory than that of Sir Henry Maine. But the theory does not depend (as Mr. Baden-Powell seemed to think) on any such generalization. It is, if I may say so, a pity that two facts were never recognized by that practical expositor: first, that there was a middle way, and, second, that in Hindu legal literature the same work will not only contain contradictory statements, but also imply different economic conditions. A very good (and for my present purpose important) illustration of this may be found in what Manu has said about boundary laws and what Mr. Baden-Powell has said about Manu.

To take the latter case first, as the remarks on Manu are very short, Mr. Baden-Powell declared, with a simplicity almost too forced, that "rules for settling boundaries are given;" and then used this presentation of the facts as an argument against the view that village holdings are known to Manu, and as a proof of exclusively "private ownership." [1]

[1] The Indian Village Community, p. 207. In the same author's Land Systems (vol. i. p. 227), the wording is "boundary of estates or holdings."

It is doubtless true that Manu recognizes boundaries of private estates; but it is quite as important to notice that he not only recognizes boundaries of villages also, but devotes to the latter his chief care. In fact, the whole subject of boundaries in his law-book opens with elaborate rules for the adjustment of boundaries between "disputing villages;" and it is only as an after-thought or appendix that he adds to these rules the subsidiary law in regard to "boundary lines of a field, spring, reservoir, garden, or house." Previous to the curt statement that in such cases the boundary shall be established "by an appeal to the neighbors," comes a long description of the formalities to be observed "when a dispute has arisen between two villages." This description extends over seventeen paragraphs and closes with the statement that "as the witnesses declare, so shall the boundary be between the two villages." According to the commentator's reasonable explanation, there are two advocates or special pleaders, each representing one of the two villages, but the whole village takes part in the proceedings. The rule of Vasishtha, who quotes Manu and is not a very early writer,[1] speaks only of the second kind of boundary. Still more noteworthy is the absolute inversion of the order in the still later law-book of Yajnavalkya. Here the boundary rule is applied first to private fields and then to "gardens, villages, and reservoirs." Virtually, the elder lawgiver says: "This is the law in regard to the disputed boundaries of villages," and then adds, "This law applies also to fields." The later jurist says: "This is the law in regard to fields," and then adds, "The law applies also to villages," — rather a significant alteration.

It is of course true that this passage does not prove communal ownership in either village; but the inference from the prior description would not seem to be that the ownership

[1] The law-book of Vasishtha is a mixture of prose and verse, of old and new. Like the later writers, he prescribes, for instance, that a proof of ownership is a *lekhya* or "writing," and enjoins the use of documents in case of disputed ownership (xvi. 10, 14). The earliest Sutra lawgiver, Gautama, has no rule at all in regard to boundaries, though he recognizes enclosed fields and private ownership in land.

spoken of is one of private fields; and it was certainly going a little too far for Mr. Baden-Powell to cite the passage as evidence of exclusively private property. The inference to be drawn is, I think, neither that of Maine nor of Baden-Powell. This village is not a "village community," but it is also not a Raiyat village. It is a joint-village. The garlanded witnesses, marking out the lines in the presence of "all the inhabitants," point to the recognition of proprietary rights in those inhabitants as a body. Further, in the early law, we hear of the much-despised "priest of a whole village," who, like the "priest of a corporation," apparently officiates for a corporate body. Now such village corporations are expressly recognized in the later law-books, and Professor Jolly, Recht und Sitte, p. 94, cites a text, found in commentaries but of doubtful authorship, which says that a field cannot be sold without the consent of the village.

The habitat of the joint-family village seems to be in the agricultural districts of the Punjab. It is therefore interesting to notice that the people who are spoken of in the early Brahmana period as living "without kings" are inhabitants of the northwestern Punjab. But the epic, besides these, speaks of a people whose only name is "villagers" or "village-head-man people." They are great warriors and "live on the banks of the Indus."[1] To my thinking, Manu, whose law-book originated in what is now the southeastern Punjab, stands between two geographical and historical extremes; and in his work, as in the early epic, which came from the same district, there are traces of two forms of holdings and two forms of inheritance and family.[2]

It is a curious fact that the British have not yet been able to decide whether they are drawing a tax or a rent from the Hindu farmer. Some, like Mr. Chesney, say that the

[1] People living "without kings" are frequently mentioned in the epic, and always as if they were well known though much despised.

[2] I may add that Mr. Baden-Powell's notion (in support of his theory) that Manu's law-book comes from Oudh is utterly without a basis in fact. Manu praises only the Delhi district. The eastern districts he knows only as the home of impure castes.

land has always belonged to the crown, and the farmer pays rent for his land. Others, like Mr. Baden-Powell and Lord Salisbury, prefer to regard the revenue as a tax. Mr. Hyndman says that "the matter is too clear for dispute," and that the land-revenue is a tax. Both sides appeal to ancient authorities and ancient ideas of the Hindu state; while, on the other hand, M. Senart thinks that the ancient Hindus had no idea of a state at all. Some of the Greek authorities speak of taxes in India, and others speak of rent, even declaring that the whole country belonged to the king, and that no individual owned land at all. The Greeks, however, may be ignored, for the reason that in many of the economic statements they make they can be proved to be utterly untrustworthy, and therefore in others are as likely to be wrong as right.

Nor do I think that we can treat the words of the Hindu law-makers as we should those of modern economists who make a sharp distinction between rent and tax. In fact, though I do not know that the idea has been suggested before, or that it would receive the approbation of scholars generally, I am convinced for my own part that the true solution is to be found in the explanation that the revenue in ancient times was regarded as a tax, but that in regard to ownership the old Hindu legislator held (without raising the question which is now put first) that ownership in land was double.

Incomprehensible as is this attitude at first sight, it is not incompatible with a doctrine both sound and natural. In the first place, the Hindu without doubt owned his land. To take the simplest case, he owned new land which he made (cleared of jungle), "as a hunter owns the deer he shoots," to employ the native parallel. On this land he paid a sixth of the crop as tax "in return for protection," as is stated over and over. If he did not get the protection the tax was not due. If the king took it "he incurred a sixth of the farmer's sins;" that is, translated out of the eschatological balance-sheet, the king at his own death owed the farmer the tax unjustly taken. It is clear, therefore, that the farmer or joint-family, as the case might be, owned the land. The only restriction was that his son ("a part of himself") divided the ownership. Hence he could not alienate his land, but it was handed down from father to son or descended to the joint-family's heirs, alienable only by consent of the joint-village if the case was one of joint-village ownership.

But, on the other hand, it was as unquestioned that the king was the master of all. The king is not only over-lord, he is owner, and one of his old titles is, "The one owning all the land." On this point I am compelled to differ from Mr. Baden-Powell, who claimed that the idea of land-ownership vested in the crown is a late growth. The king in the earliest period (in the recorded ceremony of inauguration) is expressly said to be the devourer of his people. This is no isolated phrase, nor are the people other than his own Vaiçyas. The Aitareya Brahmana says that a priest's function is to take gifts, while the Vaiçya's peculiar function is to be devoured by priest and nobleman. The only difference recognized in this early age between slave and farmer is that the latter, being Aryan, may not be killed at pleasure.

Now I submit, in the first place, that it is nonsense to suppose that a peasant proprietor, openly described as fit only to be robbed by the king, could have had any secure hold of his landed property. The king's ownership extended to all property except a priest's, which is especially described as the only land in his realm "outside the king's district," *āçā*.

But we find the same view also in the legal literature. Mr. Baden-Powell asserted, indeed, that the only authority for the idea that the state was considered superior owner of the soil, is a modern digest of the last century.

But Brihaspati, whose code was written 500–600 A.D., says that the reason why the king becomes heir to property left without another heir [male issue, wife, or brother] is that he is the "owner of all;" and Narada, who wrote his code about the same time or a little earlier, says that real estate held for three generations cannot be estranged except by the king's will. Again, Brihaspati, who lived when the village owned by one man was customary, says in speaking of such a village: "Suppose land is taken from a village belonging to one man and transferred to another man either by [the action of] a river or by the king [to which man does it belong?] It belongs to him who gets it from the river or from the king." The only reason is that the king is the supreme owner of the land.

In the earlier period the question as to who owns the land is simply not discussed. In every reference to the subject it is said, as if it were a matter of course, that (with a constant exception in the case of priestly possessions) the king is the owner of everything. He is not only the over-lord, but he is the over-lord as owner. Thus, as owner simply, he gets half of all treasure-trove; and that this is the true explanation is evident from the fact that, when the king gives a village to a priest, he gives him as owner the right to all the treasure-trove, — that is, the king's ownership has passed to the finder, who is now the owner. In regard to the interpretation of the legal passage I do not stand alone. The late Professor Bühler, of Vienna, one of the foremost scholars in this line, declared long ago that he regards the rule just cited "as a distinct recognition of the principle that the ownership of all land is vested in the king." The epic also has many passages showing that, while the priest claimed a divine right to possess everything in theory, he has abrogated this in practice, and in consequence everything belongs to the king to give. "Only a warrior [king] may give land to a priest," it is said; and, conversely, it is said again: "Land may be taken possession of only by a king." "It is a Vedic utterance that the king is owner of the wealth of all save the priests," is another statement made alike by law and epic. Furthermore, although the epic kings are perpetually admonished by the sages not to do wrong to the people, and although various sins against them are enumerated as possible, — such as oppressive *corvée*, over-taxation, and the like,—yet it is not once hinted that a king should not rob his subjects of land. If the land were regarded as originally the peasant's own, we should surely meet somewhere in the vast epic literature and wide range of legal Çastra some such note as we hear in the modern peasant's defiant cry that "the king owns the tax, but the peasant owns the land." It is not till the fifth century of our era that the king is admonished "not to upset the two fundaments of the peasant's life, his house and field."[1] As I have already observed, in the period just preceding this the inhabitants of the country are represented as easily moved to leave their homes and go elsewhere. They are, in fact, especially told to do so, if the soil or the king is "bad." "One should leave his king or native place if they are bad [poor], and take that to be his country where he can earn a living," is an epic dictum.

Nor are the laws of this period regarding the rights of kings contradictory. The king is declared to be the "preserver and destroyer" of his people, who are still, as of old, to be "devoured" by taxes or otherwise, as the king sees fit. When he needs it, "the king may take all the possessions, small and great, of those who break the ten commandments [of morality]," and "any possessions of any one save a priest." The king further gives and gambles away fields, villages, and whole districts at pleasure. Nor is such a gift of a village a presentation of the right to tax alone. The recorded copper-plate grants of the first centuries after Christ explicitly declare of what nature was this ownership. The grantee is made absolute owner, not relative, as in the case of an over-lord. We must, I think, interpret the *agrahāra* land-grants mentioned in the epic in the light of those actually extant. It follows that while the king had every reason to let his subjects be owners practically, it was always acknowledged that he owned the land so far as right of dispossession went. He owned it, but he let his subjects live on it, for to them he was as a "father to sons." But, in that he protected them and needed money, he

[1] Narada's Law-Book.

made an agreement that while they lived on his land they paid him for living there securely. In other words, just as the king might take all a farmer's flocks if needed and annually took part of the flocks as payment (tax) for guarding the farmer, so he took part of the crop as payment for protection, not as rent, although as universal owner the land was his if he chose to take it.

We may then assert that, according to the notion of the time, the king owned the land, but did not draw rent for it. It was taxed for protection only. Yet it may be seen even in the law-books that there was a gradual decline of the view that gave all to the king, and a gradual growth of the view that the field was more and more owned altogether by the peasant proprietor; the king's "ownership of all" declining just as his "right to plunder his farmers" was restricted by advancing civilization. In the later law the king's ownership disappeared except as a theory.

But a good deal of it is left in the epic, and we may thus interpret the power and ownership of kings in the light of such callous remarks as meet us in that literature. One passage of the epic declares: "All property is the result of conquest and robbery. The best property is that which one gets by taking it from another. When kings conquer earth, they speak of the land just as sons do of their father's property and say: 'This land belongs to me.'" Of the "king-devoured people" the king himself was absolute master, and it seems almost unnecessary to urge that the land was his or his subjects', in accordance with the tyrant's will. Sages admonish, but the kings steal and give and take as before. To them in their power there was but one rule, — that enunciated again as a proverb in the epic: "To the mighty all is proper; to the mighty all is right; to the mighty all is their own." That is to say, the *force majeure* was the determinant factor. Let us imagine a state where the king was answerable only to his own conscience for compensation given to a dispossessed peasant, and we have the Hindu's earlier rights of possession. He owned land as against his fellow-subjects, but he owned it as against the king just as the jackal owns what the tiger wants.

In the preceding paragraphs I have referred to the growth of land-giving. It begins with a kingly gift of a field to a priest. The early law does not approve of such gifts, but the later law praises them. The epic extols them as in the highest degree meritorious. The practice appears to have grown up in the large eastern kingdoms and is a feature of Buddhism. The epic says emphatically that all property belongs to the king "and to no second person"; while it mentions several cases of *agrahāra* land-grants, though it does not know the copper-plate grant, which appears first in the law-book of Yajnavalkya. These grants, as described in the epic, are made either to priests or to personal friends of a king or queen. Land-giving on a large scale is called an "earth sacrifice." In these cases the recipients become actual owners, not over-lords.

We may now turn from this sketch of the past and see how the literary evidence is borne out by the state of affairs that exists to-day. To do this, it will be necessary to mention briefly the facts as given in Mr. Baden-Powell's comprehensive description of present conditions.

The first blow to the old interpretation of sociological phenomena in India was given by the discovery that, instead of a community (in the strict sense) being *par excellence* the village of India, throughout the greater part of the country nothing exists that even resembles such a village. All over middle and southern India, in the east and also in the west, there is one common type of village, the Raiyat ("ryot," subject, peasant farmer) or severalty village. Only in the northwest, in the Punjab, is there to be found the kind of village which was mistaken by Sir Henry Maine for a "village community."

To understand the force of Mr. Baden-Powell's objections to the theory of Sir Henry Maine, we must comprehend clearly the essential points of difference between the types of villages referred to. There are two main classes of Hindu villages, the severalty village and the joint-village. These differ in their constitution as follows: The severalty or Raiyat village is characterized by having a "head-man" (who is selected from one of the leading families), and by an allotment of shares of land to each member of the group. In this kind of village every member is responsible individually for his share of any tax that may be levied on the village. The holdings are periodically distributed, but this is only to insure sooner or later a fair deal, so that each villager, turn and turn about, may get as good a farm as his neighbor. This redistribution has been claimed to be an indication of an early communal holding, but wrongly; for the privileged families do not and never did own the village or share it in fractions as do the members of a joint-village. Four peculiarities distinguish this type of village from the most perfect kind of joint-village. The former has a Patel "head-man" (*pâtêl*); the latter has none. The former has holdings which have always been separate; the latter has holdings which are only inherited shares of an original single estate. The former has no mutual liability for taxes, but each holding is assessed separately; the latter has a joint liability, the revenue being assessed in a lump sum. And, finally, the Raiyat village has no common land, whereas the joint-village owns a common land, though it is liable to partition.

Such is the one general form of the severalty village. Of the joint-village, on the other hand, there are three species. The first, or most perfect kind, is the Pattidâri, or "shared" ancestral village, where the community are the descendants of one man or of brothers; the second is the Bhâiâchârâ, or "brotherhood" tribal village, where a tribe, or it may be a clan, holds land under joint responsibility for the taxes; the third is the associate village, where different families make up a united group simply for defence in holding their land against outsiders. A moment's consideration of the conditions under which land is possessed in each of these groups shows that the tribal and associate forms are not in any sense a body of communal owners.

In the tribal joint-village the shares have always been held separately, having been originally allotted to each member of the group. The members are joint only in their united ownership of waste land and of the village site, together with a united responsibility for taxes. This kind of joint-village is really a sort of severalty village, and such a tribal allotment has actually been the starting-point of the true severalty village, as shown in the primitive (matriarchal) Kolarian village.

In the associate joint-village there is still less of real joint-ownership. Here the shares are equal, and, as in the last case, are not derived from a common ancestor. The village is founded by families or colonists who take up land and allot it at once. These families or colonists may or not be of the same tribe. They associate only for mutual protection, and are joint only in assuming a united responsibility for taxes.

The villages of these two species are chiefly quite modern. They belong to the western and eastern Punjab respectively, and their inhabitants are Jats and other non-Aryan tribes. The severalty village, generally speaking, is Dravidian.

There remains, as the only unit resembling a village community, the ancestral joint-family village. But here all the shares are inherited portions of an estate originally owned by one man (or two brothers), who became the rulers of the village. His property, the village, passed to his joint-heirs (agnates only, in itself an argument against communal ownership), and might or might not be divided at the option of the heirs. Sometimes part is divided and part not. In any case, the heirs hold the property always liable to division, so that even in their case there is no communal holding. Still less does the whole village own the land, which is generally rented to tenants, the rents being divided among the descendants of the original lord of the manor. Even when the estate is undivided, each heir is actually in possession of a special part and holds it for his own benefit.

We are now able to understand just what the indications and express statements of ancient literature imply (for even express statements about real estate are not explicit as regards communes). We find there a joint-family and also an undivided family. Some of the property is partible. Some of it is not. A field, it is said, is impartible. But the later the legal authority, the more inclined is he to find ways in which property formerly impartible can be made partible. The originally impartible condition of landed estate is evidenced among other things by the fact that it cannot be lost to a family by an outsider's possession. All the inhabitants of a village are responsible for its debts. They have a common meadow-land for grazing, but separate fields for the individual villager whose property is demarcated, and whose right of possession ceases at the boundary or is shared (as in the case of fruit-trees growing on the line) by his next neighbor only. A field may be rented for half its yield by the individual villager. But a field cannot be sold without the consent of the whole village, or at least of the family.

Such are the data of the legal literature, and they are supported by the evidence of the earliest inscriptions. It follows that while a common ownership was exercised by the village, there was within the village private ownership of land, which was inherited as impartible property by the sons (and widow). But alongside of this was also the severalty arrangement, which in many cases overthrew this joint-ownership. The types then were severalty and joint villages, and not communal types. The most communistic form is the still undivided inheritance of a joint-family; but this is an estate which is always liable to partition. As it seems to me, the joint-family with its original common ownership of land is sufficient to account for all such traces of communistic land-ownership as we have any record of, and the joint-ownership of the village had only the form of the modern "joint-village." As to-day, so of old, villages were of the joint and severalty class, but they were not communal in the strict sense.

## THE CAUSE AND CURE OF FAMINE.

To venture to address even the most intelligent or dispassionate audience on any phase of England's responsibility toward India (such as her responsibility for drought and famine), is, I fear, sadly like the recklessness of the man that should intrude himself between the devil and the deep sea. For on the one side stands the pessimist, who holds England guilty of grave crimes; sees no virtue in her, and expects only future ill from her future rule; while, on the other, stands the optimist, who brooks no adverse criticism of England's actions and maintains that her rule is as beneficent as it is benevolent.

But it is neither as a reviler nor as a defender of England that I have accepted the invitation to speak to you of famines in India, but rather as an historian, who sees in sundry statements made by well-meaning partisans certain points capable, perhaps, of being put more clearly than any partisanship can put them. It is then rather to the past than to the present that I shall invite your attention, and if I speak of the future it will be only as a picture which may be drawn in the light of the past. For this reason I shall pass over altogether certain features, such as the recent demonetization of silver, which lie outside of my point of view; nor shall I descant on the horrors of famine, of which you have doubtless already heard more than enough. But, to begin with a subject remote from all possible partisan interest, let me first call your attention to the Bengal tiger.

For many centuries the most useful beast in India was the tiger. The Hindus preferred the gentle cow and finally deified her, not exactly as the Golden Calf, but at any rate as the Divinely Useful; for in their time the Hindus too have been utilitarians. But they were rather inclined to ignore the tiger (except for a significant exchange of compliments in calling a king the tiger among men and a tiger the king among animals); nor did they even vex themselves with the question why the tiger was created, for their sufficient philosophy taught that he was made to enjoy himself. So they never really appreciated his function in the scheme of creation, — an ignorance the more remarkable since they were on the edge of discovering the truth, when they epitomized his work in the verse:

The wood doth guard the tiger as the tiger guards the wood.

The tiger guarded the wood, and in guarding it he helped for many centuries to save the Hindu and the cow from extreme drought and famine. His place in the economy of Hindu civilization was to keep man and man's destructive axe out of the great reservoir of rain, the primeval forest, and if we may trust the literature, which reflects the fear man felt when wandering in the tiger's domain, the latter played his part pretty well. All that great bare belt of country which now stretches south of the Ganges — that vast waste where drought seems to be perennial and famine is as much at home as is Çiva in a graveyard — was once an almost impenetrable wood. Luxuriant growth filled it; self-irrigated, it kept the fruit of the summer's rain till winter, while the light winter rains were treasured there in turn till the June monsoon came again. Even as late as the epic period, it was a hero's derring-do to wander through that forest-world south of the Nerbudda, which at that time was a great inexhaustible river, its springs conserved by the forest. Now the forest is gone, the hills are bare, the valley is unprotected, and the Nerbudda dries up like a brook, while starved cattle lie down to die on the parched clay that should be a river's bed. A little later than the time when the heroes of the epic, as is narrated therein, first set fire to the tiger's lair, there were roads and settlements here and there through the great forest.

The heroes had broken out the path for civilization and the civilians followed, but slowly and cautiously, for the tiger still guarded the wood. But in the end man triumphed over Nature's other children, and in burning and felling the forest of the Deccan planted the seed of famine over a wide area; whereas hitherto this noxious plant, though by no means unknown, had been restricted in its growth.

For in India famine is the child of drought, and no one need starve who has enough water, unless indeed the crop be stolen after the water has done its work. But this *unless*, it must be added, shows that famine may be due to something besides drought. And as it would be only a half-truth to state that famine is due in all cases entirely to drought, so it is just such a "veiled lie," as the Hindus call a half-truth, to say that either deforestation or robbery (whether in the guise of dacoits or tax-collectors) is alone the cause of famine. For despite the good work done by the tiger, there were droughts that produced famines or ever there were tax-collectors.

This would seem to be so much a matter of course as to make insistence upon the point quite unnecessary, did we not constantly hear expressed the half-truth that famine is a modern invention resulting from British oppression. Drought there may have been in ancient times, says the stanch opponent of British wrong-doing, but famine never; for the cultivator, not having his crop stolen, was able to draw from his store and weather the weather till the rains came again.

But as there are various sides to this question, so there are various half-truths, concealments of facts and distortions of history, which must be examined in the order in which they arise, before we can even begin to come near the cover of bare facts which compose the body of truth itself.

First, then, as regards the proposition that famine is the result of British oppression solely.

That British rule is oppressive, is granted even by the British, who, indeed, are wont to admit it very cheerfully, for, as Lord Salisbury has implied, "India must be bled," and bleeding a body half dead from inanition it is no exaggeration to describe as a form of oppression.[1]

But it is one thing to say that there is oppression and another to affirm that it is universal, and that as such it is the sole parent of famine. The first famine-cry comes from the most ancient records of India: —

The waters of the upper sea in heaven were prisoned by the gods,
But the wise priest released them all (removed the drought, and wet the sods).
He, praying, sang the magic verse; the rain-compelling voice had he,
God, free us from the Hunger-ill and give that magic word to me[2] —
Let loose for us on earth the rain — the waters of yon heavenly sea!

Here the descendant or imitator of the ancient priest, who had the "rain-compelling voice," calls to mind the famous famine of old, and in his present distress, with the artless simplicity of the virtuous, begs from the highest rain-god that gift of speech which, with magical power, shall force the gods to give up the rain they have withheld, and preserve man from the Hunger-ill that will follow the drought. But this is only one of many voices raised in the Rig Veda in supplication to the gods, who are over and over besought to drive away the plague of hunger:

O Indra (rain-god), give food and strength to us who are hungry.

[1] Lord Salisbury's remark, however, was in defence of the praiseworthy idea that the cultivators should be spared at the expense of the towns. That India must be bled follows from his further reply, "We cannot afford it," to the suggestion that the tax on the cultivator should be limited to "fifty per cent. on the gross produce" (*sic*) of each farm. The former passage is as follows: "As India must be bled, the lancet should be directed to the parts where the blood is congested, or at least sufficient, not to those which are already feeble from the want of it."

[2] The place of this verse in the original is before the others; literally, "the voice that has strength (to) free from the hunger-plague and win rain."

Help us with thy help, powerful god, save us from this (present) plague, hunger and wretchedness.
Indra, do thou keep drought and hunger from our pasture.

Compare also this significant remark:

The gods did not give hunger as the only death.[1]

So general, in fact, was this cry, that the word "plague," *amīvā*, as used above, became synonymous with "famine," *anaçana*.

And beginning with this remote age, we can trace the same cry down through the centuries, past the Atharvan poet, who prays that the sun may not ruin his crop, to the epic period, when we observe that the gods were no longer trusted over-much. For besides the system of irrigation, which was introduced in the earliest age and is alluded to in the Rig Veda, we find the belief that it was necessary to help out the ever-dubious intentions of the gods. Even in the Vedic verses just cited, the gods, not the usual devil of drought, are represented as imprisoning the waters. But in the epic, a sage says to the king whom he is visiting: "I hope all goes well in your Majesty's kingdom and that you do not trust in the gods for harvests." The implication is that a king would not leave the gods to provide water for the farmers. For the good kings of the epic, far from trusting too much in the gods, built canals and reservoirs as their first duty, irrigating the country as well as they could. But when their gods, who, like Herakles, were pleased to see them exert themselves, rewarded them with extreme favor, then it was said in laudation of such a king, and as a proof of his extraordinarily good fortune, that "in the reign of this king there was no famine."

But, as is implied even with this praise, famine in other reigns was no rarity. Nay, not once, but repeatedly, we find allusions in the epic to "a drought that lasted many

[1] These passages will be found in the Rig Veda, x. 98; i. 104, 7; viii. 66, 14; viii. 60, 20 (*anirā* and *kṣudh*); x. 117, 1.

years," *bahuvārṣikī*, and again, more specifically: "Now at that time there was a twelve-year drought." This last expression, though it is, I confess, a close parallel to the preceding, may possibly be taken in a sense other than that usually given by the poets themselves to the adjective "twelve-year;" namely, in the sense of the drought which comes every twelve years. As is well known, a drought does come about once in a dozen years. Thus "the twelve-year drought" may refer to such a phenomenon as well as to a drought lasting twelve years, just as "yearly," *vārṣika*, is used either of something lasting for a year, for example, a food-supply for a year, or of something which comes once a year, for example, an annual tribute.[1]

Now it may be said by those who believe that drought does not necessarily entail death, that here also there is no proof of drought resulting in famine. But the answer to this is that whenever such mention of drought occurs, the next thing noticed is the famine that followed it. Thus, in one account: "Now at that time came a (or the) twelve-year drought. The store of food was exhausted, and there was no food." The descriptions of such famines are sufficiently vivid to make it certain that the scenes were drawn from life. Proverb-literature, too, than which nothing more faithfully reflects the face of the times, assumes that drought, famine, and the ruin of a district is the ordinary sequence of events: "Happy, indeed, are they who, when their district is smitten by drought, and the grain is all destroyed, do not see their district ruined and their family exterminated." What, I would ask, can these words signify, if not that it is a rare event for the peasant to survive unharmed through the famine that naturally follows drought? Even the law was changed to suit famine-times, and though the

[1] The poets, indeed, employ the adjective "twelve-year" as if it implied a period of twelve years; but it would have been a simple matter to use a phrase of one meaning in the other sense, which was possible and much more picturesque for the poets' purpose. The Sanskrit word is (*anāvṛṣṭir*) *dvādaçavārṣikī*. There is, however, as noticed below, a record in more modern times of one drought that lasted twelve years.

usual rule is that a man may not take his wife's property, we read that, "In famine, if a man has taken his wife's property to support life (that is, probably, sold her silver bangles, as many have had to do in the recent famine) he is not obliged to refund it."

We must conclude, then, that not only in the Punjab, whence perhaps came the earliest hunger-cry, but even in the tiger-districts along the lower Ganges, drought and famine were painfully familiar before the British took a hand in starving the peasants. The forest and the rivers, as shown in the literature, prevented an effect so wide-spread as is customary to-day, but the destruction of forests was the work of the Hindus themselves.[1]

Thus we see, on the evidence of the Hindus' own ancient literature, that famine obtained in India from the earliest times. The claim, therefore, that drought is converted into famine only under British rule may be set down as simply preposterous. Nor do we even have to revert to the evidence of the earlier literature, for the same conditions existed from the fourteenth to the seventeenth century, when the British were as yet unconcerned with taxation in India. That these historical cases have been ignored altogether, does not redound to the credit of those who have discussed the subject. For it was, perhaps, not to be expected that an English statistician should be conversant with ancient Hindu literature; but that any one who can read English should insist that famine was unknown in India prior to the assumption of power by the British is quite unpardonable in the light of records accessible to all. The very worst famine known in Hindu history came in 1396. It is known as the "dreadful famine," and according to native accounts it lasted for twelve years (unless this again was a

[1] I pass over the case of famine resulting not from drought but from too much water, since, so far as I know, the British have not been made responsible for this form of distress. It is referred to in a proverb, which deprecates "too much" (a native μηδὲν ἄγαν): "Through too great cold the wood is burned, through too much rain the famine comes; *too much* is ever bad" (*ati kutrā 'pi na 'ṣyati*)

case of the twelve-year famine). At any rate, its effects were felt in "very scant revenue" for thirty years afterwards, and "whole districts were entirely depopulated," according to the native historians of Maharashtra, where this famine occurred, as is duly set forth in Grant Duff's History of the Mahrattas. Then there was another famine north of the Godavari at the end of the fifteenth century; while in 1629–1630, "famine and pestilence" ensued upon a drought in the Deccan (more particularly in Bombay itself in 1618). So under Moghul rule, we have this testimony of Antonio de Mello de Castro in 1662: "The Moghuls have destroyed these lands, through which cause many persons have died from famine."[1] And before leaving this side of the question, since the benign rule of the Moghul is often contrasted by native writers with the inhuman rule of the British, I will notice the words of an unprejudiced witness cited by Sir Alfred Lyall in his Rise of the British Dominion in India (p. 34). In a letter to Colbert, Bernier writes: "The country is ruined. . . . No adequate idea can be conveyed of the sufferings of that people."

We are now in a position to view with more critical appreciation the statement that famine to-day in India is caused solely by British taxation. After Mr. Hyndman's diatribe, entitled The Bankruptcy of India, which was published many years ago, Mr. Romesh Dutt, in his recent book, Famines in India, has taken up the task of proving that if not too heavily taxed by the British the native farmer would never suffer from famine. Mr. Dutt goes to the extreme of saying that there would be no famine at all, but only a scarcity easily borne by the thrifty farmer, who would save enough in years of plenty to tide him over the effects of drought. The proof of this is drawn from the cases of famine in the last century, and the assertion is made that there has been no famine where the tax has been light.

There is quite a difference in the way in which various parts of India are taxed. Generally speaking, the northern

[1] Da Cunha, Origin of Bombay, p. 247.

part is lightly taxed, and the middle and south are heavily taxed. The last famine was most severely felt in the middle part, one illustration of the theory.

But where are the other necessary illustrations, and is even this one convincing? The latter question may be answered first. In stating that the excessive severity of famine in the Central Provinces, in 1897, was due entirely to the fact that they were more heavily taxed than were the Punjab and Bengal Provinces, the following items have been altogether omitted from consideration: There was much greater drought in the Central Provinces, it began earlier, continued later, and was more severe.[1] There is a superb system of irrigation in the Punjab, but none in the Central Provinces. The soil of the northeastern part of the country is much richer and the harvest larger than in the Central Provinces. The people of both the northwestern and northeastern parts of the country needed only to be invited to come to the relief-works (they are a much more intelligent class); whereas a large proportion of those who died of famine in the Central Provinces were half wild, only lately touched by civilization, and it was almost impossible to get them to leave their villages and come to relief-works.

That these are rather important items, will, I think, be admitted, and to omit these factors in considering the reason why the Central Provinces suffered most is to weaken the force of this illustration to a minimum. Then for the other illustrations:

The terrible famines of 1770 and 1784 were caused in part by maladministration. But at that time all taxes were severe, and they were all but a portion of a far greater burden. The famine of Bombay in 1803 was aggravated by the Mahrattas, who devastated the country and prevented the planting of crops. In 1804 there was a famine in North India, but the ravages of a native army had here also devastated the coun-

[1] The Viceroy, on his trip early in the winter, while still in the northern part of the country, could still say, "There is no famine so far as I can see," while peasants were already dying of hunger in the Central Provinces.

try. So terrible were these ravages that maladministration and mistakes made in land revenue administration can be counted only as very subsidiary factors. The heavy tax of two-thirds the rental in North India was modified in 1855, so that in 1860 the moderate tax, which is now looked upon as an effective antidote to famine, had already been in force for several years; yet in 1860 there was a very severe famine there. In 1874 there would have been in Bengal a million deaths from famine, had not the government foreseen it and provided assistance. Yet, strange to say, the fact that the people, when aided by the government, did not starve under the permanent settlement, as they would have done if left to themselves, is not ascribed to the beneficent intervention of the government, but to the permanent settlement. So the absence of permanent settlement is made the cause of the great Orissa famine in 1866, though in that case death was due to the fact that there was no railway to carry a food-supply, and the people were killed by floods as much as by famine. This particular famine is ascribed to British oppression by Mr. Dutt, as opposed to the light taxation of the Bengal Zamindar, so that it is interesting to see that the same famine is ascribed by Mr. Hyndman in his Bankrupcty of India (p. 52) to the Zamindar himself. Then, again, there was a drought in 1876 in North India, when, as the conditions were those in which, according to this tax-theory, no famine can arise, famine surely ought not to have followed. But what happened? How did the greatly improved rate of taxation affect the country? There was a very severe famine with an "excess mortality of 1,250,000." How much better showing is this than that made in the over-taxed Madras Province in the famines of 1889 and 1892?

A review of famine-conditions during the century fails to establish that smaller assessments of taxes have in themselves made famines much less fatal. Famines have been more fatal in over-assessed districts because the heavier tax has always coincided with more important factors; that is to say, the district where the tax, owing to amount and permanency, is least heavy is the most fertile district of India or the best irrigated. But even in these districts, notwithstanding fertility, irrigation, and a light tax, millions die of famine. There may be more who die under a heavier tax, but the proportion is not strikingly different or greater than can be otherwise accounted for. In fine, the tax itself is only one factor out of many.

As long ago as the law-book of Manu, it was asserted that famine is the inevitable concomitant of bad government,— a view that is insisted upon also by the epic writers. But those enlightened writers of antiquity did not teach that over-taxation caused famine, but that famine was caused by drought, and that drought was to be avoided by good government, as shown by irrigation and the construction of artificial reservoirs. They taught, moreover, that when, because of insufficient provision against drought, famine resulted, then it was the business of the government to remit taxes and advance loans to the cultivators. This was insisted upon less from a philanthropic motive than on the economic ground that ruined cultivators ruin a realm.

When, however, we turn to the ancient records of India to see how the Hindus governed themselves, we find at once that we must make a sharp distinction between the reign of law and the savage period that has left its traces on the antelegal literature. I say savage, for though there were cities and a kind of civilization, yet the kings of this period not only were savage as regards their attitude toward the farmers, but they were told (by the priests) to be so; whereas, on the other hand, in the later legal literature, the cruel king who devours his people is referred to only as a horrible possibility. We may take the praise of kings *cum grano salis*, and admit that even in the legal period there were probably bad rulers, as, indeed, it is frankly admitted in epic poetry of about the same time that bad kings still devoured their people, and that the rich man feared the king as he did death itself.[1] But at this time there was strenuously inculcated at least, not only as a duty but as a precept of common-sense, the rule that the people are not made to be "eaten," but to be protected, "for by heavy taxation the king cuts his own root." So it marks an advance when we read on the one hand that the people are there only "to be devoured" by king and priest, and on the other that "the king who devours his people by unjust taxation goes to hell." In treating elsewhere of land-tenure, I have spoken of this very savage time, when the kings were "tigers among men" in more senses than one. I refer to it here only as a not surprising historical item, reflecting neither praise nor blame upon those valiant kings who, as might have been expected from the age they lived in, were frank practisers of the doctrine taught them by the priests (as any one may read in their sacred books) that the agricultural class existed only to support the aristocracy of nobles and priests and might be plundered at pleasure. When, therefore, our modern native authors, in their most laudable zeal to improve the state of their poor fellow-countrymen, tell us that the good old Hindu kings never over-taxed, we must inquire which kings they refer to.

For there were good kings in India. In the legal period, which is still remote enough to claim an antiquity of over two thousand years, there is every reason to believe that the earlier rapacity of the kings had been in part checked by the growth of the third estate, through developed agricultural and mercantile life, and that kings were rather protectors than robbers of their people. To these kings and their times it is perfectly legitimate to refer as an example of the way the people were treated by ancient native rulers.

The tax in old times under these native kings was sixteen

[1] "As living creatures fear death, so the rich fear a king," Mbh. iii. 2, 39. Elsewhere, ib. xiii. 61, 33, it is said that a rascal-king, *rājakali*, who fails to protect or taxes too heavily, "should be killed like a mad dog," *nihantavyaḥ çveva sonmāda āturaḥ*.

and two-thirds per cent. of the gross produce. This is not a mere theory or legal fiction, for so regular was this rate that the king, and in no other way could he have received this *sobriquet*, was known universally through legal and epic and later popular literature, as the "sixth-taker." One sixth, *ignoring his agents*, was the *king's* share till the time of the Cholas, a thousand years ago. It was increased only when the existence of the state was imperilled, at which time twenty-five per cent. might be taken as an extreme measure, though not as the most extreme; for it is expressly stated that if a king absolutely needed it, he might take what he chose from his wealthy subjects. But, having defended the people by means of the funds raised in this way, "the king should resume his lawful tax." On the other hand, if it is the husbandman who is in distress, or his lands are too poor to yield a surplus, the rate is lowered to twelve and one-half, ten, or eight and one-third per cent., according to circumstances; or may even be remitted altogether.

Contrasted with this, the British rate of taxation is from one quarter more to double the amount regularly demanded by the ancient Hindu kings. The average British tax is about the same as that demanded by the ancient Hindu kings as an extreme tax, warranted only by the necessity of "taking from the farmer to defend the farmer." But a tax not at all uncommon under British rule is even more than this, and sometimes reaches quite a half of the gross produce of any one field.

But this half, as contrasted with the old sixth, is not a British invention; and from the historical point of view, to make a special point against the British on this score, as if they had invented some new method of torture, is quite unwarranted. One third or one half the produce is too high a tax (or rent, as it is sometimes facetiously called), but it is not a tax invented by the British. The Cholas of South India took half the produce as a regular tax, and the ideal formal tax of the Mahrattas was forty per cent. of the gross produce. Moreover, it must be remembered that this latter was merely the scheduled rate, instituted by Çivaji, the great founder of the Mahratta state, in antithesis to the rule of Todar Mall (adopted by Shah Jahan), whereby (nominally) one-fourth to one-half the gross produce (one-fourth with permanent settlement) was taken as tax. Çivaji, on the other hand, adopted the arrangement instituted by Dadaji, whereby the farmer gave the government two-fifths of the produce (in 1637). But under Çivaji's successors, "the revenues were farmed (as they were not to be, according to Çivaji's rule), many of the raiyats fled from their villages, and speedy ruin threatened the territory."[1] According to Lyall,[2] the Mahrattas "rackrented the land scientifically," whenever they settled down upon it; though, as a matter of fact, they were mainly occupied with pillaging and devastating the country.

Thus we see that the good old Hindu kings, who took only one-sixth of the crop, came between two sets of native Hindu kings who were not so virtuous. Before them were the kings who held the farmers to be the "food of the nobility" and good only to be robbed at pleasure;[3] while after them came the "plundering robbers" of the South, as Judge Burnell called the Vijayanagara Telugu kings, and the Mahrattas of the Deccan. Moreover, under native kings sixty per cent. of the actual yield has been taken from the threshing floor even in the past century.[4]

[1] Grant Duff, *op. cit.*, i. pp. 125, 232, 319.

[2] Lyall, *op. cit.*, p. 158. According to Hunter, Gazetteer, India, p. 440, the native tax is sometimes one-half and sometimes three-fifths of the produce. In Orissa, the native Raj took sixty per cent., and Hunter himself saw this taken in other cases.

[3] Even as late as the epic, viii. 38, 17, there is a casual allusion to "fat peasant villages, good for a king to devour," which speaks for itself.

[4] Compare Hunter, *loc. cit.*, and Robert Knight's Land Revenue of India. These statements are not theoretical, but are based on what has really occurred. It can scarcely be doubted that the mild demands of the old Hindu kings were made with the knowledge that the middleman, who collected the revenue, took part for himself. One would think from the current praise of these kings that they collected direct from the farmer. But in fact they collected through "centurions," "thousandmen," etc., the numbers representing villages under an officer, as may be seen in their laws.

Nay, it is by no means so certain that even the older Hindu kings did not at one time look on a rent of fifty per cent. as equitable. In view of the fact that there is no such legal provision, I should not insist on this. But as an interesting bit of antiquities it is at least worth mentioning that the payment of half a man's crop as rent was actually recognized in ancient times; though the practice is, as it were, fossilized in a phrase. This is the expression "halfer," or "half-plougher," well known to students of legal literature, and implying a man who was expected to pay half of his crop for the use of the field it grew on. It cannot be said that such a man was a mere servant, for the native commentator is careful to point out not only that the "halfer" might not be a servant, but that the half-produce of this term covered cases where the man lived either on private property or on a field belonging to the king, in which case he paid as rent to the government just fifty per cent. of his produce.[1]

But not to dwell too long on a doubtful past, besides the heavy taxes of the Chola in the South and the Mahratta in Central India, there were the Moghuls. They held North India, and their grasp was tight. There was only one of them who was not a tyrannical oppressor. Nevertheless, when the accuser of England wishes to demonstrate the peculiar enormity of British misrule, he utilizes the eternal Akbar (who, by the way, was half-christianized), to mark the contrast between ill and good. Thus Akbar, says Mr. Dutt,[2] took seventy-seven million rupees where the British take one

[1] The rent of the "halfer" probably represented the ratio paid before the period of the formulated law which we now possess. In the extant law-books, the term is usually applied to a servant, a fact that may show the condition to which a "halfer" was inevitably reduced. The half-produce rent of such a man, when he was a servant, might, though not necessarily, be offset by his rations. But the commentators, as already mentioned, admit that he may not be a servant at all. The facts that this rent is illegally high, and that in legal literature the name has become almost synonymous with serf, seem to point to older conditions intervening between the sixteen and two-thirds per cent. tax of the law-books and the unlimited rapacity of the kings who, in the earlier holy books, are told that farmers are only fit to devour.

[2] Civilization in India, by Romesh C. Dutt, p. 121.

hundred and twenty-four million rupees. On the other hand, Akbar was the only lenient Moghul,[1] and it is doubtful whether even the *laudator temporis acti*, unless himself a Mohammedan or a Mahratta, would be willing to exchange the rule of the British for that of his predecessors, either Moghul or Mahratta. But besides this, all estimates of revenue in Akbar's time depend upon uncertain money-values, the relation between the *tankah* (*dâm* or double-*dâm*) and the modern rupee and pound; not to speak of the difference in the purchasing power of silver and value of land three centuries ago. That these factors make the ratio in effect quite different to what it is in appearance, may indeed be offset by the statement that Akbar's tax was not so rigorously exacted. But at best this statement is based on a presumption,[2] whereas it is known that, of all the Moghuls, Akbar was the most considerate of his subjects, and that under his successors the Hindus were simply pillaged. When Mr. Dutt says that Akbar's tax was "meant to be an ideal demand and could never have been strictly enforced from year to year," and so leaves the matter, we can say only that Mr. Dutt's zeal makes him an unreliable witness. The single fact (in his economic statement) that he here avoids all reference to the farmers of the Moghul's revenue disposes of Mr. Dutt's claim. Akbar got one-third; but between him and the cultivator stood the agent. How much did he take from the raiyat before he passed on the third to Akbar? Can any one suppose that the Zamindar who farmed the revenues, and became a prince in power, built up that power on a salary? It is quite safe to say that, when the Zamindar passed over a third to Akbar, another third went into his own purse. Under Akbar, as under all native rulers, "Landholders and revenue

[1] The land-revenue exacted by Akbar was more than doubled under Aurangzeb (nineteen million pounds raised to forty-three and a half millions). Hunter, The Indian Empire, p. 356.

[2] A fact, however, not mentioned by Mr. Dutt is, that, besides the revenue, the cultivator under Moghul rule paid not less than forty assessments of a personal character, on trees, cattle, poll, marriage, etc. Hunter, India, p. 462.

officers," to cite Hunter again, "had each their own set of myrmidons, who plundered the country in their name." According to the same authority, Akbar's tax amounted to about three times the British tax.[1]

But I must say a word more in regard to this native landlord known as Zamindar, about whom, for he is still the landlord owner in Bengal, the native reformer is wont to publish the most extraordinary statements, both historical and economic; for he not only holds him up as a model landlord, but as an original institution. One naturally sympathizes with the under dog, but it is a chill to this emotion to find it has been given on false pretences, and the discovery of one or two misrepresentations, even if not intended, is liable to breed a doubt of all statements not verified. In this regard the Hindu reformer, whether he speak from the platform of his Congress, or through the medium of a book, is peculiarly liable to shock intelligent sympathy, because of the national lack of historical instinct. India has always cultivated a kind of tropical history, but it is not the same species with that recognized as history in the Occident. In ancient days it consisted of extravagant stories about the vanished felicity which men enjoyed under the rule of still more ancient kings, and this conception of history still obtains, though modified by the influence of English education. But the modification has been far from altering the national inability to take a critical attitude as regards the facts of history. Thus, of the many Hindus who cite history to show how lenient were the ancient kings, not one, so far as I know, has ever called attention to those kings whose rule was to devour their people. In the same way, the native historians are unwearied in stating that "according to Megasthenes" the Hindu of 300 B. C. never worried the farmers in war-time, and that, according to the same authority, the Hindu had no famines; but they either are ignorant of or ignore the fact that, according to their own traditions of the same age, the

[1] Hunter, The Indian Empire, pp. 351, 352.

Hindus are especially told by their priestly authorities to devastate the land and ruin the crops of their enemies; that they are enjoined not to spare the land *at a time of famine;* and that, in regard to the other point, their own literature shows that they always had famines. Megasthenes' authority also is not always credible. His countrymen said that he saw little of India, and his own testimony shows that in many instances his account does not reflect actual conditions under Brahmanic rules. Thus he tells us that there were no money-lenders in India, and that the Hindus did not even know what interest on a loan meant, — a statement which must shock even a Hindu historian, since it was made after the legal rate of interest in India was fixed at sixty per cent. per annum, and centuries after the figure of the usurer was familiar to the Hindus.[1] Or shall we say that the Greek portrays only Buddhistic conditions, too ideal for Brahmanized kings to maintain?

The unhistorical attitude which characterizes the reformer appears again when, to laud the ancient *régime*, he tells us that the Zamindar is the hereditary owner of the land and always has been "from remotest antiquity," besides being an exemplary landlord. The fact is that this Zamindar was originally the publican or revenue-collector for the Moghul emperor, from whom he frequently freed himself and became landlord by right of might. All that can be said is that he was sometimes a Hindu. But generally he was an alien (Mohammedan) officer. When the British took possession, they ignored the peasantry and established this Zamindar, a mere factor, as landlord-owner. "Any one," says Lyall, "who had money or credit might buy at the imperial treasury a Firman authorizing him to collect the revenues of some

[1] If Megasthenes is to be cited, he should be cited entire, and we should be informed that, according to him, that which the native reformer to-day insists should be called a tax and made below one-fourth of the produce, was not a tax but a rent and above a fourth (a fourth, with extra cesses), — points which, so far as I have observed, are passed over in silence by Mr. Dutt and others, who are perhaps a little inclined to draw on Megasthenes only for what pleases them.

refractory district" (*op. cit.* p. 124). In the course of half a century, as it was known to all that this exemplary landlord rackrented his peasantry, the British themselves mitigated the woes due to his inhumanity as well as they could (having surrendered landlord-rights to the Zamindar), by enacting that the sum paid to the Crown by the Zamindar should be reduced, with the understanding that the latter should demand less of his peasantry.[1]

The Zamindar, of course, saw to it that the first part of this new arrangement was carried out. He gave from then on only five to six per cent. of the value of the gross produce to the government; while he himself was and still is supposed to take only twenty per cent. of the gross produce from each cultivator, as rent.

Now, one-fifth of the gross produce is regarded as an ideal payment for the cultivator, and since it can easily be shown that where the British government levies its own tax it often takes one-third of the gross produce, the reformer would like to see just such a permanent settlement introduced all over India, a Hindu landlord by preference, but failing that, an unalterable rate representing one-fifth the produce.

On the other hand, it may truly be said that the Zamindar arrangement is probably the most unjust, as it certainly is the stupidest, in India. For not only are the cultivators deprived of their rights in the soil, but they are exposed to unlimited rackrenting at the hands of unscrupulous Zamindars, who can demand whatever they choose of the peasantry. The history of the native's dealings with his poorer brother does not favor the idea that the Zamindar, when at liberty to do as he pleases with his hinds, will be a shining light of benevolence. Stupid, too, is this arrangement, for Bengal is the Eden of India, the richest and most flourishing province, the best able to pay the government for its share in the increase of value arising from improve-

[1] The government was placed in the hands of Commissioners (with a Governor-General) in 1784, while the British Crown has been in possession of India only since 1858.

ments. But of all this increase never a penny comes to the government, and when taxes are increased it is the poor provinces must pay them.

Nominally, however, Bengal is the peasant's paradise. He has a benevolent native landlord and pays only one-fifth of his crop as his rent. He ought never to be troubled with famine in such circumstances, but this is only in theory.

Without going into details of arrangements, it suffices to say that in the Northwest and Punjab Provinces the cultivator pays about the same or a little more than he is supposed to in Bengal,[1] while in the Central Provinces and in South India he pays from one-fifth to one-third of his gross produce, sometimes as much as one-half the net reckoned as one-third the gross produce, but under such circumstances as, it is claimed, make the sum total (extra cesses, etc.) about equivalent to fifty per cent. of the gross produce.

The farmer then (and this is the great example of the reformer) who in Bombay pays direct to the state, pays as a minimum what is paid as a maximum in Bengal to the native landlord. The difference is further accentuated by the fact that in Bengal the landlord at any rate, and it is supposed his tenant also, has always the same tax or rent to pay, while even in less favored districts the rate is changed only once in a generation (thirty years); whereas in the Central Provinces and in the Madras Province the assessments are frequently changed so suddenly that the ratio is made one hundred per cent. higher in a single re-assessment. Under these conditions a nominal tax of twelve to twenty per cent., such as is found in the Madras Province, may and

[1] In thus estimating the cultivator's rent, I accept for argument's sake the amount stated to be the rent (or tax, according to locality and interpretation of the Crown's position) not by British officials, but by the reformers, whose argument for reform is based on their own estimates. Officially, the cultivator's tax in this and other cases cited is much less than here given, except in Bengal itself, where rackrenting is still supposed to exist. There is no reason to think that either side is right in details. The government minimizes its estimates, and the reformer's figures favor his plea. But in general it may be said that in North India the revenue is reasonable, if not so elsewhere.

undoubtedly is in the end a real tax of fully one-third. As an instance of oppressive taxation may be cited from Mr. Dutt's last book the implication conveyed in a speech made a year ago by the Maharaja of Darbhanga, who in the Council of the Viceroy pleaded with the government "not to draw from landholders more than sixty per cent. of the village income."

But there is this to be added in regard to the general outcry against British taxation in India. The reformer calls for twenty per cent., but the peasant enjoying that tax already is as loud in his protests as is the peasant oppressed with a rate of one-third instead of one-fifth. One needs only go among the Punjab peasantry to learn this. The root of discontent is not with the tax so much as it is with the way in which it is collected. And again: the charge is made that the British tax in general is excessive, whereas those who make it demonstrate, as soon as they exhibit their statistics, that even at their own interpretation of these statistics (I mean that, refusing to take the official statistics at their face value, they interpret them as really signifying to the farmer something quite different), the British government has already partly complied with the demands of the reformers, and the tax which they ask for is the tax actually in force over a great part of India. Thus Mr. Dutt himself says that the state of affairs in Bengal is ideal; that there is no fault to be found with the tax as collected in the Province of Oudh and the Northwest; and that even the Punjab now presents conditions scarcely open to criticism. But under these ideal conditions what has been the last famine, and what would it not have been had the government not had relief-works and canals?

There is then, and thus far attention has been called perhaps too exclusively to this point (but justice should be done even to the upper dog), no cause of grave complaint against Great Britain for the manner in which, in general, the government has treated its Hindu subjects. In sum, in what has been said already, two misapprehensions have been cleared up. It is not true that famine was unknown in India before the British entered it. It is not true that the British have taxed their subjects more heavily than have modern native rulers or the Moghuls. It is even possible that they have not taxed more heavily than did the "sixth-taker" of antiquity.

Now, however, let us turn to the other side. We will begin with the conditions in the Central Provinces and in South India. It is here that the tax is heaviest and misery like a plague has here become endemic.

The first thing that strikes the attention is that this woe has fastened itself upon just that part of the country to which the officials point with the greatest pride; where there has been the most exhaustive examination of conditions; where the sagacious (and I will add conscientious) expert has made his most careful analysis and estimated most scientifically just how much every field ought to produce and ought to be enriched by a rise in prices and by local improvements; on the basis of which calculations is fixed the revenue to be derived from the field. In a word, the British tax is meant to be a carefully estimated fair quota of the crop.

Herewith we are, as it were, illuminated at the outset with the light of the knowledge that the red-tape of scientific guesswork is the efficient cause of the trouble. Subtract the actual average yield from the expert's prognostication, and the remainder approximates to the total of the farmer's misery.

This misery is appreciated by the British, and is not passed unfeelingly, as testify the large sums involved in the annual remittance of taxes. But remittance is not made systematically nor in accordance with any fixed principle. For the taxes (or in general the sums the farmer has to pay) are not remitted often enough to prevent the over-burdened farmer from selling out and giving up his farm, which, as farming is his only occupation, he surely would not do unless forced to it. During the recent famine, many more farms have been abandoned to the tax-collector; but even before the famine began, so terrible was the pressure that in little more than a decade two million acres were thus abandoned, representing hundreds of thousands of small farmers. And the proof that the reason for their abandonment was over-assessment is that more than half of these acres failed to find purchasers and had to be bought in by the government.[1]

But before we penetrate deeper into the misery of the present, let us cast one more glance back at the past. The peculiarly simple and helpless Hindu farmer was of old guarded against himself in three ways: first, by the custom that prevented him from alienating his land; second, by being allowed to pay his rent in kind and in proportion to his crop (that is, if he had no crop, he had no tax); and, third, by laws which put some limit to usury.

Now, as contrasted with this, under British rule, the peasant is first allowed to alienate his land; second, he is obliged to pay in money, withal whether he has any crop to sell or not (in other words, he is obliged to sell his land to get money to pay his tax); and, third, until lately the usurer has been permitted to take any sum he pretends is due him, although it is well known that this particularly vulpine native is accustomed to falsify his accounts, which is easily done with ignorant peasants.

This three-stranded rope first entangles and then chokes the peasant. The expert comes, says the farm must yield enough to pay a tax of so many rupees more than before. The sullen peasant protests, but that is useless. Comes rain, a good harvest, the expert is not far wrong; yet a little less is got than is expected. But somehow, let us say, the peasant worries through the year, though much scrimped and unable to spend anything on fertilizers; a vital point, for starved land makes starved farmers. Comes next a drought. All the seed-corn is parched. There is no crop. The rupees are few, and when the tax-collector comes the rupees go. Then comes another drought. Already starving, the peasant is visited by the tax-collector, who insists on having the

[1] On these points, see Mr. Vaughan Nash, The Great Famine.

annual tribute, perhaps arrears as well. The only alternative to loss of the farm (for on failure to pay, the farmer is ousted) is the usurer. So with the government and the usurer together the peasant really has no choice. Thus it happens that already a large per cent. of farm-land is in the hand of the money-lender; that is to say, the most unscrupulous and worst element in the state is rapidly becoming the real landlord of the country.

So much the worse for England. But in the mean time what becomes of the wretched peasant? He would die, but that the same government that has kicked him out picks him up and puts him on relief-works, where he lives or dies as may be.

Such are the chief strands in the complicated cause of every recent famine in India. There are others which, like these, the reformer imputes to wilful wrong-doing. Native arts, they say, have been destroyed; the great industries are in British hands. So they are, so they will be, till the Hindu becomes the equal of the Englishman in industrial pursuits. Nor is it a crime on England's part that she does not subsidize native artists. Then they say that border-wars are a costly and needless extravagance; that is, a crime. But the point lies in determining whether they are needless. If they are not, are they criminal? For myself, I think they are worse than useless, an exposure of India. But is not this a question of policy, to be answered by persons qualified to judge? Can it possibly be imputed as a crime that Great Britain sacrifices her own soldiers to maintain her prestige?

There are charges made against England besides these, of economically criminal character. But most of them are incidental rather than perennial. They are of the past, and though they are blemishes there is no use in dwelling upon faults long since committed and in part confessed. Yet not to mention them would be to place England in a false light before the world. Such are the exorbitant demands made upon India for the payment of expenses in foreign wars. It could be said that India was interested in the

Suez canal, but it was flagrant injustice to make India pay more than a million pounds, while England paid but half a million, for the expense of occupying Egypt. This injustice is frankly admitted by the British themselves, although it has never been rectified. Another case of the same sort is thus summarized by the Englishman who was Governor-General at the time (of the Perak expedition): "I cannot conceive any one doubting that India has been hardly treated. The law was broken, and the charge so made upon India has never been repaid." Mr. Dutt, who cites these cases, is quite right in bringing them up against England. Among many charges of more doubtful nature, these stand confessed.

More dubious is the charge that the Famine Relief Fund was misappropriated. Certainly, the million and a half annual reserve was not forthcoming when the last famine came, as India, perhaps, had a right to expect. But there was a large margin of discretion left to those who had the spending of the moneys raised by extra taxation, and I cannot admit that there was in this case any criminal misappropriation of a trust fund, as is maintained by the Hindus themselves. The fact is, doubtless, that the money was spent on wars and other improvements, unnecessary railways, and similar public works; but these were all provided for by the terms of the agreement, and there was no fund really set aside for famine expenses, only a fund from a possible surplus, which, owing to the fact that the money was spent on other things, for which allowance had been made, never actually existed.

In the same way, it has been charged that railways have been built for speculation more than for actual need or for famine relief. There is, perhaps, some truth in the charge that what Mr. Hyndman harshly calls the "corrupt, unscrupulous, and jobbing" Public Works Department has not been free from connivance with reckless speculators. Such speculation or investment, whichever it be, has cost India millions of wasted pounds.

But these ills are ephemeral. More lasting is the ill that arises from the home charges and the drain from India in paying pensions. Here, again, however, we pass outside of the category of "wrongs," although the native reformer appears to make no distinction between one and another of these ills. Money had to be borrowed to improve the country and now interest must be paid on the loans; while the simple fact as regards pensions is that they are merely part of the salaries. In other words, no man devoid of common-sense ought to be made an Indian official, and no man with common-sense would live twenty years in India except with the understanding that, after he had given the cream of his life to India, he should at least be assured of the skim-milk on his return home. The alternative is to *cubbonize* India, to appoint only natives as officials. But this is a change to be made with caution and it is already making. Nor is it a moral wrong to keep the most important posts in British hands. So with the cost of the army. No doubt India pays heavily for the rule that keeps the Sikh from the Babu's throat and the Mahratta from the towns he was wont to devastate in Rajputana. But she would pay still more heavily were that rule removed.

Nevertheless, although the British are not criminally responsible for the extra expense of home charges, any more than they are criminal in having in India a soil that through ages of misuse has deteriorated, deserts that ages of deforestation have created, and over-population due partly to the thriftless character of the peasant and partly to the lack of wars in the last few generations,[1] — they have to face the conditions thus created and to recognize that if the home charges are not immoral, they yet make a terrible addition to the burden borne by India. No one can demand of the British that

[1] Two centuries ago there was too much land for the inhabitants in Bengal. To-day there is not enough, because the population has increased six-fold owing to the Pax Britannica. In this case, we may say that Great Britain is responsible, but surely not criminal, in having created an over-population. Plague and famine have their terrible utility — for those who survive.

they should settle in India, like the Moghul; but no one can deny that the Moghul in spending in India what he stole from India did much to lessen the weight of his crimes.

Therefore, it becomes a moral question with England whether there is any use in comparing her tax with that of the Moghul or that of the Mahratta, and assuming that her tax is just because it is relatively low. Much more has she to see to it that extensive irrigation shall be strengthened by laws against self-selling on the part of the peasant; and, above all, that irregular taxation shall meet the exigencies of an irregular climate. Irregular taxation may sound absurd, but it is the old rule, the only rule the peasant understands, and the only natural rule to follow in a country where crops vary by ninety-nine per cent. A fair proportion, even as much as twenty-five per cent., of the crop, when there is a crop, is just; but, on the other hand, the same rule when there is no crop. Even Dadaji, because the people were distressed, laid no tax for years — and shall England be less merciful?

What the Englishman owes to India is, in short, what he owes to himself, not only as the mighty lord of India, but as a self-respecting Christian. There is no use in asserting that a tax is humane and that subjects have nothing to complain of, when year by year they are forced out of their farms and starve perennially. Neither Hunter's complacency, Chesney's arrogance, nor the fair figures of the Statesman's Year-book, can alter the fact that something is rotten in the state of India.

So far all impartial judges must agree. But let us not exaggerate. Threefold though the source of famine be, the three efficient causes, — lack of water where wells should be, lack of restraint where restraint should be, lack of means to improve the land, because the usurer devours the cultivator, — all these three revert to one, over-pressure. Unselfish as are the servants, the master demands wealth, and it must be forthcoming. Nevertheless, this corporate master not only has large desires, as he has great needs and selfishness, but he has also a conscience, the existence of which has been proved on many occasions. Furthermore, he has no little ignorance of how his desires are obtained. If it could be effected without serious loss, there is no doubt that, with the realization of what his demands entail, he would no longer exact bricks without straw. But from the Nerbudda to the Godavari, India to-day is a sweat-shop, where lives are sacrificed and men drag out miserable days, not simply because God has sent a famine, but because peasants are ignorant, because wells are few and usurers are many, and because the master, also ignorant of what his need produces, always needs more money.

Still, although one rarely sees any admission of the fact in the diatribes against English policy, attempts have already been made to rectify some of these evils. There is even a law against the ancient right of the usurer, and this law confines somewhat the inherited power of this long-legalized robber; but it is not a sufficient guard, for the usurer continues to fatten and the peasant to starve. Irrigation has done wonders in the North, and the British may well be proud of their achievements in the Punjab; but what has been done in the Central Provinces, and why not? For what little has been done in the way of well-making, when set against what might have been done to save the peasants there, weighs very light on Justice's waiting scale.

So much I grant, and I will add this, that as matters stand now, it is merely a question whether Lord Salisbury's answer to a proposed reduction of taxation, *We cannot afford it*, is to prevail over the moral instinct which should reply, *We must afford it.* England is master and can take what she will. But, believe me, robbery, whatever you hear to the contrary, has not been England's Indian policy in the past. If it had been, rackrenting would not have been stopped by England, nor would there be those easy taxes, which even the native agitators praise as perfectly satisfactory, in the North. If she has sometimes made India pay too much and if rigorously regular in her annual demands, England, on the whole, has nevertheless dealt moderately with her subjects. Of the wrongs scored against her by Hindus and by her own people (for though I have cited the reformers as chiefly natives, it must not be forgotten that they are just as apt to be Englishmen, not to speak of those Americans who seem never to be quite so happy as when they are mourning over England), some of these wrongs exist only in that confusion between rights and privileges to which I have already alluded; while many are due rather to lack of familiarity with Oriental ways than to oppression. Do you doubt this? I will make the statement still stronger, and it shall still be true. The British have done much to reduce the peasant to starvation, not only because of lack of familiarity with Oriental ways, but because of their sense of law and justice. Let me give you some illustrations. The British, then the East India Company, as I have already told you, reduced the peasantry of Bengal to the state of rackrented subjects of the Zamindar. Why did they do so? Because, although they had the power to take the land, they did not take it, but looked about for the natural and legitimate owners of the vast estates of which they found themselves suddenly possessed. Now you must remember that to the British of that day, — this was in the century before the last, — the natural owner of land was the baronial lord. And there sat the baronial lord in possession, drawing his rents. He was the Zamindar. Was it to the interest of the British to put all the rents back into the Zamindar's pocket and acknowledge, what the latter claimed, that he was the owner? Not at all. It would have been much more profitable to have ousted the Zamindar and made England landlord. But the British knew nothing for a long time afterwards of estates in severalty and joint-villages. They gave up the lands, as they thought, to the rightful owner, and therewith they relinquished their hold on the rents he drew, taking from him only a very small tax, and leaving him to draw a stipulated rent, which fifty years ago they fixed low. If the Zamindar has rackrented his peasants, is that England's crime? Is it not a fair illustration of my first statement, that wrong was done through ignorance?

And now for the stronger statement that wrong has been done from a sense of justice. I am not trying to establish a paradox or whitewash the devil. The British for the first time, at least in centuries, have introduced into India and maintained courts of justice, where suits are decided, as in Europe, by the testimony offered and according to what is supposed to be the law of the land. Now, apart from those cases where injustice has been done merely because the British did not know that the priestly codes are not the law of this or that district, the Hindu usurer, in his cases against the farmers, had the whole law on his side. He could come into court with his falsified accounts and his perjured witnesses, and win his case every time against the poor and simple peasant. Did the British conspire with the usurer to oust the peasant? No. They upheld him to their own disadvantage (for the usurer is baleful to the country and the British know it perfectly well), because he was in his legal rights. Any wealthy man in India can get as many perjurers as he can afford. Law-cases have been time and again decided legally but without equity, because the British have been unable to make their own legal machinery work in that country.

As I said before, it is not the tax, so much as the regularity with which the tax is exacted, that makes the trouble in India. The five-acre farmer makes just enough to live on when he is lightly taxed and the harvest is good. When the harvest fails, he has nothing to live on. But the British tax is exacted, harvest or no harvest. Here you have another illustration of the neglect of native methods in favor of the more advanced methods of the Occident. The British assume as a matter of course that the tax is to be drawn regularly every year. It is their home custom. But the villager has been accustomed for a long time to be heavily taxed, or robbed, once every few years and then to be let alone, and he likes that way; whereas he considers a regular tax not only a regular nuisance but a great wrong, simply because it is regular. He regards a tax anyway as a sort of whipping which he has got to take, and he would much rather have one good beating and be done with it, than to have a man come around and give him a blow at regular intervals. Then to return to the usurer, he gives another illustration of the British sense of justice. For why is it that the usurer has all of a sudden got possession of ten to twenty per cent. of Indian farm-lands? How has he grown wealthy? Because, while the old laws let him exact tribute from the peasantry, this was only another method of the state's getting its own revenue. The fact is, the state gave license to the usurer, but when the usurer had got the money the state made him disgorge. The Hindu law says expressly that when the king needs money he may take it from the middle-class moneyed men; and nothing is said about repayment. But the British let the usurer keep the money as well as get it. Why? As I have said and I think now proved, because of their sense of law and justice. To rob even the usurer is not British practice.

You will, I think, admit that this whole question as I have presented it, and I have tried to present it fairly from every point of view, is an exceedingly complex as well as a very grave problem. It is one that every free-and-easy railer against England can, of course, answer off-hand. He need only take the admissions I have made, ignore all other considerations, historical, economic, legal, shout Fie on England, and the thing is done. But to one who knows India in its past and in its present, who has seen it and viewed what has been done there, — and I will add, what is to be done there, — abuse is no adequate critique of the situation. I have said that what the Englishman owes to India is what he owes to himself. But the rectification of wrongs involves as much study as it does generosity. There are wrongs, and a great sacrifice is needed to correct them. The remedy is more than heroic, for it is the application of Christian principles to statescraft, withal at a time when it is especially hard to make it. I do not speak here of righting the wrongs of the past, but of systematically remitting the tax when there is a drought, leaving the peasant enough to live on, and seeing that his livelihood is not taken from him even by law. This means, however, not only a great reduction in revenue, but a slow bettering of the economic conditions. As to the former, it implies perhaps the sacrifice of some imperial power, and certainly of some imperial rights, for the sake of moral right. I may be too sanguine, but I think not; I believe England will yet make the sacrifice. As to the betterment of conditions, I only wish that I could tell you half of what has been done already. England's officials in India have been striving for years for the redemption of a land long weighted with crime, poverty, and disease; a land divided against itself by caste and sect and nationality; a land of insolent aristocrats and degraded peasants, with no strong middle class between them. You have no idea what England has accomplished there. Her noble officers, English, Scotch, Irish, as well as the best Hindus, the toilers rather than the talkers, with untiring energy perform to the full and overflow the wearisome task committed to them. Not only have these servants of England established a marvellous machine for provincial government, which has not had its equal for efficiency since Rome collapsed, nor its equal for honesty in any system of holding subject provinces, but, high and low, they labor with the devotion of missionaries; and if sometimes they curse their fate, for it is not an easy one, they are indeed, profane or not, the missionaries of Christian civilization. No one who has seen the good works they have accomplished can question their zeal or their ability eventually to lead depressed India up to a higher plane of life. Reflect for a moment on only a few facts. Sixteen million people, formerly wild-men, now brought under the influence of civilization. What Raj save the British ever cared for them? Slaves made into free men. When you read of the kind kings of old, remember that the slave population was not included in their kindness. Established peace and its burden of hunger. In ancient times, perpetual wars, perpetual robbery. To-day, over all India, an efficient rural police, unknown before. Shall all this count as nothing? England has made India as a whole more prosperous, more stable, more a nation, than the country ever was before; given even her meanest subjects equal justice in a law-court, — a privilege the native agitators may ask the Brahmans to look for in the records of their past and they will look in vain — educated the lowly and made the high wise in their own conceit; taught the Babu his wrongs and given him permission to proclaim them; lowered the taxes and raised the depressed and the oppressed. Never before has a poor man received sympathy from the ruling class; never before in India has a man grown rich with impunity. Let the barren optimist say that England has no mistakes to correct and no wrong to right, and I shall insist again that a scientific forecast of what a farmer's field should produce, with an imperial government urging the expert to raise his estimate and an unchained usurer around the corner, is a mistake and a wrong. But when the pessimist, that unholy person, says that the British have oppressed India as has no other Raj, and that all is mistake and all is wrong in India, then I answer that he neither understands the conditions, historical or present, nor estimates fairly the ratio of wrong and right.

I make no charges of intentional or malicious wrongdoing; but I say that there are two sorts of people (and they will talk to you most on this subject) who, given the right topic, simply cannot speak the whole truth. One is a Hindu talking about India, and the other is an Anglophobe talking about England. From the latter you will hear all England's sins detailed, but never a word of what England has done as standard-bearer of the highest civilization. As to such a man's views on India, the test is easy. Ask him whom you hear descanting on British wrong-doing in India how England stands in other regards. After all, he is a guileless, shortsighted person; and when you have heard him explain that England has invariably done wrong, in all places and at all times and to all men, then you will know what weight to lay upon his one-sided opinion in regard to India. As to the Hindu, so extraordinary is his patriotic lack of veracity that he not only falsifies history, of which, to be sure, he is usually ignorant, but he even misrepresents the most evident facts of the present, not alone in regard to Anglo-Indian relations, but in regard to any point in which he wishes to exalt his native land. A pardonable weakness, but to what absurdity does it not lead? One of these virtuous impostors, for example, has recently informed us that the position of Hindu women is better than that of American women, though the press is scarcely done ringing the shameful but verified charges against the foul abuses practised by the husbands of Hindu children, the murderers of Hindu girls, the degraders of Hindu widows. And remember, these are not the sporadic villanies of such wretches as, Heaven knows, no country is free of, but they are deliberated usage, sanctioned and upheld by the very Hindus who to-day declaim against England. But all these points touch our present topic. For what power first put down the practice of burning widows? Not the Hindu Raj, who invented it; not the Moghul, who vainly tried to stop it; not the Babu and the Mahratta, who defended it; but England. And what power alone has exerted itself to stop girl-murder under native Rajas? England, again. And what power is even now slowly but surely mitigating the awful lot of the child-wife, whom even the Moghul sought to save, and that of the child-widow, whose blood and tears have been the one unfailing rain of India for more than two thousand years? God and England. And these, my friends, are but items of a long account. Even if you cast the account in money alone, you will find that the Englishman has sinned less through cruelty than through ignorance of the people's ways and of their inability to fit themselves into even the most equitable scheme fashioned according to Western ideas. For it is false that the British tax throughout India is in itself iniquitous. Apart from a restricted area and exceptional circumstances, it not only is a lower tax than the Hindu was wont to pay, but it represents a fair percentage of the farmer's income. But if you cast the account in other terms — and are we to look only on the rupees? — what then? I tell you, there is no Raj in the annals of Hindu history that has done so much for India as has England; not her old rulers, for they ruled for the Aryan alone, nor did they ever have placed before them the complex problems of to-day; not the Moghul, for, with rare exceptions, he never "considered the good of India as his duty;" not the Mahratta, for his hand was armed against every man save a Mahratta. So I say to the optimist: You are mistaken. The usurer is a wrong. To tax paupers is a wrong. No law is right, no rule is without fault, under which the burden of any thrifty peasant is greater than he can bear. But to the pessimist I say: Have at England if you will; only good will come of it if the truth be told, and truly she is not impeccable. But have at England as you will, without knowledge and without regard to truth, and you make your pleading a veiled lie and your cause ridiculous.

And now in closing I feel as if I should offer excuses for an address which I am afraid will have neither satisfied those who hoped to hear England defended nor pleased those who like to hear her abused. But it has been impossible for me to "take sides" on this question. It has too many sides. So I have spoken according to the facts as I see them, good and bad.

## THE PLAGUE.

"Prévoyant que si je survivais à cette aventure j'en ferais l'histoire."

THIS plague is the last of a number of such visitations since Christ's birth, the earliest of them, barring those of 166 and 250 A.D. and the one that occurred in Egypt and Persia and along the Mediterranean litoral in the sixth century (for no one knows whether these passed through India or not), being the plague of the thirteenth century, and the general pest following it a century later (1344–48). But even in this case, though the two may have come from the same source, yet only of the latter is it known with certainty that it passed through India, having first started in China. The plague which ravaged London and other parts of England in 1665, resulting not only in countless deaths, but in important social and political modifications, may have been the plague "which few escaped" in Bombay, in 1618. It was in India till 1630. The same plague reappeared in 1684 and 1690 in Surat, and in Bulsar in 1691. In Bombay itself the plague lasted from 1689 to 1702; while in 1720 Marseilles was attacked by a plague said to have been imported from Syria in silk-goods, though the opinion that the plague is not conveyed by merchandise at all is strengthened by the observation that in Marseilles not a single porter of the silk bales died of the disease.

As plague is probably endemic in Egypt, it is doubtful whether its successive circlings there are not links in the same chain. Such a round occurred when Napoleon was in Egypt, and again in 1835 in Alexandria. But these cases may have something to do with the fact that outbreaks occurred in India almost immediately after each in Egypt; in 1815 there was plague in Kutch and Kathiawar, and in 1836 in Marwar.

Since then plague has broken out in Garhwal (Gurawal) in 1852 and 1876; in Baghdad and other cities of Mesopotamia in 1876–77; and in Hong Kong in 1893–96. In Mesopotamia, Garhwal, and Yunam the disease is endemic. In Garhwal it is a local disease engendered by dirt, and is the true *maha-mari* or Great Death, which is said not to be identical with the bubonic plague. Be that as it may, the plague has been called the Great Death by the natives here since its first appearance. Only the up-country hotel-keepers, whose bungalows this year of fear are nigh empty of guests, have euphemistically changed the name, and when one goes from Bombay into the Mofussil (country-districts), one is greeted with the absurd question, "How is now the little-death?" (*echota-mari*).

Since 1720 plague had not desolated a Continental city. For sixty years it had not invaded India, but it is endemic to the east in China and to the west in Mesopotamia, it has always hung about the edges of the country and is supposed to lurk in some of the hill hovels on the northern border. What was more important, there was constant shipping between Bombay and the home of the plague, and it was well known that the plague was a filth disease.

Bombay is not the dirtiest city in India, but its uncleanliness is probably exceeded in quality by that of Calcutta alone. Yet Bombay possesses more dirt and it is more compact, as the city is the largest in the country, containing, according to the last census, 821,764 souls, while of these about 770,000, the native inhabitants, are for the most part crowded into an area of but four square miles; and in some parts of the city there are 760 people to the acre, the densest population, it is said, in the world.

In 1661 the city had a population of 10,000, and in 1673 of 60,000, if travellers' estimates may be trusted. Filth has been gathering in the town for centuries. To the Portuguese, the town was still *a ilha da boa vida*, "the island of good life;"

but by 1706 Waite called it an "unhealthful island," and in 1707 he alluded to it as "this unveryhealthful (*sic*) island." But the systematic accumulation of filth is a later growth, which arose in this way. The upper part of the city, which even now is swampy, two centuries ago was almost all bog. The town is on an island (originally seven islands), which like New York is pointed at the south and gradually broadens toward the north, the Battery being represented by the ward or district of Kolaba, and the Harlem Flats by the northern swampy district, which is known in Bombay also as the Flats. The lower end too of Bombay is rocky, as in New York. But a large part of the interior of the city is below the mean sea-level. Other parts formerly below have been filled in and raised, but not with sweet soil. For the present city is largely built up on hollows filled with refuse, partly undrained. The Fort, the southern part of the town extending nearly to the Victoria Station, then the native town, in the middle of the city, and eventually the districts originally outlying but now in the town were thus reclaimed. One of these reclaimed tracts, for example, is the present Kamatipur Ward, where the plague, when it came, raged most violently.

The city grew rapidly and, as it increased, the city sweepings and other fouler matter were utilized to make new building-lots. Thus on a foundation of mud and manure were created hundreds of salable acres in Byculla, in Mazagon, in the Oart (the cocoa-nut plantations), and still later in the fashionable northwest quarter of the town, Malabar Hill and Breach Candy (i. e. *khinda*, Pass).

This practice was discontinued in the middle of the present century, but in the sixties the city authorities resumed it, converting acres of swamp into valuable property by filling them up with decomposing filth.

Such drainage as there used to be in the city was effected by means of a main drain about a mile long, which was in reality an elongated cesspool, since there was not fall enough to carry off the stagnant matter constantly accumulating in it. The sewage was at first conveyed into the Flats, then into the harbor. At present there are some open and some closed drains in the city, but there are whole districts which have none. Mandvie Ward, where the plague first appeared, has no proper sewerage, but only water-drains, constructed in 1871, which are intended to carry off the surplus water that falls in floods during the monsoon season, June–September. The whole district is water-logged, owing to the constant silting up of the drains, some of which have not been cleaned for twelve years. Complaints about them have been frequent for fifteen years.

The fashionable drive of the city is an intra-mural Appian Way bordered with graves. On the one side is the Bay, on the other the burning-ghats of the Hindus and a burying-ground of the Mohammedans. The heart of the city when the plague entered it — how shall one describe it? The streets heaped thick with foulest stuff, the houses not free of it; the native town, a labyrinth of malodorous lanes, which connect streets or run into other lanes, or form blind alleys; and besides these lanes, very close tunnels, known locally as gullies, which perforate the filth, and are intended as alley-ways between the tenements. These buildings are indeed not like our sky-scrapers, but, rising as they do to a considerable height on either side of a two-and-a-half foot gully, they cut off all sunlight from the narrow sty below.

Bombay, like New York, because of its horn-like shape, has no room for expansion to east and west, and as there is no rapid transit the poorer people are necessarily herded together, and they naturally prefer this to the toil and expense of a northern journey on the slow tram. In Calcutta, which is all built on a mud flat (or, as the inhabitants call it, an alluvial plain), there is room for the poor, and they still continue to live, more or less separate, in small groups of low hovels, *bustis*. But in Bombay's congested middle the tenements, or *chawls*, as they are called, are as large if not so high as our own tenement houses, though within there is the difference between the Orient and civilization. There are, indeed, besides these structures, which contain several hundred inmates, smaller *chawls*, holding twenty to fifty people, and in some districts there are single houses of the poor. But to describe the most characteristic of them will suffice. They all have two things in common, — darkness and dirt.

In small houses, such as are found chiefly in the northern districts, the family practically live in one dark room, out of which, however, may open a darker closet for water-pipes, where washing is done in perpetual dampness and gloom. The floor of these shanties is usually of mud, and the mud is usually wet with all kinds of water and filth.

The smaller *chawls* are built all over the native city. They are often situated two or three feet below the level of the street or lane. Not seldom is there a cluster of them, bordering a network of intricate little lanes, in some of which there is not space enough for two persons to walk abreast. Lanes and houses are alike evil to see, and more evil to smell.

But of the big *chawls*, where land is more valuable (one hundred dollars or more a square yard, for it is sold by this measure), some accommodate, or at least contain, a thousand grimy tenants. These caravanseries are the especial feature of that part of the city where the plague first started, Mandvie Ward. From without they are fair enough to see, and at first one is astonished that these should have been the lair of the plague, for if the street is unclean and the gullies on either side of the *chawl* are indescribable, the buildings themselves are substantial, and seem to be roomy. But the manner of their iniquity is this: The *chawls* are six or eight stories high, with a six-foot hallway from bottom to top through the middle of the house, where a stair takes half the space of the hall; and a series of black cubicles, eight or ten on either side, fronts on the hallway in every story. The hall on the ground-floor is lighted by the entrance doorway; the hallways above, only by the dim light from below, or in some cases by narrow slits in the back wall of the hall. The air which comes through these slits rises from the common opening intended as a closet in the rear of the main building. The little cubicles along each hallway are eight by ten feet. They have no ventilation and no light. Each is usually occupied as a sleeping and eating room by a family of five or six, though sleeping-space is generally sublet to as many more as will fill the floor. The floors of these "better-class" *chawls* are of cement, not mud. The walls used to be of bamboo, but are now of wood and plaster. When the cubicles get too dirty, they are subjected, generally in view of a visit from an inspector, to the *gobar* process. This consists in smearing both floor and wall with cow-dung, which is then allowed to dry. It purifies the air to some extent, and has a pungent odor agreeable to the natives. On this carpet of cow-dung new filth then collects daily as before. There is in such a cubicle no furniture save bedding and a cooking-pot. The smoke finds its way out as best it can. In the corner of the room is a small receptacle called a *nahani*, pronounced *nanee*, which is connected with a down-take pipe without, and is intended only as a sink, but it is habitually used for other purposes. Everything to be got rid of is thrust down the *nahani* pipe, so that it is frequently clogged full. Since the only light in the cubicle comes from a dim, unventilated hall, this also is dark, close, and foul, a noisome den. The tenant will not seldom refuse to clean the hall, even with *gobar*, for he regards that as the business of the landlord, who, however, is generally content if his rent is paid, and cleans nothing. Nor will the tenants cease to dirty the gullies. But, in a word, to make a short cut through nastiness, the personal habits of the natives of the tenement class are not much better than those of animals, which indeed share houses and even cubicles with them, and help to render these unfit for human habitation. Sixteen to twenty of these cubicles on a floor, six or eight stories of them, constitute a typical Mandvie *chawl*. Not the poor only, but also rich native merchants are found in such habitations. A few tenements erected on sanitary principles are to be found in the city, but almost the only houses of this sort are those erected by the Tramway Company, which is under the superintendence of an American, whose decent *chawls* have been notably free from plague during the whole of the pestilence.

The "gullies" alongside of a *chawl* are dirtied not only by irresponsible people, but even officially by the *halalkhores*, or *bhungis*. These are the regularly appointed employees of the municipality, night-workers, whose business it is to remove the night-soil accumulated through the day and carry it away in carts. Instead of doing this, they are apt to pitch it into the nearest water-drain or into the house-gully. At the very beginning of the plague it was stated that hundreds of complaints had been made in regard to this practice. But the *halalkhores* continued it long after the plague had broken out, as may be seen from many reports and complaints made at intervals all winter. These reports show, too, the general condition of the streets, where *cutchra* (street-sweepings) had been allowed to collect for years. A month after the plague was known to be in the city, a native physician, at a meeting on October 19, thus describes the appearance of the streets: "The dust-bins are not only full of *cutchra*, but filth and garbage are lying in heaps on the roads, emitting a stench which is highly sickening." Another says: "Coomarwada Second and Third lanes are in a most disgraceful and filthy condition. The side gullies are full of all abominations, and the whole length of the drain is choked up with sullage and night-soil." Still another physician describes Lohar street, "where sullage water collected itself on the public road, and ran in streams on to Kalbadevi Road," and adds, "The attention of the Health Department had been repeatedly drawn to the nuisance" before it was cleansed.

Man having prepared a place for plague, Nature, as it were, induced the monster to enter it. But Nature had helped man long before. During the summer of 1896 the rains, usually distributed over four months, were concentrated in the first three with a total excess of twenty-seven inches (above the normal fifty-eight inches for the three months). This was followed by a partial drought in September and excessively hot weather in October. As a result the subsoil, though the surface was flooded, was less evenly and thoroughly soaked than usual. Consequently the noxious filth which had been accumulating about the neglected drains in the subsoil was not held thoroughly in solution, although the total rainfall for the year (up to October), 87.65 inches, exceeded the evaporation, and was in fact fifteen inches in excess of the average. But to ensure the health of the city there should be ten inches of excess of precipitation annually, as against the evaporation, whereas since 1887 there had been altogether only seventeen inches, including that of 1896. There was then, given an accumulation of filth in the subsoil, in the very excess of evaporation for a decade past the meteorological prelude to the drama of death.

It is a curious fact, shown in the Bombay Observatory,[1] that there is an excess of vapor pressure about once in ten years, corresponding with the phase of "maximum sun-spot area." In 1896 there was a minimum period, hence evaporation was at a maximum, for it varies inversely as the vapor pressure. With a soil fairly clean, the effect of the decennial fluctuation is slight; but when excessive evaporation leaves a soil surcharged with filth, there is a parallel excess of escaping foul gases and a perfect environment for disease.

Ten years before the plague arrived, the death-rate of the city was but 24 per thousand annually. Some months before, it was 40 per thousand. The mortality had increased steadily for six years. In the previous year, October, 1895, to October, 1896, it was nearly two thousand more than in the year October, 1894, to October, 1895, being in the year ending October, 1896, about 27,000. The press had raised in regard to neglect of sanitation a warning voice six months before the plague came. The municipality, however, had taken no steps to meet the coming emergency, although they had twenty lakhs of rupees at their disposal.[2]

[1] These observations are taken from Mr. Baldwin Latham's Report on the Sanitation of Bombay, and those in the preceding paragraph, with the notes on drainage and sweepings, from the Times of India.

[2] A *rupee*, divided into sixteen *annas*, was, in 1896, equal to nearly one-third

Under the government there is a municipal corporation of seventy-two members, the chief executive of the city being the municipal commissioner. Europeans are apt to neglect the meetings of the corporation, partly because their vote does not count for much when opposed to that of the natives, who have a two-thirds majority, and partly because they "have no time to spend on politics." Subordinate to the commissioner are the various heads of departments, for example, the officers of the harbor, police, engineering, and health departments, with whom the commissioner usually consults, but to whom in the end he issues peremptory instructions. To an American, the most astounding fact in the constitution of the city government is that the health officer, instead of being dictator, as he should be and is with us when public health is in question, is without power, being subordinate to the municipal commissioner, from whom he virtually has to receive orders.

The plague entered the city, as nearly as can be reckoned, in the last week of August, 1896. In the first week of September the health officer was informed of the fact, but, according to his own statement, he had already known of it for some time. By September 3, certain physicians who were members of the corporation were already treating the malady as true plague.

The first cases appeared in Mandvie Ward, a district of 37,000 inhabitants, in the middle of the city. It spread rather slowly at first, but before September was half over the native population had become frightened, and prominent native citizens were shortly organizing such measures of relief as the divines of the Orient deem sufficient to prevent the progress of plague. An exodus from this ward and even from other parts of the city had already begun. But the health officer still officially ignored the whole matter. Not yet had the commissioner taken any steps to prevent the spread of the

of a dollar, though its nominal value is about half a dollar (two shillings), and it has been as low as a quarter. The *anna* may be reckoned as equivalent to two cents. A *lakh* is 100,000. One hundred *lakhs* make a *karor* or *crore*.

disease; nor had the press spoken. Though the presence of the plague was known to many, silence was the rule.

But when three whole weeks of September had passed and, as nearly as can be estimated, between two and three hundred people had died of the plague, the matter was casually mentioned at an ordinary meeting of the standing committee of the corporation, held on September 23, when a private physician first called attention to it, and on the spot named the disease by its true name. Referring to "the existence and prevalence of a dire malady on the Port Trust Estate and its vicinity," he said: "The malady is the bubonic plague. . . . I think it is caused by the putrid emanation from the putrefying and decomposing matter in the sewers on the Port Trust Estate, which are choked, and can only be called cesspools. . . . I have more than once called the attention of the corporation to the great danger." Another gentleman stated that he had heard of the prevalence of the plague "about twenty days ago," and continued: "I at once communicated with the health officer . . . and furnished him with the numbers and descriptions of houses where the epidemic had broken out. . . . I am informed that between two and three hundred men have died from the plague during the last fortnight, and panic-stricken residents of the locality have been migrating to Kutch and Kathiawar and other distant places."

The health officer, when he had been requested to make a few remarks, cautiously said: "In regard to the occurrence of cases of a peculiar type of fever referred to, it may be mentioned that the type is of a suspicious character," adding that he had known of the matter for some time before any one had spoken to him about it, and that he had been taking "special precautions." It would be interesting to know in what the precautions consisted; certainly not in any of the preventive measures usually taken to avoid infection.

In regard to the filth spoken of, it may be remarked once for all that when the plague appeared in a new district it appeared in filth. Thus when it moved north and attacked the people at Grant Road, the first case reported from there was "in a hovel in one of the rows of particularly filthy hovels;" and the first cases that were noticed in the city, in Clive Road, Argyle Road, and Broach Street, were in general in an unusually unclean environment. The only apparent exceptions were the cases in "large commodious corner-houses exposed to the sea breeze." By them, and they were many, who were pecuniarily interested in proving that insanitary surroundings were not conducive to insanitation (for nearly half of the municipal corporation are owners of *chawls*, and in fact some of the most disreputable tenements in the city are owned by members of this body), these cases were cited as proof of their contention. What the commodious houses of this district are, I have shown above; the fact that a cold breeze made the half-naked inmates liable to catch cold, and that the plague began with pulmonary trouble, may have offset the hygienic advantage of salt in the air. But the accident of position was not really a very important item in a town where the vilest alleys border on the best streets. The Parsee temple near the Post Office is on a fine avenue, but beside it is a horrible little lane, and the temple itself till late in the winter contained a very filthy well, so that it was not surprising that plague broke out in the little lane early in the season, though the lane runs up to the west, which in Bombay is the windward side of the city, and the house of plague was within a few rods of a broad drive, apparently clean but invisibly diseased, like the temple, the worshippers at which were sorely smitten.

Testimony as to the wealth or poverty of the first victims, as also in regard to the religious community to which they belonged and their nationality, was very contradictory, because each reported according to the few facts he knew, or perhaps according to his prejudices. Only one general statement remained undisputed, and this was that the victims were at first chiefly young people from five to thirty years of age. In respect of the disputed points, judging from the most reliable testimony given on several occasions and from what I heard, the earliest victims would seem to have been neither wealthy Hindu merchants nor Jains, as was variously asserted, but first of all poor Hindus and then Jains and Mohammedans. But the item of wealth makes little difference, since, with some exceptions, personal cleanliness amongst the natives is not up to the standard demanded by hygienic laws, even in the case of the well-to-do, for often even the wealthy live in opulent squalor.

Before the municipality had officially heard of the plague's existence, the common citizens had invented, or more strictly imported, a cure for it, and made preparations to ward off the wrath of Heaven, whom they make responsible for everything.

In respect of the cure, the natives had observed that the slight pain in the groin on the first day and the enlargement of the glands on the second were usually followed by high fever and delirium, and that on the third day the patient died.[1] They therefore endeavored to check the appearance of the bubo by applying a hot iron to the groin and removing the cuticle. Acting on the suggestion of some Bhatias, who had described how cautery was practised in Kutch, the Indian

[1] The symptoms of the plague described above in outline were retailed at length from personal observation by Dr. Atmaran Pandurang in October. With the addition of other (bracketed) tokens, specified in a later report by Dr. Jas. Cantlie, they are as follows: "A peculiar discoloration of the skin, prostration, countenance stupid, expression of apathy, fever frequent and feeble pulse [delirium, vomiting, cardiac distress, terrible thirst], enlarged lymphatic glands in the groin, the arm-pit, and the neck, those in the groin usually forming a large swelling painful to the touch, the bubo; no diarrhœa but bowels costive, liver and spleen enlarged, but no change in the urine in quantity or appearance, hurried breathing, not answering readily questions put, drowsiness running rapidly into coma and death; but in quick cases, feeble pulse, hurried breathing, drowsiness, coma, death, without fever or enlargement of glands. Other cases take two to seven days; quick cases, six to twenty-four hours." The "quick" cases, though infrequent at first in Bombay, became common in the course of the winter. At Karachi, on the other hand, the plague appeared at the very first in the quick form, and the first victims there lived only a few hours. Patients that recovered were sometimes left in a paralytic state. The plague which devastated middle India at the close of the seventeenth century was "so violent that in a few hours it depopulates whole cities," as is reported, in 1695, by Dr. Careri. It was called *goli* (ball, bubo) by the natives and *carazzo* (implying the bubo), by the Portuguese. Dr. Da Cunha, Origin of Bombay, p. 191.

doctors thus put their patients to useless torture and cured none. But there were many quack cures which the natives adopted in lieu of better instruction, for the municipality appointed no special physicians to see to them for some time after the meeting of the 23d, and the poor, so far as the authorities were concerned, were allowed to die unattended. But from the time the plague broke out, the *vaidyas* (doctors, literally wiseacres) of the Hindus and the *hakim* of the Mohammedans might be seen sitting on the curb-stones, selling powdered lizard and other antidotes, not always so harmless. For both in Bombay and in the Mofussil, where also the plague soon appeared, it presently became a crying evil that these unlicensed quacks were murdering men with many decoctions. But the half-educated as well as the ignorant believed in them.

On the very day on which was held the municipal meeting referred to above, where was uttered the first warning of coming trouble, there was another meeting in Bombay. The native merchants, more alive to the danger than were their official protectors, assembled at the office of a Bhatia and invited subscriptions "for the poor who were afflicted with the scourge," and for the performance of religious rites to propitiate Kali, the dreaded spouse of Çiva, for to her anger the Hindus attributed the plague.

The press and the municipal authorities said, "Hush! lest the world hear of it and business be injured," but the Hindus, and the Mohammedans also, were already crying aloud for aid. A series of religious processions followed.

First, the Brahmans attempted to appease the wrath of Kali, and three days after the municipal meeting they paraded the streets where plague was well known to be at work, marching in solemn procession, clad in gay robes, and reciting Sanskrit verses. It was supposed by some of the lower classes that Kali had been angered through the rejection of the old metal anklets, such as the women used to wear, in favor of dark-green *bangris*, or *patlis* (bangles) of glass, which had recently been introduced into the city.

It was said that cows' blood was used in the manufacture of the new bangles, but very likely the whole tale originated with the rival manufacturers of the metal anklets. However that may be, there was now on the part of the women, chiefly mill-hands, a general return to the holy ancient way, and a great breaking of glass. So, after the Hindu women had broken all their bangles, and the Brahmans had recited their Sanskrit verses, the priests proclaimed that Kali was angry no longer. Then for a few days the Hindus believed that they were saved.

But the Mohammedans, who do not believe in Kali, had their own rites, and three days later, that is, on September 29, they too held a religious service, similar to that of the Brahmans. For after a band of fakirs had assembled on the seashore near the Churney Road Gardens (by the Queen's Road) and offered prayer there, they began to march, and in an array similar to that of a Greek chorus, namely, in files of three (their number too was fifty), paraded together to the Field of Death, for so Mandvie Ward was already called by the poor (though the municipality had not yet recognized that there was any plague in the city). Through this ward, with heads uncovered and bare feet and to the music of a bagpipe, they marched first, and then in the same way visited in order all the other places where the disease was known to be, for it had spread even outside the limits of Mandvie. They thought that the holiness of their presence after the performance of the rites would tend to allay the malady, and, like the Brahmans, they really did do some good, for they helped to still the popular fear. But to the stranger they were less imposing on account of an innocent error which they were led to commit. For though they bore themselves not unworthily of their sacred mission, yet the leader, who made the music, having been at some time, as it would seem, a musician in a British regiment, played on his bagpipe only Scotch jigs. He played with great solemnity as well as ability, but the effect was risible, and the number of the band also suggested comedy rather than tragedy.

The next day, for the native town was now in great terror, and those who had not participated in the first celebration were glad to take part in the second, the Hindus again entreated their gods. But the chief suppliants were not the poorer classes, for only wealthy merchants and their friends and families were engaged in the ceremony itself, which differed from the former Hindu rite, and in preserving many ancient superstitions, such as those of holy numbers and the circumambulation of fire, was of peculiar interest. It was carried out in the following manner. First of all, at the entrance to the lane called Dariasthan in Mandvie, there was erected a golden entablature of welcome to the invited guests, who were more than a thousand in number, and were to pass through this lane to the temple of the same name situated there. The whole rite was at the cost of a pious Hindu, who had bidden his friends to this ceremony, which might almost be called a feast, since, though the function was essentially an intercessory service, it partook of the nature of a festival, as will be seen. For when the guests had passed the sign of welcome and were come through the lane, which was further decorated with banners and variegated bunting, they entered the temple to the sound of music, which was made by a band of native musicians. Most of the women remained in the entrance-hall or went to the galleries above, but some went into the inner temple with the men. There rites of prayer were first performed, but not such as call for further notice, save that they were invocations directed to the assuagement of Kali's anger. Then, however, the priests turned to a huge kettle, which stood in the middle of the square of the inner temple, and having placed in this the feast agreeable to the goddess, cocoanuts, melted butter, and rice, together with costly incense and many fragrant drugs, they covered these things with vermilion powder, such as the Hindus use to mark the sacred *namon* on their foreheads, and then burned all the contents of the kettle as an acceptable sacrifice. It was burned by seven priests, which is a sacred number. Then these seven circumambulated seven times the place of sacrifice, keeping their right side toward the fire. Girls also, decked in garlands, followed the priests, for Kali has female servitors. Then prayers were said, and there was a great noise from the cymbals, in making which, or other music, each musician strove to produce as much racket as possible with his brass instrument, since in this way the lesser spirits of disease, as they believe, are frightened away. Thus this worship of Kali combined elements the most diverse. For with the self-same music they believed that they were both pleasing the goddess and dismaying her attendants. There was nothing more done in the temple; but subsequently, towards the cool of the afternoon, these people and a good many more, all wearing holiday clothes and ornaments, proceeded through the stricken district, priests first, then the men, and finally women. They thus passed by the way of Kazi Syed Street, and the Musjid Bunder Bridge, through Argyle Road and Broach Street, where the plague was worst, to the waterside at Carnac Bunder, and there, after singing and praying as they had done upon the route, they cast oblations into the sea, and having prayed again, went home.

But after this there were no more superstitious rites for a long time, partly because to the Hindus so much of the following month was a time of regular continued sacrifice, and partly because all hoped that what they had done already would prove efficacious. Only the Roman Catholic and Protestant churches had services for the same purpose of averting the wrath of the Deity, first in the cathedral at Magazon, on October 5–7, and again on the 11th at the same place in connection with a High Mass in honor of St. Sebastian. And between these, intercessory prayers were offered, in behalf of the sufferers from the plague, at the Protestant Missionary Conference. But these familiar services need no description.

At the meeting of the standing committee on September 23 a private physician had demanded "isolation" of plague-patients. No attention was paid to him. Before the end of the month the Times of India, admitting that plague was in the city, called for proper segregation. This, by the way, was the only paper in Bombay that then or afterwards envisaged fairly the facts of the situation. Two days after the meeting of the committee a prominent physician said that he "knew personally" of fifteen to twenty deaths a day from plague. No medical man of any repute denied that the "peculiar fever," so lightly treated by the health officer, was bubonic plague. Yet no arrangements had been made for a plague-hospital. The Health Department continued to pooh-pooh, and insisted that the trouble was confined to one community, though physicians bore direct testimony to the contrary. The municipal commissioner exercised none of the powers which had been conferred upon him by the Municipal Act to prevent the spread of disease, though he was advised to apply for more power by the government committee appointed to inquire into the plague. The word "plague" was officially tabued. The little-death, as the hotel-keepers called it, was known to the Health Department also as bubonic "fever" only; nor for a month after the meeting of the standing committee on September 23 was plague under any name allowed to stand in the official records. The first entry was for the week ending October 20 (as "bubonic fever"). Even after this, most of the plague-deaths were distributed under the captions of pulmonary diseases, phthisis, old age, and the like.

The reason for this concealment was tersely stated in the municipal corporation: Bombay was a trading city; knowledge of the plague would hurt trade. For this, amongst other more personal reasons, the commissioner and his subordinates concealed the truth. For this reason also the chairman of the Chamber of Commerce, a month after the pest appeared, declared that there was no such thing as plague in town; naïvely adding that, as Colombo had already quarantined against Bombay, any one might see how inimical to the welfare of the city were revelations so untimely.

The health officer's only move to meet the plague in battle was to remove filth. Other members of the municipality, on the other hand, were rather inclined to the opinion that filth was innocuous. The police commissioner, who had a great deal more to say about sanitation than had the health officer, made some remarks on the subject at the next meeting of the standing committee. He was convinced, he said, that the plague was due to sugar and silk. Date fruit came from Baghdad, and silk came from Hong Kong. These places had had the plague, and were responsible for its presence in Bombay. Filth had nothing to do with it. Perhaps rats were responsible; on the whole, he thought rats were responsible; perhaps rats and sugar and silk were all alike responsible. He was not sure, but he inclined to sugar and silk; anyway, drains and filth had nothing to do with the matter; but perhaps it was rats.

On the same day, September 30, the municipal commissioner informed the government that in his opinion "there was no cause for very serious alarm." The question of rats *versus* drains was agitated for a long time in the city, for it was supposed that the plague sprang up in the town spontaneously, and it was not known till long afterwards that early in August a band of pilgrims had come to Bombay from a Himalayan village where the plague is endemic. Therefore they may have brought the disease with them; but as to the other causes, as has been said already, merchandise cannot carry the germs, and the plague always sprang up in the filthiest environment. But rats have the disease, and when dead rats were found on a place plague followed, yet only if the place was quite filthy; for dead rats were found even in the hotels without plague following.[1]

On October 5 and 6, respectively, the government proposed that the sanitary staff of the municipality should be

[1] Among the odd statistics published during the year it was shown that while respectable women died as easily as the men, the prostitutes were almost immune, not because the wages of sin was life, but because these women kept themselves cleaner, and were better fed; for which reason, perhaps, the Europeans also were spared. How absurd were some explanations given in regard to susceptibility to the disease, was revealed by another statistical report which stated (in April) that, whereas native Protestant Christians died at the rate of 16 per thousand, Roman Catholic Christians died at the rate of 40 per thousand; whether because of cleanliness, robustness, or creed, was, however, not stated.

increased; and a Notification was drawn up by the municipal executive, the terms of which were interpreted to mean that the segregation of plague-patients would be made compulsory.

This Notification of October 6 immediately became a bone of contention. It was six months to a day before the most recalcitrant natives were brought to see that English authority could enforce segregation. But this was under the pressure of a stronger hand than that of the municipal commissioner.

The municipal commissioner received an extra grant of 100,000 rupees for sanitary purposes (for which he had applied on September 30), but about a third of it was spent in making manholes. The remainder was sunk in work neglected for years, such as the excavation from the drains of a thousand tons of silt, which, though disinfected, still "emitted sickening smells," the flushing of drains, and cleansing of alleys. Most of the appropriation was gone in three weeks (October 19). There was soon more muck dug up in the city than could be carted away. It stood for days heaped in offensive mounds, while the upturned soil reeked with foul gases. As to the segregation of plague-patients, the health officer had not only taken no interest in it, but had expressed it as his deliberate opinion that it was "impracticable, out of the question." In this opinion he was supported by influential members of the municipality. For instance, the chairman of the standing committee, a native Hindu physician, declared at a meeting of medical men that segregation was cruel and useless; and the meeting applauded him. The most done to prevent the spread of the plague was to try and catch plague-patients as they ran about the city, and disinfect them. They were continually flitting from one part of the town to another. But the arrest of such persons was always regarded as a happy accident; no system was employed, and thus from infected localities the fleeing natives shortly spread the plague over districts not before contaminated.

The health officer's published statements that segregation was an absurdity played directly into the hands of the natives, who immediately protested against any form of general segregation, not only because in their opinion it was merely an English fad, but particularly on the ground that the holy privacy of the Hindu or Mohammedan home was thereby invaded. The judgment of a committee of physicians (who had been especially appointed to report and advise), to the effect that segregation was a necessity, here went for naught. Few natives have yet learned that there is nothing holy which is opposed to the public weal.

Another religious phase of the opposition to segregation was the *kismet* theory of the Mohammedans, which has its parallel among the Hindus. According to this theory, it is impious to try and escape from the fate prepared by God. Moreover, it is useless, and hence precautions are vain. Amongst both divisions of Indians the practical result of this theory is to make them not only scorn segregation, but also disregard all laws of health. No importance is attached to the sanitary condition of houses or towns. Disease and death are gifts of God. They hold in this regard that Christians are cowards; that it is a craven fear which induces them to clean houses and streets; and care of health is an impiety which would obstruct God's will.

No sooner had the Notification of October 6 been signed, and a few patients had been removed to the Arthur Road Hospital for Infectious Diseases, than the health of the town unfortunately began to improve. The municipal commissioner at once concluded that the plague was not going to amount to much after all. For a few days, however, segregation was enforced, though it was afterwards asserted that no formal order requiring such enforcement had ever been issued. But the natives, Hindus and Mohammedans, were clamorous for the repeal of the obnoxious measure. The health officer had, besides, enough to do in accomplishing the undone work of a decade, and could spare no men or moneys for other things.

With the news that plague was to be opposed with segregation, and the ensuing diminution in plague-cases, hope had sprung up in the breasts of the European residents. Moreover, they expected much from a change in the weather, not knowing that cold aided the plague. On the other hand, the Hindus, who to a man believe in astrology, had their own reasons for feeling encouraged. There were five Tuesdays in the month, the new moon came on a Tuesday, the Sankranti Feast came on a Tuesday. When these ill-omened Tuesdays were past and the (Hindu) month came to an end, then, they said, the plague would go. But instead, more trouble both abroad and at home. Aden, belonging to the Bombay Presidency, Colombo in Ceylon, Naples and other European ports quarantined against Bombay. The merchants began to feel the pinch; but their dependents and smaller local tradesmen felt it more. And, despite official reports, the plague kept spreading.

On September 20 a man had died of plague in Mandvie. Four days later a boy was taken from this man's house to Kamatipur Ward. He was removed while suffering from the plague. In less than a fortnight Kamatipur, thus infected, had as many cases as Mandvie itself. The streets of this new district were indescribably dirty; the gullies were not flushed; the filth was so great that even the common people fretted at it. Complaints had been made to the Health Department, but up to October 5 the only thing done was to remove one patient. In this case, as in all others, the health officer, instead of preventing, walked behind the plague.

Before the middle of October, plague was firmly fastened on Mandvie, the Fort, Kolaba, and Kamatipur. On October 6, the very day of the Notification, a man came down to Bombay from Poona. He had the plague, which he had first carried from Bombay to Poona, and then brought back to Bombay. From this time on Poona was infected, two fatal cases being reported there by October 14. In the North, emigrants from Bombay had already infected Ahmedabad (October 5). Karachi quarantined against Bombay on October 13. But it was of no avail. No real quarantine on the railways was introduced till months afterwards. A careless inspection of outgoing passengers was begun at Bombay itself. But this did not hinder the exodus of plague-cases; and till January the Mofussil districts continued to receive uninspected plague-stricken patients from the Presidential town.

For no sooner was the Notification put in force than many of the unwilling natives, who would not submit to it, prepared to flee. Thousands had fled from fear of the plague alone, but thousands more fled in dread of the hospital. By the middle of October the population was already sensibly diminished. Starvation prices began to obtain in Bombay, and curiously enough, famine abroad, instead of deterring refugees, in the end helped to increase the number of emigrants. For just as soon as relief-works were opened for sufferers from famine, the day-laborer of Bombay could leave a town where he paid double for grain and lived in fear of death, and enroll himself amongst the "famine-stricken" in the country, exchanging starvation and fear for hope and food.

So the lower classes streamed out of town, travelling by rail, by steamer, and by bullock-cart. The last was the favorite conveyance when there was a case of sickness to conceal. Stowing the plague-patient, the small kit of the family, and wife and children in the cart, the astute native crept out of town by night, easily escaping the vigilance, such as it was, of the police. All winter long these carts went south, crawling slowly up the Ghats through Poona to Satara, Belgaum, Kolhapur, and other towns of the Deccan. Others sailed away in private craft. To many it was merely a return home. For a large majority of the laborers of Bombay do not regard the city as their home. They come from the Deccan, from Gujarat, from Sind, to find a livelihood in Bombay, but "home" to them is where their fathers lived and they themselves were born.

At the end of the second week of October the formal announcement was made that the plague had been brought under control. Perhaps it was so. But on October 14 the officers of the municipality, who, according to their own declaration, already had their hand upon the throat of the foe, relaxed their hold, and in an extraordinary memorandum to the health officer, subsequently confirmed by the Act of October 30, decided, because of protestations on the part of tenants in Mandvie Ward who objected to compulsory isolation, that the terms of the Notification ostensibly compelling segregation "should not be stringently put into force," as its provisions wounded the religious feelings of the community, and many petitions on the subject had been sent to the commissioner. In fact, inflammatory placards had appeared in the city, tending to excite the hostility of the people against the government, while articles of the same sort were constantly appearing in the public native press, some of them ascribed to members of the corporation. Letters on the subject appeared daily in the papers. The Act of October 30 declared that "no case where proper segregation and treatment can be carried out on the premises will be removed to the Arthur Road Hospital," and that the health officer had been "instructed accordingly." Then in the first week of November formal instructions were issued to all the executive officers of the municipality not to execute "stringently" the Notification of October 6.

With the order not to interpret this Notification stringently, that is, to interpret it loosely, there was an immediate cessation of all attempts to segregate in the hospital or isolate at home. There was no case where (in the judgment of the family) "proper segregation" could not be effected at home. In fact, any other segregation was regarded as improper. Only waifs went to the hospital. So ended all segregation, and instantly the death-rate increased.

The last week of October had shown the result of segregation quietly discountenanced, but the mortality of November and December showed the effect of its formal discontinuance. There was an ostentatious report of "marked improvement" recorded on October 24, before the order for segregation had been really rescinded. Thereafter there was a steady increase in the deaths from plague.

It was most unfortunate, in view of the imperative necessity for segregation, that just this measure was most repugnant to the natives. They loathe the hospital. To eat food prepared by foreigners is sinful. Those cared for by outsiders become out-castes. The natives felt themselves outraged at every point. Their houses, when they were cleansed, were entered by Mahars, whose touch and presence are contamination. They themselves were carried to a strange place to be attended to by polluting strangers. The ignorant masses knew nothing of sanitation, but they knew their own ancient customs and laws. To them all the decent etiquette of life and the religion of their social intercourse were at stake. It is not too much to say that the members of the chief native communities would rather have seen their dearest relations die than have suffered them to be examined by inspectors or taken to a hospital. And what they felt for others they felt for themselves. To be removed from those who alone in their estimation could with propriety attend to them was the passage not only to humiliation, but even to an indignity worse than death. And they proved this by their acts. The patients at the hospital, though they knew that they would starve without it, spit up the food forced upon them. Several attempted to kill themselves. But it was in the case of *purdahs*, the "curtained" women, that the national feeling was most outraged. That a stranger should touch such a woman, handle her, whose face even no man save her husband had been allowed to see, was to them as terrible as would be to us the extreme affront of woman's modesty, even the violation of her honor. This is, in fact, the only analogy that represents correctly the sentiment of the Indian in respect of medical examination. When inspection was insisted on without due regard to his feelings, there was not lacking the stern act that seemed the only means of escape. Thus at a later date one native, whose wife was publicly inspected on the northern frontier (not in Bombay, as was erroneously stated in the papers), deeming no relief possible, drew his knife and stabbed her to the heart, then smote the inspector, and tried to kill himself. We may say, "What fanaticism! What bigotry!" but it is simply the persuasion of convention long fixed as a moral law, and it cannot lightly be set aside. Between sanitation and the *purdah*, however, there is no reason to find only a dilemma to be abandoned. For woman physicians would answer both the requirements of modern life and the demands of the natives.

There is, moreover, but one way to meet a plague in India, and that is to have the different communities segregated in their own hospitals, the women under the care of women alone. Yet in Bombay there was no inspection of women by women at this time; there was but one general hospital for epidemic diseases. The suggestion had indeed been made early in October that a special hospital should be built in accordance with the social requirements of the country; but the municipal commissioner refused to consider it, on the ground that the plague was already under control. The first private hospitals were started, that is, subscribed for, about the first of November; but the city authorities had nothing to do with these.

But there occurred on October 16 an incident which, strange in itself, redoubled in its effect the fear of the native in regard to segregation. Before this he expected death as the alternative to being fed by strangers; but now he feared lest these strangers should kill him. He believed, in fact, that he was carried to the hospital for one reason only, in order that he might be tortured and cruelly slain.

At the south end of the Esplanade, where the road leading to the Apollo Bunder[1] meets the road to the Secretariat, there stands a noble statue of the Queen, gift of the Gaekwar of Baroda. It is a familiar sight to Europeans, — a thing to be seen by the stranger. But to many amongst the natives it was a sort of idol, for to them the Queen Empress of India herself was the image of divinity, a view held not by the uneducated alone, but by the more religious of the half-educated Hindus; for according to their law-books the ruling power is the visible person of the Divine, whether the ruler

[1] Anglicized, with popular etymology, from Palva (Pala) Bandar, "boat-harbor."

be native or foreign. But in other cases also, as in that of great men to whom statues are erected, the uneducated, whether Mohammedans or Hindus, look upon the statue as the effigy of a sacred person, and sometimes put offerings of fruit and flowers before it, as the latter do on the shrines of gods, and the former on the tombs of saints.

It was, therefore, not only with a feeling of indignation on the part of the Europeans, but with a thrill of horror as at a sacrilege on the part of the mass of the population, that the inhabitants of the city learned that on the night of October 16 some miscreant had injured and disgraced this statue of the Queen. In the night it had been daubed with tar and around the neck had been hung a string of native slippers, adding deepest insult to irreparable injury. It was supposed at that time that the tarring of the statue was the outcome of disaffection created by the sanitary measures just adopted. The perpetrator of the deed was not discovered, but the act made a deeper impression on Bombay than the mutilation of the Hermes once did on Athens. For from that time on strange rumors were ever afloat in regard to the object of segregation. Before long, in utter oblivion of the fact that the plague had been established in the city before this rascally deed was done, it was repeated about, and firmly believed by the many, that the plague had been sent by the Queen Empress in revenge for the insult offered to her statue, and that they who were taken to the hospital were taken there to suffer her divine revenge. In accordance with ordinary Oriental notions in regard to the punishment of traitors *en masse*, the native population conceived out of their own imaginings the fearful idea that the Queen had demanded to see the livers of thirty thousand inhabitants of Bombay as the sign of the death of that number of male victims. They said that patients were bled to death in the hospital, being hung head downwards on hooks; that their livers were cut out even before they died, and that their bodies were hacked to pieces afterwards.

Other stories, too, were widely spread about. One physician reported that his poor patients believed that the doctors in the hospital deliberately poisoned the sick to prevent the growth of the plague. That this tale contradicted the theory of revenge made, of course, no difference in the eagerness with which it was received and disseminated. Then it became known amongst the people that blackmail was practised by some *badmashes*, or knaves, who in the guise of officials would threaten to have their victim taken to the hospital unless he paid them *cherry-merry* (that is, a bribe) to be silent. The common people immediately came to the conclusion that every inspector who tried to get a patient to the hospital was a blackmailer posing as an officer. Moreover, they regarded municipal physicians, especially the European, as in league with the hospital to avenge the Queen, and would not call in any one to attend the sick.

One of the most interesting superstitions connected with the hospital was the revival in Bombay of the ancient and widespread belief in *momiai*, or the efficiency of blood in welding together the foundations of new buildings. The Hindus were wont of old to kill and bury under new foundations of bridges, houses, or towns a certain number of victims, and to this day when a bridge is building in parts of northern India, as was reported on this occasion by various correspondents in the newspapers, the natives keep their children out of sight lest their bodies be used as *momiai*. The victims are supposed to be stewed, the top of the brew being placed on the foundation. This is *mom-i-ai*. The word is Persian, and designated originally a kind of mineral pitch ("wax"). In Bombay it was said by the vulgar that the hospital-patients were used to make *momiai* for bridges washed away in the last monsoon.

Besides such idle tales, the belief was prevalent, even amongst the half-educated and universally amongst the ignorant, that unless the relatives kept constant watch of their sick, the removal of the latter to the hospital precluded in all cases not only every further meeting, but also all further information in regard to the patient. And in some cases it was true that the patients were burned or buried without information being given to the family.

Toward the end of October, riots began to be as frequent as were prayers in September.

The Arthur Road Hospital, at that time the only hospital for plague-patients in the city, is situated not far from a large mill, somewhat back from the road, in a large compound[1] (yard) near the race-course, about half-way between Jacob's Circle and De Lisle Road. The yard is protected by a wooden gate at the entrance to the compound, and by glass-tipped masonry walls. On the afternoon of October 28, a riotous mob tried to force an entrance, but they were repulsed, extra police having been called in, and on this occasion no damage was done, though it was said that the mob consisted of at least five hundred mill-hands. These mill-hands, owing to the blackmail practised particularly upon them, and to their organized hate of the hospital, were the most dangerous element opposed to the execution of sanitary laws.

The next morning passed quietly enough, but at noon another crowd assembled, this time numbering about a thousand, and demanded the reason for the presence of the yellow hospital-van in front of the building. It was subsequently said that the hour and absurdity of the pretext for violence showed that there had been no premeditation on the part of the rioters, who were mill-hands coming from work for their nooning. The sight of the hated van probably acted as a spur to their sluggishly ugly temper, and the appearance of the vehicle, which was not only rough and uncomfortable, but also of a forlorn aspect, was indeed not likely to allay the wrath of any one prone to criticise the Health Department. For it was the saddest-looking cart that ever carried dying men to their death, and the complaint that in the case of weak patients its jolting hastened dissolution was not altogether unfounded. The municipality did not even soften its roughness with rubber tires, which the general government, when at a later date it took control of everything, immediately did, as it per-

[1] Anglicized from *kompong*, enclosure.

formed also many other gentle acts calculated to soothe instead of irritate.

But the cart of death at the door of the human shambles, for so the people named the van and hospital respectively, was pretext enough; and had the crowd discovered what was actually the fact, that at that very moment the van contained the body of one of their own number, a mill-hand stricken with plague, there would doubtless have been much more trouble. But what occurred was that their attention was first distracted by the coming of another crowd from another mill. The few Sepoys (police) on the scene, scenting danger, attempted to keep the two gangs from joining in front of the hospital. But in vain, and the two bands next became one mob. But they did not injure the Sepoys very much, being not yet fully aroused, and having no particular quarrel with them, their own countrymen. So they let the police off easily with a few blows, and were crafty enough even to allow them to arrest one or two individuals. For with these prisoners the Sepoys' hands were full, and they could do no more. But the two mobs, amicably united, now rushed at the gate-keeper, and by stoning him (they were otherwise unarmed) effected an entrance into the compound. Now, in the hospital besides the patients there were only the few native assistants allotted by the municipality to help the one doctor who was employed to do all the medical work; for the hospital was not only in a very insanitary condition, but it was miserably equipped, and one doctor was all the staff.[1]

The one doctor was not present. His Hindu assistants came forward bravely enough, but being greeted with the ferocious cry, "We will kill you as you would kill us," they naturally retreated, some to the dispensary and some to the back yard. But they acted for the best as they saw it, and

[1] The mortality of plague-patients at the hospital when most crowded, in December and January, was 74.12 per cent., as against 65.50 per cent., the average when not crowded. The hospital was a disgrace to civilization; but till February it was not even subjected to criticism.

characteristically telephoned, not to the police, as any but a native would have done, but to their chief, the health officer, and inquired what was to be done in circumstances so unusual, for they had never been instructed as to the proper procedure when people threatened to kill them. But the health officer rang up the police. Meantime the mob made an assault on the hospital; though, being cowardly, they only stoned it. Nevertheless, as there was a ridge ventilator and holes in the roof besides, and stones fell thick, several patients were wounded, and in the end one man, who was not very ill and would not have died otherwise, having been struck severely, perished of the wounds. So the mob hurt only their own friends, but they stole whatever they could find, till armed policemen, and amongst them forty cavalrymen, arrived before they could do further damage.

A direct raid on the police took place the same day on Tardeo Road, where late in the afternoon some five hundred mill-hands attacked two native policemen. The latter were supposed to be municipal officers engaged in ferreting out plague-cases and were at first merely accosted angrily. But when they explained that they were Sepoys off duty and going home, the mob thought they were trying to escape, and set upon them. An inspector interfered, but idly, and when one of the mill-owners came to the rescue and hid the men in a wooden *chowky* on the mill premises, the crowd grew furious and attempted to kill them. By a wise prevision on the part of the government no native may bear arms of any sort, so that even a crowd can do little against armed men, and usually it suffices to summon only a few Sepoys to rout a mob of a thousand. The Sepoys were at once summoned. But this day the mill-hands refused to disperse when the foot-police came, and the latter attacked the rioters without avail. Then the mounted police arrived. Yet the mob resisted even the horse, who to be sure went at them rather gingerly at first. But at last the troopers, becoming angry in their turn (for they had been beaten back and the whole mob was stoning them and two of their number were badly hurt by the workmen), rallying again, rode the malcontents down, and quickly pacified them after the English fashion.

This was a lesson which it is a pity was not generalized. But apparently the English were shy of arousing hostile action and dreaded fanaticism. They had seen a little of it three years previously, when their cannon had to sweep the streets of Bombay and kill some natives in a race-riot; and besides, there are some who still talk of '57 and think all that may come back again; while there are others who believe that sympathy is better than force. And on occasion this is so, but never when sympathy may be mistaken for fear. With a mob and with fanatics force is best and kindest in the end. But at first the English bungled the whole business, not so much as to mobs as in regard to all their recalcitrant subjects. For, to begin with, they forced the natives into the hospital without sympathy for their prejudices, and then sympathized so with their prejudices that they used no force to get them into the hospital, and this, too, after the natives had threatened. So the latter naturally concluded that bluster would prevail, as it did for some time. But the lower classes of Hindus, both real Hindus and Mohammedans, can be controlled easily enough if they are convinced that their rulers will stand no nonsense, as was shown in the spring. As long as they think otherwise they will resist, for they are like children.

The situation in Bombay, however, was extremely difficult, and while it is easy to criticise, it was harder to manage. For though the officials were English and affairs might have gone better had they insisted on modern methods, yet the government itself was in the hands of the natives, who, though they were educated men, did nothing in an enlightened spirit, but sided with the ignorance of their own people, openly protesting and secretly instigating resistance against every civilized means of meeting such a crisis. And so it was all over the country; for the native editors also tried to influence opinion against reform and against the English, the two being grouped together. But probably there was more than bigotry in all this, for in Poona things finally reached such a pass that the plague was openly utilized for a little bubble of sedition. This collapsed, however, at the first prick of power, though not before an English officer had been murdered.

Before the events of the next months are reviewed it will be necessary to consider a few statistics. By the end of October about eighty thousand people had fled the city and thus slightly diminished the total population, on which is reckoned the average death-rate of preceding years. The year of plague was remarkably free from other infectious diseases. Few cholera cases or small-pox cases and no epidemic of any kind except the plague occurred during the whole winter in the city, though small-pox was common in the country and country cholera cases also were often enough reported. It will, therefore, be an entirely reasonable assumption that the increase in mortality apart from that due to the plague was not greater than that in the years before, especially as the latter was reckoned on a full population and the former is taken from a population rapidly diminishing. In the autumn of 1896 the total mortality for a week will then represent the average mortality plus the plague mortality, if allowance be made for an increase of about two thousand deaths for the whole year due to other causes than the plague. But this corrected estimate is likely to be far under the truth when the population becomes appreciably diminished and may in fact be disregarded entirely from the end of September.

Some such calculation as this, rough though it be, is made necessary not only because of the fact that the health officer neglected to make any entries of deaths from plague prior to October 20, but also because of the incorrectness of the official records. Errors, if space permitted, could easily be proved by setting the official returns against the undoubted statements of physicians. In some cases it would be seen that one or two physicians reported in their own practice alone more deaths from plague in a week than the Health Office under the control of the commissioner recognized as occurring in the same week through the whole city. The only figures that can be relied upon from September to April in the official records are those giving the total mortality of each week.

In the following table the plague mortality is obtained by subtracting the "average weekly" mortality from that of the current week of 1896. The system here adopted was recognized in Bombay itself, and worked out by the Times of India, as the only one likely to give a basis for the investigation of the real mortality due to plague. To understand the table it must be remembered that the column headed Plague Mortality records the number of deaths above the average of the previous five years, for the corresponding week. This plus is about the plague mortality for the week in 1896. About 160 deaths may be subtracted in September as due to regular increase in mortality. The remarks in the right-hand column explain the figures, which, as below, are those of the Times.

| Week ending | Total Mortality. | Plague Mortality. | Remarks. |
|---|---|---|---|
| Sept. 8 | 593 | 62 | No segregation. |
| " 15 | 618 | 126 | |
| " 22 | 647 | 141 | |
| " 29 | 720 | 193 | |
| Oct. 6 | 791 | 300 | |
| " 13 | 634 | 136 | Segregation enforced. |
| " 20 | 606 | 129 | |
| " 27 | 698 | 228 | Segregation almost abandoned. |

It is unnecessary to dilate further upon the incorrectness of the official reports. A careful exposure of them was made by the editor of the Times of India from week to week as they appeared, and that journal may be consulted for details. In partial excuse for the Health Department it may be said that the municipal physicians would not recognize that true plague could exist without the bubo, so that the Department unwittingly called by other names a large number of cases of plague. But other cases were *de industria* given incorrectly by the officials, by the native physicians, and by the families of the deceased. An official acknowledgment that the municipal reports were not trustworthy was made by the municipal commissioner and the police officer, before the standing committee of the municipal council, on December 30. It seems otiose to take other testimony. In regard to the numbers leaving the city, tables carefully compiled by the Chamber of Commerce eventually showed that in November, December, and January alone, 358,852 people in excess of the usual numbers left Bombay by rail and steamer alone. Previous to the publication of these tables there was only the haphazard statement of the municipal commissioner to go upon, who confidently stated that "only a few thousands" had left the city. If to these three hundred and fifty thousands be added the unknown thousands fleeing in September and October, the more than a thousand a day that were still fleeing in February, and the uncounted numbers that slipped away in carts and private boats all through the winter, the commissioner's estimate will appear at its true value. There is unfortunately no confidence to be placed in any statement made by the municipal officers of Bombay in regard to the plague. The official records consist in careless errors and deliberate falsifications. Oddly enough, this appears to have been the opinion of the very officer who was responsible for these misleading reports. For when the plague first broke out, the health officer, knowing that every one was asking why the city was in a condition so insanitary, and being eager to screen himself, formulated a bill of indictments against the municipal commissioner, in which he charged the latter with neglecting the useful advice given him heretofore, and alleged that he himself, the health officer, had in years past vainly urged several points; to wit, the completion of the drainage, the flushing of gullies, and the *non-acceptance of the evidence of municipal officers.* There were other minor points, but none so important as the last.

The beginning of November was looked forward to very anxiously. The weather was normal, but the plague, which had already fastened on seventeen different districts, from Kolaba in the south to Byculla in the north, was still advancing. Its trend had been west, south, and north, and every one wondered now in which ward it would appear next, for by this time all knew that the Health Department were helpless before it, either to control it where it was or to prevent its going whither it would. The fact also, at last universally recognized, that the official reports gave no real knowledge, in respect either of the death-rate or of the direction taken by the plague, caused general apprehension. For it was seen clearly that each fresh case of plague, when entered as old age or phthisis or remittent fever, if brought from a newly infected house or ward, increased the danger to the people in the locality thus infected, in proportion as they were left ignorant of the truth. The municipal corporation were known to be averse to sanitation; the municipal commissioner had notified the town that his former Notification was not meant to be taken seriously; and the natives unanimously opposed any reconsideration of the subject.

But these were not the only grounds for fear. For it was pretended by certain of the natives that some terrible catastrophe would come upon the city during the feast of Divali, *dīpālī*, the "lamp-row-festival" in honor of Vishnu's spouse. The first and second days of this festival, at the beginning of November, were named as the days of danger. The prophecy was said by some of the Hindu and Parsee papers to have been declared by Pundit Guttoolalji; while the so-called Maharaja or Guru, that is, the pontiff, of the Vallabhacarya sect of Vishnuites, Devakinanda, was also reported to have frightened the populace by foreseeing the coming disaster. Both these statements were denied by the persons implicated, but the hint of harm given by the papers was enough. The common people believed that some untoward event, even greater than the plague, was about to happen, and that, in the quaint imagery of the Orient, "the Sirkar (imperial government) had withdrawn its umbrella from over their heads."

As a foretaste of new trouble, three great conflagrations occurred in the city. They were regarded as ominous. As Divali drew near, the crowds of terrified natives fleeing from town exceeded every precedent. They that were well went, taking with them, if they could, their sick; and many plague-patients easily succeeded in escaping the notice of the officials, for the rush to be saved was greater than the police could oppose. Every train was full, and every steamer; private craft and bullock-carts took away thousands.

Ordinarily, Divali is celebrated with brilliant illuminations. Lamps are burning everywhere, fireworks are set off, the whole town is a blaze of light. This year it was to be a dark failure. Fear reigned. One fiction fought another. Now the story was rife that there was to be a general slaughter of the native inhabitants, ordered by the Sirkar to avenge the Queen for the insult to her statue. Again the Bazaar (native town) was horrified by specific prophecies of earthquakes and universal ruin to take place during the festival. Scarcely an hour passed that some fresh rumor did not terrify the Indian's credulous heart as he heard of new woes coming. Before the fatal days arrived (November 2 and 3), in fact, before the month began, half the population had left town, while half of them that remained trembled because they had not done likewise. When Divali dawned the natives hardly dared to breathe.

But the days of harm passed harmlessly. No earthquake shook the island; there was no massacre of natives; and the children of the Orient breathed again. Half of them that had fled without preparation in the final panic returned within a week and packed their things together, encouraged, but ready to flee again at a moment's warning.

The death-rate increased steadily. About a quarter of the population was gone from town. Silent witnesses to this fact were the empty houses, empty streets, wellnigh empty wards. Shops began to be closed everywhere; the busiest lanes were still. An irregular exodus began again. Long processions passed through the streets. They consisted of refugees escaping in a slow unbroken stream. Most of them were unable to read English; they did not know that the official reports were most encouraging. They knew only that their friends and neighbors were dying as they had never died before, and that plague ruled the town. So passed November's dreary days.

But Mandvie Ward was now free of disease. No death had occurred since November 21. The health officer said that he had got control of that district. As a matter of fact the plague had killed those whom it had caught and the rest of the inhabitants had run away. The whole ward was practically deserted. There was nothing more there for the plague and it went elsewhere.

The heaviest mortality in the city was among the Mahars first (the cleansers of filth), and then the Jains, who now died at a greater rate than did the Mohammedans. Till the end of January the mortality among the Mohammedans remained higher than among the Hindus.

The city corporation, who were pleased to shift upon the health officer the blame for apathy in the past and ignorance in the present, signalized their appreciation of the gravity of the situation by creating toward the end of November eight new health officers. But they did no good, for they were subordinates. The hospital at this time was strengthened by the appointment of some new assistants. Six assistant surgeons were also appointed. A sub-committee already had in hand the re-organization of the Health Department, but the corporation did not wait for its report, for in this week the mortality was 760, or 314 above the average. By this time most of the native medical men had run away. The native members of the corporation also ran away to the hills for safety, returning to town only to attend the meetings. The loquacious leaders of the people, the orators against segregation, took to flight, too. Holding the fort was left to the English. November's record is as follows:

| Week ending | Total Mortality. | Plague Mortality. |
|---|---|---|
| Nov. 3 | 668 | 225 |
| " 10 | 623 | 174 |
| " 17 | 704 | 242 |
| " 24 | 760 | 314 |

To explain the higher death-rate, the Health Department, amongst other curiosities of statistics, gave 127 deaths in the week ending November 24 to phthisis alone, double the usual amount, though reputable doctors knew of no increase in that disease. According to the same official authority, 161, more than double the average, died of remittent fever in the week ending November 17, and just 161 in the next week. This monotonous disease had already carried off 107 people in the week ending November 3, and just 107 again in the week ending November 10. But, as I have said, epidemic diseases other than the plague were rarer than usual. The plague seemed to absorb every other illness. The fewer deaths in the week after Divali are due to the tumult of exodus at the last minute and the slow return in the next few days of half those who had gone. The figures represent a sudden drop in the population.

Though segregation was officially abolished, inspection was not. Concealment of cases was still regularly practised. No punishment rewarded the concealer when the act was discovered.

By the beginning of the next month there were about forty-five deaths a day from plague. One physician alone treated one hundred cases in the first week of winter.

December was a month of terror. In the first week the mortality was the greatest ever known in the city, exceeding even that of any week of the great famine of 1877. From 772 deaths (plague mortality, 315, the record for the week ending December 1), the mortality rose to 1051, an increase of 279 in one week, and 591 above the average taken on a full population. Even official returns recorded 55 deaths in one day from bubonic fever. The daily average due to plague was really about 84. An appeal was made that segregation might be tried again, but the municipal commission, despite signs of yielding on the part of some of the natives, made no effort to re-introduce the measure. Kamatipur, which with its 30,000 inhabitants had now taken the place of Mandvie as the headquarters of the Great Death, more than quadrupled its mortality in eight days, and soon there were few houses in the whole district that had not the red ring of death upon their front. The commissioner in this month had ordered the red ring to be painted upon every house where a death from plague occurred. Some of the houses had half a dozen such rings. Later on some had many more than this. One had more than thirty. Deaths from other causes were marked with a cross. For every cross appeared a dozen rings.

By the middle of the month, the different sects of Jains, Parsees, Hindus, and Mohammedans, had committees in hand to see to the erection of special sectarian hospitals, which the more enlightened leaders of the different communities had persuaded them to agree to as a substitute for the hated Arthur Road Hospital. The Jain hospital was ready first, early in the month. The Parsee hospital was formally opened on December 18. Some of these hospitals, however, were long in building and all were long in filling, for the natives did not like them. That of the Khojas was not ready till March; that of the Bhatias was not even begun till then. These hospitals, though that of the Parsees was better built and well appointed, were usually cheap buildings of mats and bamboo. Voluntary segregation was now recommended even by the natives, though at a meeting held December 11 they still protested against enforced segregation. Voluntary segregation was, in point of fact, all that was necessary, but the trouble was that it could not be enforced! Very few went into the "voluntary" hospitals. The Governor placed at the disposal of the municipality the park connected with the Government House at Parel for use as a place to build temporary hospitals; and subsequently an annex to the Arthur Road Hospital was erected there. But neither the commissioner nor the health officer liked these voluntary hospitals. They sniffed at Parel park and said it was "insanitary." The corporation did nothing to encourage even voluntary segregation. In all this time of bitter distress the native members did not raise one finger to aid or instruct their fellow-citizens. Some were apathetic; some were intolerant of sanitary reform. They met to jest and denounce sanitation. Not a single radical measure was inaugurated by them during the whole course of the winter.

The commissioners on December 16 asked for and, of course, obtained one hundred and fifty thousand rupees in addition to the original one hundred thousand granted on October 5. The Health Department still continued to oppose segregation, flush drains, and shovel up the filth of the last ten years. The corporation were at length induced to pass a resolution, December 17, to remove the town sweepings to Chimbore, instead of emptying them into the harbor. But the corporation did no more. They could not, at any rate, decide how to effect this reform, and, in fact, never did anything more about it till months afterwards, when the Governor told them that they must.

The plague struck further north. Localities hitherto unaffected now fell into its power. Outside of the city, sundry new towns of the Presidency reported that plague had appeared. To the south, Poona, the rest of the Deccan, and even the Mysore territory beyond it; to the north, Thana, Broach, Ahmedabad, Karachi, — were now infected. In Goa the authorities decreed as a sanitary measure that the bodies of all who had died of plague should be burned, not buried, whether Hindus, Mohammedans, Jews, or Christians.[1] The Patriarch Archbishop thundered against the law as unchristian, and the Mohammedan howled. But the law stood for a time and plague obtained no great hold there, till the Archbishop's thunder at last frightened the authorities. They yielded the point. Then the plague increased in Goa.

This question touched Bombay also. Intramural graves, often not covered with earth enough to prevent the jackal's robbery, sometimes but a few inches deep, seldom more than

[1] Only the Hindus, and not all of them, burn their dead. The Parsees expose them on the Towers. Some poor Hindus bury the dead, as do the Mohammedans. Cremation is often waived in the case of venerated Hindus, Swamis and the like, and their tombs become shrines.

two and a half feet, thousands of such graves, corpses buried one on top of another, in graveyards crowded, and to a great extent over-crowded, with the corpses of plague-stricken Mohammedans, in short, a trench of shallow graves to the windward of the city from its middle to its northern limit, — such was the state of affairs in Bombay. For not only were there two such burying-grounds, one at Grant Road and one on the Queen's Road, but the low-caste Hindus that bury their dead had a third intramural ground at Haines Road. The Christianized Hindus, chiefly ignorant fishermen, had still a fourth, though undetermined ground; for they dug shallow pits near their houses and buried their dead there. For thirty years the closing of the Mohammedan grounds had been demanded in the interest of public health. The health officer himself said he thought that they "had been filled perhaps twenty times." At a later date, January 7, reference was made at a meeting of the corporation to graves where corpses were dug up and new interments made in rapid succession. The question of closing these grounds was one very vital to the interest of the city. There actually was a new ground which had been reserved for the Mohammedans for three years at Tank Bunder, but it was not made ready till late in January. Then the Mohammedans were politely asked to use it, but they angrily refused to do so. It was not till April that the ground at Grant Road was closed, but this was not done by the municipality. Even the crematory grounds were in bad condition. It was said that bodies lay unburned for days at Sonapur (December 10). The same statement was made afterwards in regard to the Worli ground, but the health officer denied it.

It was also said that the vultures of the Dakhmas or Towers of Silence, owing to the surplus of Parsee food given them in December, sometimes refused to do their office. These Towers rise like huge oil-tanks above Malabar Hill, hideous themselves but set in luxuriant beauty of scenery. The first, Kapiskhan's, can accommodate 237 bodies, and is used mainly by the Shenshai Parsees. The second, Banaji's, can accommodate as many more, and is used mainly by the Iranees and

Kadimi Parsees, though it is open to the Shenshai also. The two Towers of Anjuman and Manekji Sheth will hold 262 and 141 bodies, respectively; while the Modi's Tower is for the family of the founder only.[1] Most of the bodies are devoured on Kapiskhan's Towers. According to the report published at the time in a local paper, there are between three and four hundred vultures, but many of them were busy among the shallow graves in the neighborhood and perhaps for this reason none was so voracious as usual. Whether any dead bodies actually remained uneaten on the Towers cannot be known. The report was denied by the Parsee priests, and only Parsees are admitted to the Towers.

There was at this time and afterwards no little distress on account of the increasing lack both of those whose business it is to bear the corpses to the crematory or cemetery, and of those who there receive them. And in this distress the Parsees shared, for though they had enough *nasasalars*, who carry the corpses into the Towers, yet there were not enough *khandias*, who bring them up to the Towers. Much unhappiness was caused by this, as well as by the absence of other requisites in the final care for the deceased, and even by the cost of fuel wherewith to burn the dead. For everything was dearer than usual, owing to the famine and the lack of laborers, and so great an amount of wood was required for the consumption of so many bodies that the price rose, and the poor had often to pay their last coppers to get sufficient fuel for their need. As an indication of the scarcity that resulted from extra demand, but also as a proof of the great number that died, one religious community alone used seven and a half times as much fuel per week for burning their dead as they do ordinarily; nor was it, as compared with others, a community very heavily smitten by the plague. Moreover, this was when less fuel than usual was burned for any one funeral, since even the rich economized and the poor used only as much as decency

[1] This was the first Tower built in the city, in 1670. Two more are mentioned by Dr. Da Cunha, Origin of Bombay, p. 299, where Kapiskhan appears as Kapuskao, and Anjuman's Tower bears a different name.

required, and when the city was emptied of many of its inhabitants.

For between the middle of December and its awful close some third of the natives had again left town. In many ways this was the most painful as well as the most exciting period in the progress of the plague. For the mortality leaped up higher and higher as the colder weather strengthened the malady, and all classes were fleeing, the wealthy with the poor. The latter packed their little bundles, and with their goods on their head and their children in their arms went out for the last time, some, already infected, to die of the plague, some to subsist on charity, some to starve, and some to live on hoarded or borrowed money, till spring and the decline of the disease moved them to return. But some, and amongst them even former policemen of the town, became robbers and added to the terrors of the year of plague and famine by swelling the bands of dacoits, brigands, who, during this winter especially, ravaged the country from Delhi to Hyderabad.

But the wealthy natives who hitherto had lingered (because they feared to leave their houses and goods in a city so hampered and undone), now fearing death more as it stood more imminent, sent their valuables to the bank and hired houses in the suburbs, Andheri and Thana, and in other more distant places up and down the coast or in the hill-country, whither they removed their families, servants, furniture, and horses, settling down for what length of time the plague should remain. And the vaults of the banks became so crowded with safes and boxes that no more goods could be received.

By Christmas time every suburb about Bombay was overfilled, and there was not a house in the Konkan to be had for quintuple its ordinary rent. Then no houses remained to be rented for any money, unless one fugitive bought another off who had rented an asylum before him, and he gave forty-fold the rent given by the former tenant. Many of the poor could find no refuge at all. Even sleeping-room on a veranda in a suburb that was deemed healthy cost more for a night than a poor man earned in a week.

The last week of the old year (but chiefly the first month of the new) was marked by the spread of panic among the mill-hands, who, though contumelious and aggressive in respect of compulsory segregation, had in some instances consented to make use of safety camps of tents or *cadjan* (huts of bamboo and matting). The mills, being well ventilated, large, and kept in sanitary order, were particularly free from plague, and no special panic had hitherto arisen, as there had been no unusual number of deaths amongst the hands. Yet they remained not so much because they were not afraid as because they could not get their money. For it is the practice at all times to hold back the pay of the mill-hands for a whole month, in order to ensure their remaining till substitutes can be got. But in this year, in view of the fact that operatives who did not wish to die of the plague might be tempted to sacrifice their month's pay and leave without warning, the overseers kept back the pay for two whole months. And the same trick was played on the hotel servants also by their masters. But the mill-hand thus treated was in a very bad way. For ordinarily he lives without any store of money, but the Marwaris,[1] or money-lenders, and certain usurious grain-dealers called *shroffs*, knowing him and the circumstances, usually lend him grain to eat and even advance him small sums as he needs from day to day. And at the end of the month their agent is present at the gate when the man is paid and takes from him what is owing, and the interest, before he can spend it. But now the *shroffs* and Marwaris had closed their shops and fled from the city, and the poor mill-hand whose pay was not paid could find no one to lend him grain or money, for even regular usurers would not lend to one whose wage was held back for so long, since he could give no security and might die of plague the next day.

The mill-hands, therefore, agitated for daily pay, or at least for pay at the end of the month. One mill actually paid at the end of a month, but the next day it came near to closing,

[1] Literally, "people of Marwar," but used as a common noun to designate small money-lenders.

for most of the hands, to escape plague and debts, had decamped in the night. But the other mills refused. Moreover, the native managers themselves fled from the plague, and this added discouragement and new fear to the anger of the workmen, so that some fled, giving up all their pay, and some, thinking it as well to die of plague as of starvation, remained to agitate for their claim of daily paid wage. By the end of the first week of January, forty thousand spindles had stopped, and it seemed probable that in a few days more a quarter of a million skilled workmen would join those who had fled, and like the latter be begging for their life, or working for two annas a day as charity-laborers on relief-works in the country. The mill-owners, however, eventually managed to keep a large number of them, for though the former mutually agreed (January 26) not to yield to the men's demands, yet as each owner was more willing to cut the others' throats and save himself than abide by his pledge, sundry of them secretly yielded and gave daily pay. But this resulted only in the rapid exchange of good workmen for bad, since in the increasing panic the old hand would often flee at the day's end and some raw workman would be put in his place to bungle and break. But enough remained to avert a general closing of the mills, though the agitation of the men caused a great deal of trouble. The whole matter, however, belongs rather to January, though the agitation began in December. The rights of it seemed to lie with the men, though, indeed, to grant the demands made by them would doubtless have resulted badly for the mills. But if the owners, considering the great scarcity, had themselves lent food or money to the workmen and raised their pay a little, the latter would probably have remained. But the owners and stockholders appeared to think differently.

The end of December, when plague and famine ruled the town, was to many the breaking point of an endurance long strained but firm till then. In the case of countless artisans and domestic servants, the usurer now ruled them as the viceroy of famine. For in India, servants find themselves, and the workmen, all living from hand to mouth, suffer most on a rise of prices and are driven to the usurer. But they have to pay him 180 per cent. interest and in reality more, for after a little time they are unable to reckon this (compound) interest and must take his word for what is due to him. But when once the usurer has the man he never lets him go, and even in ordinary years most of the servants and workmen, both in town and country, are in this bondage (I inquired particularly and found this to be the case everywhere). Whence it happens that all the poor man gets he gives to the usurer, save what little is requisite for him to live on till another pay-day. But in this year, with the *shroffs* gone, who are concealed usurers, it was still worse, since the poor were so completely in the hands of the money-lender that they could not live without him; and there was great distress amongst all the wage-earners. Then, too, because their *shroffs* had fled, even the *halalkhores* early in January threatened to go on a strike, but the intervention of their *muccadums* — that is, the bosses of the gangs of workmen — prevented this calamity, which would have been serious, for had the *halalkhores* left town there would have been none to cleanse it.

Before the year ended, Bombay was in all respects a most woful city. Little discomforts filled up the crevices between big sorrows to make one solid block of misery. The wheels of every business were clogged. All labor was at a high premium, and to get any work done was difficult. Domestic servants left without warning; in the hotels the "boys"[1] begged for wages long due which they could not get, and then gave up the struggle in despair. The coolies and carters were few; the barbers and the *dhobis* or washermen were hard to find, and the latter were not to be depended on even when found, for they would die on the clothes they had taken to wash, and both linen and *dhobi* would be burned. The regular purveyors of the city, — milkmen, butchers, bakers, and the like, — had run away in large numbers; industries were stopped; trade was almost at a standstill. The cloth-shops and grocery-shops of the *vanias* were bare storehouses; the piece-

[1] Anglicized from *bhâi*, "brother" (fellow, and so servant).

goods merchants had practically shut up. The shops of the yarn-merchants, of the metal-merchants, of the merchants of brocade, of silk, of goldware and silverware, stood empty all day. The booksellers of the Kalbadevi Road put up their shutters. None bought what was not absolutely requisite. The laughing bazaars were now like cemeteries. Distress came with especial hardness upon the clever workmen, whose wares attract both the fashion of Bombay and the taste of tourists. The gay world bought no gewgaws; a few tourists had indeed come, but almost none remained. Most of them had fled from the country; nearly all were gone to safer towns at least. Momba Devi[1] protected her children no more, and the workers in brass and copper had naught to do. The carvers of sandal-wood, of blackwood, and of ivory, the fine craftsmen in gold and silver, all these could but starve or flee.

Now too began the on-fall of "quick" cases of plague, such as obtained in Karachi when the disease first broke out there. The hale laborer suddenly died at his work; the runner dropped upon the street; the servant in good health an hour before expired at his master's side. The policeman fell dead on the corner; the bearer of the corpse became a corpse.

The number of funerals was dreadful to witness. They never ceased. To burial or to fire, the dead were borne every hour, and these swift journeys (for the frightened bearers ran with their load) continued day after day for weeks together. In the second week of January an observer saw enter one graveyard no less than a funeral a minute, and the crowded pyres of the dead were always burning.

[1] The Mother Goddess of Bombay (Momba), whose title of Great still remains in the name of the district Mahim. Momba Devi district in the present town includes the copper bazaar. Da Cunha says the name of the town was spelled both as Mombaym and Bombaym. Momba was a Kôli (Dravidian) autochthonous divinity. Her old temple on the Esplanade has been razed. The modern one has shrines to Çiva and other (Aryan) deities, as well as to Momba-devi. Mahim, however, was afterwards settled by the Prabhus of Gujarat, and their Aryan temple was sacred to Prabhadevi. But her present abode is in turn shared by older deities, Çitaladevi and Khokaladevi, the goddesses of small-pox and of cough, respectively.

It was not strange that in the excitement weird thoughts and fancies obsessed even the soberer citizens. Where segregation-camps were the only hope of safety, faddists among the English prevented unanimity by raising one objection after another and proposing all sorts of absurd panaceas. Some queried, and it was gravely debated, whether the whole principle of segregation, as hitherto understood, should not be inverted. "Segregate the healthy," they cried; "let the sick stay where they are. Isolate all the hale members of the community, put them under guard, confine them to certain districts." One sage laid the whole trouble to the Flats and wished to have these five hundred acres of filth piled with wood, to be burned for a healthy covering. Others seriously desired in December to consume Bombay itself with fire, apart from certain localities. This suggestion was renewed in January. At that time, Malabar Hill, Camballa Hill, the Docks, the Marine Lines, Tardeo, the Market, Upper Kolaba, the Mill Districts, the Esplanade, and a few groups of buildings, like the Grant Buildings, were fairly free of plague. It was proposed to burn down the whole city with the exception of these, chiefly outlying, parts, all the citizens to act as firemen to guard the rest of the town. Another proposal was to "establish a general funk" by means of inflammatory placards and proclamation by *bakari*, that is, by drum and crier, among the illiterate, as if there were not sufficient fright already. But the proposer of this scheme argued that too few natives had fled, that the sole means of safety was in laying the plague as it had been laid in Mandvie Ward by giving the foe no food. If all the inhabitants were to flee, the plague would be starved out. So all talked, but nothing was done.

The deaths still increased daily in number. By the end of the third week of December, the total weekly mortality was 1416, with 946 as the mortality due to plague. The next week, ending December 29, the plague mortality alone was about the same as the total mortality of the week before.

The health officer had at last concluded that a house-to-house inspection was imperative (as indeed it was), but when he found that his department could not attend to this and disinfect the slums, and that native officers were not obeyed by the people, he called on the British, namely, the Bombay Artillery Volunteers, for the delicate and dangerous work. Without hesitation they accepted the risk and went unquestioningly from house to house, from *chawl* to *chawl*, arguing, persuading, and insisting on the necessity not only of sanitation, but in some instances of proper isolation. For the peril of the hour forced one fear to yield to another, and cases were now quietly segregated even against expostulation, — a task rendered easier by the fact that most of the native agitators had run away, leaving their poor compatriots to settle the question of segregation or death as best they might. The work of the Volunteers began on the first day of the new year, and as the Health Department had left them to their own devices, they were able to enforce of their own Sahib authority the principle so long neglected. Much honor is due to them, as their act was a willing offering of health and life. For at this time, though Europeans had not been much attacked, yet no one supposed that they were immune, since there was no dearth of fatal cases which, through kindly consideration for the bereaved, had been reported as deaths of Europeans, though most of them were in reality amongst Eurasian or half-breed families; nor was it possible to suppose that any one could enter the haunt of plague, and labor scathless there for many days. But that is what these young Englishmen did; for they went personally into the dismal chambers that the Health Department had not touched, and face to face with the plague, in the presence of its dead and dying, despite resistance on the part of those whom they would save, let air and light into the foul darkness. In many cases they found it necessary to remove roof-tiles and break holes for the admission of these unknown luxuries. Then they cleaned what had never been cleaned, inspected the inmates, removed the sick and the concealed dead, and did otherwise all that ought to have been done before.

The Volunteers made some distressing discoveries, cases of

plague uncared for and bodies of plague patients dead for days but still concealed, while the relatives, fearing segregation for themselves and the destruction of their effects, waited a favorable opportunity to take the corpse in secret from the house. Ghastly efforts were made by the natives to hide their dead. The corpse would be covered up in a corner, or even held up to be counted as a live inmate of the dark hole where the family lived.

But with the renewed suggestion of segregation there came new fright into the simple heart of the natives, whom plague, famine, blackmail, usury, and the fear of gods already tormented, and when they found that they themselves were ill, or one of their family, they would on the instant leave everything to escape from the city, so that even their dead, of whom they are usually very careful, were abandoned in blind terror; and if, as they fled with him from town, the sick one died, they left the body in the street.

But in the case of those who did not try to escape, it was pitiful to see them and hear their agony, whenever one of the family fell ill in the house and was carried away to the hospital. For even when the victims were women or children, although in their case no great fear of the Queen's anger was entertained, yet the excitement was intense, as the relatives clustered about the door, wailing with all the extravagance of Oriental woe. But when it was the husband and the father, and they thought that his death was certain, if not from the plague then by the knife of the Queen's servants in the hospital, the despair of the mourners soon got beyond all control. Such little tragedies occurred daily, and one which I saw myself I will speak of, though it is impossible to depaint the distress of the unhappy creatures and the sadness of the scene.

For not only did all the relatives come out and accompany the sick man as he was borne into the street, but friends and near neighbors, who were either ignorant of danger or heedless of contagion, joined them there, and sharing in the sorrow swelled the dismal little procession, marching behind the litter and crowding beside it with weeping and all the noisy lamentation of the East. There were children in the family and three women, two old hags and one younger and not uncomely, and they all came out and were joined by about a score of friends who escorted them. For a little way they went forward uttering piercing shrieks and invoking vainly the sick man to return and the bearers to give him back to his dear ones, that they might be beside him when he died. But the bearers and the police, who were also there, advanced unheeding, and the children, falling behind, began to play in the street. Then, however, the women of the family with streaming eyes and clasped hands began to entreat the police for mercy, calling upon all the gods, their own and the gods of those they addressed, to hear them. But after they had vainly conjured the police to go no further and seen clearly that there was no hope of their prayer prevailing, they made frantic efforts to induce them to promise kind treatment, sometimes screaming to all the officials together and sometimes fastening upon one alone, as if otherwise the authorities would be relentless in cruelty. For they besought the police to save the dying man from the knife, and let him die in peace, since he had committed no crime against the Queen; but if they would not restore him, to remember to tend him well, and do this and that for him; with many incoherent cries besides. But the one that was about to die, and this was of all the strangest part of the scene, remained perfectly still, or at the most moved only his lips, as if (as they are wont to do when dying) he were muttering the name of his god, while he lay staring sideways at the crowd without any concern in the tumult of their despair, either because he was too weak to speak or too stricken with fear to know fully who they were that pressed around him.

But when they were come some forty yards, the police attempted to turn the throng back, not roughly, as they were often accused of doing, but with a great deal of pity and gentleness, for they themselves were not unmoved by the sight about them. Nevertheless, failing in this they finally resorted to pushing, and at last they were compelled to prohibit the passing of a certain spot, beyond which every advance on the part of the mourners was forcibly prevented. So at this point the mourners dropped behind, but though they had cried vehemently before, yet now when they were no longer permitted to see the dying man and knew that love could go no further, the passion of their anguish became so painful that even a stranger could not endure it. I was afterwards told by a Volunteer that one of his men had even fainted at just such a scene, and no wonder, for it was horrible.

But even apart from pity, the whole spectacle was strange and had something as if inhuman in it, for it seemed like the funeral of a man not yet dead. Nor could one in reality be sure that the sick man would have any other funeral when shortly, either before arriving there or as an inmate of the hospital, he actually died. For sometimes no notification of a man's death was made to the family, but unattended and uncared for his body was hurried to the grave or burned as quickly as possible.

Not the least striking part of the whole scene, however, was this, that except for the relatives and immediate friends no one seemed to notice or to care; and as the family came back to their home even they that had gone out with them left them; and their return was through groups of their nearest neighbors who yet, like the little ones that had remained behind, were already chattering and laughing on their verandas, just as if nothing had happened. For all had grown callous, and not knowing when they themselves might die paid little attention to others.

To a growing carelessness of this sort, I can testify from my own experience. For never having happened before to see such a sight, the first time I saw a man who was apparently healthy fall dead in the street I was much startled. But when I had roamed about the city for some time (for I was there off and on every month but one till the plague abated and especially during the great terror of December), I would scarcely notice such an accident. And, too, I found that the expectation of death, which at first terrifies, wears off just like one's horror of the sudden corpse; and though at first one imagines death imminent and is afraid, yet afterwards even in the midst of fancied danger one thinks nothing of it.

Men died swiftly in the dying of last year. But they did not die without another effort to be saved, and indeed, despite callousness, it was not wonderful that mortals should turn again to Heaven for relief. Already on December 8 there was an universal appeal to God made by sects the most diverse, — Hindus, Hebrews, and Mohammedans, who joined in one common procession by night, reciting prayers as they marched through the city by torchlight.

The English, too, had a special intercessory service on December 22, to pray for the decrease of the plague, but the week after the mortality rose to the highest point yet attained. Then, because no visible effect had been produced by the prayers of the English, the Mohammedans in turn resolved to pray. Two great meetings took place, but the first was merely to formulate the belief of the community in "prayer and not segregation" as the best means of extinguishing the plague. "The mosque is our hospital," was the cry. Plague was said to be the result of accumulated sin, and holy water sprinkled on a scapegoat was therefore recommended as a cure. It was resolved to hold a mass prayer-meeting in accordance with these principles, but the sacrifice of the goat was omitted and only prayers were held. On January 2 a vast crowd of Mohammedans foregathered for the event. As no building in Bombay could hold them, they met in the open. That scene, too, was one not to be forgotten. It was the end of the winter's day. Beyond the yellow margin of the Esplanade, where the blue grackles quarrelled in the grimy trees, stretched the bay-water dancing brightly, while far in the distance the Highlands to the west rose fairly purple under the low sun. Except for the birds it was very still. The noise of the city had almost ceased. The multitude had come together silently as if awed. They had been collecting all day. They gathered, dark-faced and sombre, in families and white-robed bands, slowly arranging themselves. But soon they were too numerous for distinction; only they kept, as they knelt compactly side by side, a sort of serried order. The service was begun by the principal Kazi, who first singly invoked God to avert the arrows of His pestilence. Afterwards the whole assembly united in prayer, at the beginning with sounds low and monotonous, but then louder and so in more varied tones, till when the mania of fervor had roused them fully, the excitement shrilled their voices and the prayer became a cry and then a yell like an imprecation. One would scream and stop and then another would scream, or a dozen would shriek together; and all the time they prayed, they prostrated themselves. So their bodies rose and fell in long rows like waves; while in regular movement each forehead would be bowed to the dust and then uplifted, the head thrown back, the arms extended to Heaven, the black features writhing with the intensity of their supplications. Raised a little above them on boxes and stools draped for this purpose, stood here and there the gaudy priests leading the appeal of the great host, as it bowed and rose, swaying rhythmically to the music of the chanted prayers.

For an hour they thus invoked Allah together, but as the sun struck level across the bay, each priest in turn addressed them, praising their piety and promising them in God's name speedy succor. So they prayed and were comforted; and after they had eaten all the cakes and dates that had been provided, and offered each for himself one last supplication, they departed.

Some of the Hindus also, who had already done so much for the gods, were now moved to sacrifice again. On New Year's day the wretched fishermen of Worli and Mahim, whose huts on the northern shore the plague had recently made more miserable, having resolved to do what they could to propitiate the deity of death, provided themselves out of their scanty stores (for they were starving as well as stricken by plague) with the offerings which their goddess accepts. After the sun had set they entered their boats and stood off, and when they were well away and the sudden darkness came on, they drew their craft together. Then lighting torches, which they held high aloft, they arose with one accord and prayed to Kali, at the same time casting into the sea their sacrifice, which was of milk and palm-juice and sweets. When this was done they prayed again, with what form of words I do not know surely, but it was reported the next day that they had charged the goddess to relent for the sake of her own offerings, which, if she should prove heedless of their prayers, they would never give her again. As a sign of this threat they extinguished their torches in the sea and so rowed home.

Shortly afterwards those Parsees who still lingered in town invoked also their own peculiar gods. First they had public *jasan* or intercessory prayers to the Sun, and a few days later a congregation of three hundred met together at Karelwady to beseech the mercy and protection of the various Zoroastrian divinities. Of all the rites this was in so far most interesting as it had to do with the oldest gods in India. For though the Parsees themselves have been in India only 1265 years, yet their gods are older than the Vedas; but the great gods of the modern Hindus are later, or at least they were received later into the pantheon of the ancient Hindus.

The fire-temple at which the ceremony was performed stands near the western sea. There the Parsees first offered prayers to the Sun and to Fire, and also to Mithra, who was once a sun-god, but is now an attendant divinity. Then they descended from the temple to the sea, the priests having on their richest robes and leading the procession, and there prayed to the Spirit of the Waters, who, they believe, is a goddess of purification. For both the Spirit of Fire and the Spirit of the Waters are in their estimation purifiers and healers. But they offer no sacrifice. So when they had prayed and the venerable priest of Zoroaster had said a few words (whereby he reminded them that the Prince of Wales had once been cured of a grievous illness by means of similar prayers on their part) the service was brought to an end. And such services were held also elsewhere, wherever the Parsees were who had fled from the city, at Surat, at Mhow, and in other places.

As I have already said, many of the natives, both the uneducated and the half-educated, believed that the original cause of the plague was the insult offered to the Queen's statue, and they considered that there had not been any sufficient apology for this act, which in their mode of thought was sacrilegious and aimed against Heaven itself. Toward the middle of January, therefore, the following petition, composed in the customary English of the better-class natives, was sent to the Governor. To understand it fully, it must be remembered that the prayers here suggested are intended as a deprecation of wrath addressed to the Queen in her capacity as earthly representative of the Divine. The petition, it will be noticed, is not sectarian, but catholic to a degree undreamed of in the ordinary philosophy of the religious world. All sects and castes are to unite in prayer to a deity named Almighty God. This is not meant as a concession to Christianity. The title is intended for a general designation of the Supreme, as the Hindus call their own Supreme God by the same name, and the formula is employed by them and by Mohammedans to paraphrase the names of Vishnu-Çiva and of Allah. The petition distinctly makes the first cause of the plague to be the mutilation of the Queen's statue.

## AN HUMBLE APPEAL TO HIS EXCELLENCY THE RIGHT HONOURABLE GOVERNOR OF BOMBAY.

To his Excellency the Right Honourable Governor and President in Council, Governor of Bombay.

May it please your Excellency, — The humble petition to alleviate human sufferings for the benefit of the public goodness and welfare of the people of Bombay and its vicinities.

Most humbly declare that at present a disastrous and destructive disease, known by the name of Bubonic Plague, is spreading and prevailing on in Bombay, and hundreds of people are dying through its effect every month. It is supposed that the cause of the above disease and plague is the rueful and abominable act of some one miscreant by doing mischief to the auspicious statue of her most Gracious Imperial Brittanic Majesty the Queen-Empress the Kaiser-i-Hind by blackening and besmearing it out of and in spite and malice and purposely to hurt and wound the natural feelings of the loyal British subjects, to insult and tarnish the glory of her Majesty's auspicious name and reign, and has also made a sacrilegious act, and blasphemed the Almighty God with irreverence, and by doing this act of high offence and infamy the said abominable mean wretch has drawn on himself the general imprecations of the loyal subjects of the just and benign British Rule. It is therefore most earnestly beseeched to his Excellency that his Excellency will be pleased and kind enough to order expressly, all and every nations and subjects of all and every caste and creed, including Europeans, Parsees, Hindoos, Mahomedans, Jews, and Hebrews, and all other nations residing under the British sway, and all the other subjects of every nations, to suspend and recede from all their worldly affairs and business, and to desist from it for a day or a few days, as long as his Excellency will think fit, and order them all to fervently pray into their public places of worship and prayer, such as in churches, agiarees, mandirs, mosques, and synagogues, and every other holy places, and keep these few days as Sabbaths, and invoke and supplicate the merciful Almighty God to get it stopped and extirpate the disastrous plague from its root, through the supernatural influence, and to preserve and spare the British subjects from untimely dying and draw out from the jaws of death, and by the Divine Will and supplication the general health, peace, and prospects of the people will be restored, and by it the lives of the people will be saved and rescued by its Divine influence. By doing this act of public charity it will be deemed a divine benediction bestowed on the poor British subjects, and all the loyal subject will heartily wish the prosperity of the British reign and will always as in duty bound ever pray for the long life of their merciful ruler the Gracious Her Majesty. AMEN.

This petition was not acted upon. But a few days later, on January 19, the Hindus performed a saving rite by themselves, which consisted chiefly in encircling the town with a stream of milk. But I cannot describe it more fully, and must omit also a few other curious rites both performed and merely proposed about this time, for there were many such ceremonies suggested as cures of plague by learned Pundits in various parts of the country. Only one incident, since it seems to me of special interest, I will mention particularly, and that is that in the propitiatory service there was not infrequently a wonderful reversion of religious belief. For as far as Indra and other Vedic gods are concerned, they are lost in the modern All-god. But in this year of extremity, the people went back to the old god of rain, for famine was harrying the folk as well as plague, and this same ceremony which I have just mentioned of encircling a town with milk was performed against the famine-demon by the Sheth of Ahmedabad. It was given out that he was praying to the great gods as he circumambulated the city pouring milk; but in reality he prayed to Indra, as I was credibly informed by one in authority who knew. And similarly, I was told by an official who knows Behar well that to this day the peasant there prays to "Indra whose wife is Kali." So changed but deathless are the old gods. But it would be too long a story to tell all that occurred between the people and their gods, and what happened as regards the famine and the earthquake — for the year was marked also by one of the most terrible earthquakes — I must leave out; only one curious fact about the small-pox goddess may perhaps be added. For there was small-pox in the Mofussil, and there is a goddess Small-pox to whom the people pray. In behalf of adults they pray, "O kind goddess of small-pox" (or more truly, "O kind Small-pox"), "keep away from us." But for babies the mothers pray, "O kind Small-pox, come soon to this baby and treat it gently." They believe that every one will probably be visited by Small-pox, but that the goddess will not be hard upon infants, so they hope she will come when the children are little. They call her Çitala, "the cool," because she brings burning fever, and "kind" because she is cruel, as in the case of Çiva.

But to come back to the plague, the prophecies of the astrologers, though often proved false, continued to find credence.

The most popular was that the plague would cease with the Makar Sankranti holiday, which occurs when the sun enters Capricorn, the middle of January. After the middle of January the most popular prophecy was that the plague would cease with the Holi festival, the middle of March. After the middle of March, "next year" was the time set. The means proposed by the native astrologer to avert the plague was the invocation of certain planets (Mars and Saturn), and the worshipping of the "wheel of the nine planets."

The total mortality in the last week of December had been 1853; that in the first week of January was 1711 (plague mortality, 1217). This seems to be a reduction, but a careful estimate in the Times of India for the week ending January 5 shows that the chief plague-hiding diseases are credited in this report with 676 deaths above the normal, withal when the population was a third to one half less than the normal. But there was for a few weeks, owing either to reduction of population or to one of the lulls which occasionally appeared in the plague, like a trough between breakers, a diminution both in the plague mortality and in the total mortality, though at the end of this lull the latter rose to a height hitherto unknown, for in the week ending February 9 the plague mortality alone was 1371 (total mortality for the week, 1911).

During January the aspect of the city was mournful beyond description. The throngs of people hurrying to the stations; the death-falls in the street, when no passer-by dared to touch the dying man; the pitiful little funerals, where sometimes the only mourners were the bearers, and they, feebly chanting the shrill dirge, would run rapidly with the uncovered corpse lest they died on the way; occasionally a funeral without a bier, but the body was slung on a pole and, it was said, even oozed blood; the starving, emaciated figures huddled together on the doorsteps of the wretched tenements; the frightened, suspicious glances with which every one looked on every one else in the street; the general air of crouching before an invisible malign power, — these were the marks of the New Year. And the physical appearance of the city did not lessen the melancholy effect. The streets, despite all the efforts of the Health Department, were a reproach to humanity; the long drought had covered the trees with dust; they stood gaunt and gray-leaved above the sickly grass. All day the sun shone hotly, all night it was bitterly cold; not with the tonic cold of the West; but with the horrible chill of a tomb, of India.

At this time voluntaryism, a phrase of the occasion, was the order of the day. In submitting to voluntary segregation there was a great difference between the communities. The Khoja sect of the Mohammedans, owing to the influence of their leader Aga Khan, showed themselves much more enlightened than the Sunni Mohammedans. The Jains would scarcely enter their own hospital. The Hindus had not yet resolved to have a hospital, but the municipal sheds were at their disposal. These, however, the Hindus, like the Mohammedans, did not want to use. The native community that acted most sensibly was that of the Parsees. They had an excellent hospital, they went to the hospital more readily, they opposed segregation less than any other sect or nationality.

But whether the gods had heard or only the Raj across the sea, better days were already at hand. The city government had proved itself incapable of wrestling with the storm of plague. So now a real gubernator took the city's helm.

The speech from the throne on January 19 (the day after Italy proposed the Venice Plague Conference) did much to keep up English courage. It said little in respect of the plague, but that little was enough: "Take the most stringent measures." The Governor at once (January 20) appointed first a special plague officer to inspect the city and "advise" the municipal commissioner; then an assistant health officer, twenty medical officers, and others deemed necessary.

In addition to the useful measure of appointing scientific experts, both doctors and officers for the purpose of facilitating house-to-house visitation, — there were thirty thousand houses to be inspected, and the four employed by the health officer had been entirely inadequate, — the Governor early in February (the 10th) published a Notification made possible by a special Epidemic Disease Act which had just been passed. This Notification authorized, and in fact directed, the municipal commissioner, of his own authority and without reference to the magistrates, to prohibit the occupation of any building declared to be unfit for human habitation; to require abatement of over-crowding, the vacation of buildings and premises for disinfecting; to enter deserted buildings forcibly (when they were locked up), and to cleanse and disinfect them; to remove the earth of floors, and to cut off water-connections when necessary; to demolish any building unfit for habitation, and to destroy infected articles. Some few of these powers had already been assumed. All of them might have been acquired long before, had the commissioner taken the initiative, or even followed the advice given to him by the government committee (appointed to report, when the plague first broke out) to apply for greater powers. February was spent in organizing and carrying out a campaign against the plague. On February 26, the Governor, Lord Sandhurst, delivered a timely speech, in which he said in effect:

"Citizens of Bombay, do not fear the cost of sanitation, nor the anger of the greedy wretches whose insanitary houses have been held together for rent. Destroy what is unfit for human habitation. Kill the plague by destroying its habitat in these rookeries. This is what I have been trying to do. Help me to continue this work, till we pull down all the foul death-traps of the town. Erect sanitary buildings. Broaden the streets. Rebuild Bombay, and let her be again in reality, as she once was, as she was meant to be by nature, Bombay the Beautiful."

This speech was received with enthusiasm. It brought back courage. People felt that at last a man had taken charge.

On March 5, the Gatacre Committee was appointed by the Governor. General Gatacre, the chairman, had been put in control of the hutting arrangements at Parel Park, where an auxiliary hospital was equipped (to which were afterwards sent the convalescents of the over-crowded Arthur Road Hospital). He was the Executive's right hand in the vigorous sanitary reform instituted by the Governor and had already done most efficient work. The city health officer was not made a member of this committee; the city commissioner was put on the committee, but not as the chairman. By the appointment of this committee the sanitation of Bombay was completely taken out of the hands of its municipality. The committee was expressly stated to be "subordinate only to Government," that is, to the Presidential government. The letter of the Governor to the municipal corporation explaining this drastic measure concluded with the bland remark: "To do this is no slur on local bodies; it is no blow to local self-government. It is simply an Imperial necessity."

The necessity was stated to be due to the fact that, as the plague was now spread over the whole Presidency, it was essential that the campaign should be conducted with military subordination on the part of local bodies. In the formal appointment of the committee, the municipal corporation were curtly directed "to carry into effect without delay any measures which may be ordered by the committee." In other words, the city corporation were reduced to a political cipher.

Under this order municipal apathy vanished. The corporation hurriedly raised legal objections to their own virtual suppression, as implied by the somewhat extraordinary wording just cited, but in the end they submitted as gracefully as they could. Thereafter, as regards the plague, the municipality dropped out of sight.

Times were changed now in Bombay. Four hospitals — the Arthur Road, the Parel auxiliary, the European General, and the Kamatipur shed-hospital — were open to plague patients, and the natives were told that the sick would have to be isolated, whether they would or no. Segregation was actually enforced. Then the plague began to decline. Other huts were erected, at Tank Bunder, Chaopatty, Kamatipur, etc. To these were sent the destitute and those who had been in contact with plague cases. But many more huts were built.

By April there were forty-one hospitals in the city (besides the sectarian hospitals) and six hundred segregation huts. The hospital staff was strengthened. Nurses from England were cabled for. Woman inspectors and physicians were appointed for *purdah* women. For the first time medical certificates were insisted on. Hacks, if used to convey plague-patients, were no longer permitted to return undisinfected to their stand, an abuse which, despite all protests, was current during the winter. Restrictions were put upon returning inhabitants liable to bring disease back with them; first on those coming back by ship, then, in April, on those by rail. An army of men were sent out to inspect and cleanse the ten districts into which, to facilitate sanitary work, the city had been divided; a responsible officer was put in charge of each district. An extra staff of nearly a thousand men was created in the health department; of four thousand in the engineering department. The idle military were put to work. Concealed cases of plague were artfully detected by means of official surprise-parties, after the locality had already been inspected. The corporation were told that if they did not at once settle the question of the disposal of *cutchra*, over which they had been dawdling for six months, the question would be settled for them. That also which the corporation had never had sense or sympathy to do, the higher government now did. It ordered compensation to be paid, not as a right, but as a grace, to "the very poor," whose infected goods were destroyed for the public weal. Finally, in the middle of April, one crowning abuse was stopped. The Mohammedan Grant Road burial-ground was closed by order of the Governor.

It must not be supposed that everything was accomplished at once. The number of cases of plague still concealed, despite the most careful surveillance, gives a hint of the numbers not detected under a less vigilant system of inspection. Even blackmail was still practiced, but the only case reported was that of municipal employees, who in April took six rupees as a bribe and let a *godown* (storehouse) go free of inspection.

The mettle of their new rein-holder was soon tested by the

balkiest of the natives, the Sunni Mohammedans. But an intimation of strength had been given before this. The great religious Valkeshvar Fair of March 1, and the popular delirium of the Holi Festival, which inaugurates the return of spring and takes place on the full moon of the same month, were both looked forward to with anxiety, as had been indicated in a letter addressed to the Governor on February 15 by the Chamber of Commerce. The former celebration, however, was now restricted by the express orders of the government ("in consultation with the municipal commissioner," for this officer figured in proclamations); while the Holi procession was absolutely prohibited. As for the Mohammedans, the imperial government itself prohibited the still more dangerous Haj pilgrimage (to Mecca), to the great grief and indignation of the Mohammedan community, who saw in this act only "an invidious distinction;" though in this the Sunnis opposed their own chief, Abdur Rahman, Amir of Afghanistan, who supported the action of the English authorities regarding the Haj. But it was left for the Sunnis of Bombay in particular to emphasize their own unfitness for civilized society. No sooner had the new law gone into effect than there began (March 15) a series of angry mass-meetings, to protest and petition against the measures of segregation and inspection. In vain the Governor, in refusing to grant the petition, explained the situation at length, and assured the Sunnis that their feelings, especially in regard to *purdah* women, would be respected. The Sunnis sent in another petition more impertinent than the first (for both petitions virtually said, "we will not"), and then had the impudence to declare roundly that nothing would induce them to yield the point. After the loss of much time spent in kind and courteous explanations the Governor, on April 5, told the Sunnis peremptorily that they would have to obey. They obeyed at once. Some of their wealthy leaders had been converted to common-sense long before and supported the government, both in trying to persuade their ignorant fellows and in generously building hospitals for them. But these gentlemen, who were really enlightened, had little influence as compared with the clerical leaders, most of whom were incorrigible. On the receipt of the definitive refusal to exempt Mohammedans from the common law of safety, "a would-be Ghazi" sent General Gatacre a letter, informing him that he would be decapitated within a fortnight owing to his zeal in enforcing sanitary regulations. But the barking dog did not bite. The Calcutta Mohammedans imitated the Bombayans on April 9, when five thousand of the former made a formal protest against the same sanitary regulations, then about to be put in force all over India.

March had opened with a drop in the weekly account with death. For the first time since December the plague mortality stood in three figures. Three weeks later the deaths had fallen from this point of nine hundred and thirty-eight to six hundred; by April 20 they were three hundred and ten; by the first of May there were only one hundred deaths in the week. By the end of March the returning inhabitants nearly balanced in number the outgoing, and after that the former were in excess. By the end of April the plague was almost extinct. Not the warmer weather alone was the cause, but the new commander and the means he used. In the latter half of March appeared a new red sign in Bombay, the letters U H H painted on the front of houses, Unfit for Human Habitation, but fit homes for plague. Hundreds of these houses were condemned, and the wretched inhabitants were hutted in the country. But the monsoon expected in June put a stop to the work, lest more people should be found to be hutted at the beginning of the rains than could be roofed again.

After the Governor took control there was less excitement, and nothing of religious moment occurred, for finding that danger was departing men no longer took the same interest in the gods. Only early in the spring some of the *thakorjis* or Vishnu idols, whom the priests had fed and prayed to all winter, till at last they could wait for succor no longer, were removed from the town, their priests fleeing just as the tide was about to turn. Yet so great was their faith that they carried with them the gods they thought had been deaf to their prayers.

In other respects also this season was devoid of memorable events, save that riots had occasionally to be suppressed. But when sanitation and segregation were resisted the rioters were put down easily, for the Governor was not afraid, and the people yielded as soon as they became convinced of this.

By June the plague was stamped out of the city. Then became apparent the danger which had lurked in the sign of recovery. So long as lasted the careful inspection of those who poured back into the town, there was no risk. Bombay at the end of spring was actually free of plague. For a whole week in June no death due to it occurred in the city.

But the end was not yet. Those thousands of refugees who had carried the plague with them and planted it over the whole Presidency, up and down the coast, north and south and inland, east as far as Nasik and the Khandeis district — but the main plague outside the Presidential town was at Karachi, Bulsar, and Poona — and still further, beyond the Presidency, at Bangalore in the south, where it had entered as early as November, at Gwalior, Agra, and even Lahore in the north — those thousands returned. And in returning from other districts, which were still plague-smitten, month after month, when no longer controlled by any adequate inspection, for the state government had accomplished its task and resigned its hold, — in returning to a populace as determined as ever to resist segregation or sanitation and to a municipality too weak to enforce either means of safety, they brought back the Great Death to Bombay.

---

Written during the winter of 1896–97 and completed the end of June, 1897, soon after I came back from India. I have since added a few notes and the last two paragraphs. Of the history of the plague subsequent to its recrudescence in the city I have no knowledge, and though I saw it elsewhere than in Bombay it would extend this sketch unduly to tell of its course through the country at large. Nor do I believe that after the first few months, barring the tragedy at Poona, where for a time all the ways of the East and West ran counter, there were either elsewhere or in Bombay the same terror and excitement or any events that revealed the strange heart of India more clearly than those I have here tried to describe. For outside of Bombay, the authorities, already warned, paid less attention to the remonstrance of ignorance and so mastered the plague more quickly; and later, when the Great Death crept back into Bombay, the doctrine of fatalism became, as it seems, the accepted faith even of those to whom it was not native, and the whole city relapsed into apathy, letting the plague do as it would and waiting till it should choose to go. But of the first few months I have ventured to write in the belief that the account may perhaps interest those who are either pleased with superstitions or curious in regard to what is doing in India. For in the latter regard, though the stage was small, there is no reason to suppose that on a larger one the political actors would play different parts, and in the former there is much to fascinate the student of antiquity, as he sees how the dead past of Europe is still a living reality in the East.

## NOTE ON THE PLAGUE.

It was stated in September, 1896, by practitioners of Bombay that ninety-six per cent., some said ninety-nine per cent., of those at first attacked by plague in the city had died. This was before any systematic practice had been adopted, and when indeed most of the cases were not treated at all. The ratio is surprisingly high, but it does not seem to be much exaggerated. The best means of discovering how many died when left to themselves is to reckon not on the basis of uncertain figures in a great city, but on that furnished by a small group, the numbers of which can be controlled and which no doctors have tampered with. At Theronda, near Rewadanda in the Kolaba District of the Presidency, there were 173 deaths out of 177 cases of plague, until the introduction of medical men (native doctors can be ignored) and sanitary regulations lowered the proportion. In Lower Damaun, a pest-hole in the Portuguese territory, even with the best medical attendance there were, in April, 140 deaths a week amongst a population of 9000. It is interesting to compare Thucydides' estimate. Out of 4000, in less than forty days 1050 died at Potidaea. Other points of comparison with the Attic plague will occur to the classical student, — its growing strength as winter came on, the synchronous famine and earthquake (in the North), the tendency of other diseases to run into the plague, the endurance of the body till its sudden collapse, the paralysis that occasionally resulted instead of death, etc. It was unfortunate that Dr. Haffkine's serum was not ready before the middle of January. When first tried on the prisoners in the jail (January 30) it seemed to be really a preventative. At least, there were 170 patients who were not inoculated, and 150 who were, and amongst the former there were afterwards twelve cases of plague and six deaths, while amongst the latter there were two cases and no deaths. Dr. Yersin did not come upon the scene with his antidote till March 5, when the plague was already in hand.

# NEW INDIA.

From the later Vedic age, when the king who was "eaten by the priests" was in turn the "eater of his people," a striking metaphor has been preserved. Taken from the chief architecture of the day, it describes the "altar" of the king's state. In this altar, the priests and the nobles are "the bricks;" the common people, the agricultural class, are only "the filling between the bricks." Unmentioned remain here those elsewhere known as "the black mass," the slaves, who have no place at any Brahmanic altar, human or divine.

Beneficent as was Buddhism, in its doctrine of "non-injury" and in its over-riding of caste-distinctions, it was routed by Brahmanized civilization, though the latter was deeply affected by it. Under the later Brahmanic kings the people were nominally protected. The king took one sixth of the farmer's grain. But the king ruled through vicegerents, military commanders who were also revenue-collectors. In Max Müller's opinion they were simply revenue-collectors, but even if this extreme view be wrong, as I think it is, there remains the fact that these vicegerents, called Supervisors, governed for the king over ten, an hundred, a thousand towns, and their support was drawn from the towns. The rapacity of royal officials was a favorite literary theme, and the whole system was one that clearly made for secret extortion. Manu says that the king's officials "are *usually* rascals, who, though appointed to protect, steal the property of others." In feudal states, the native kings sometimes took half the nobles' revenue, drawn from the doubly impoverished peasants.

The Mussulmans came next, whose rule was "anarchy and

oppression." Two Moghuls are credited with virtues, the "apostate" Akbar and his grandson, Shah Jahan. Under them flourished the Zamindars. Akbar's great revenue rose steadily, both under his son, a dissolute hypocrite, and under his magnificent grandson, whose costly military expeditions, court luxury, religious endowments, and own fabulous fortune were paid for by a tax that never ceased to increase till Aurangzeb, the "Louis XIV. of India," completed the misery of the people. There were too Afghan kings who are wished back by the believer in antique felicity. Such was Firoz Shah, of whom a modern critic of present conditions, a Hindu sighing for the past, ingenuously writes: "The historian of this monarch expatiates on the happy state of the raiyats who lived in that day, the great content of the people, and the general happiness of the realm. *This historian is said to be a writer not much to be trusted*" (italics mine). Of course, no court historian can be trusted.

So we are told by travellers, dazzled by the luxury of Oriental courts seen for the first time, that those days of rapine and oppression were blissful days, and we are given the impression that the peasant who paid for the luxury was as happy as the king and honored traveller who enjoyed it. Yet there are awkward passages even in the records of such travellers. Thus, one of them is cited to show how great was the welfare of the Hindu under the Mahratta; but midway in his tale of brave deeds and fine temples we stumble over this: "The praise of good administration is rarely merited by Mahratta chieftains."

But not all Hindus extol the past at the expense of the present. All extol the past, to be sure, and see in it virtues which a more critical view must qualify; but some, while not wanting in the pensive piety of propappolatry, so to speak, nevertheless see clearly that the best foreign Raj India has ever had is that of to-day. One of these is Mr. Dadabhai, whose words carry especial weight because he has been for more than forty years an avowed opponent of the accepted British polity. He sees, too, in the failure to appoint Hindus to high offices a violation of an imperial pledge,[1] so that he has much to blame in England's course. Yet he says, in words which I italicize because, coming from a Hindu, they more than counterbalance the many diatribes emanating from Occidental reformers: "*There has not been a nation, who, as conquerors, have, like the English, considered the good of the conquered as a duty, or felt it as their great desire.*" And again he says, speaking of his own wisest countrymen: "*They know that a real regeneration, civilization, and advancement of India materially, morally, and politically, depends upon a long continuance of the British rule.*"

This is the belief of the best thinkers to-day in India. There are Hindus, simple malcontents, who breathe out only hatred of the foreign Raj. Half-educated, they do nothing to enlighten their countrymen. Reckless agitators, scurrilous editors, disappointed place-hunters, they are intellectual mongrels, a bastard brood born of a too facile intercourse between East and West. But there are others, educated Hindu patriots, sons of their age, who weigh well past and present conditions, neither sparing adverse criticism nor withholding praise. These are they whose words should be heard, not only by the public, but in the councils that direct the fate of their country. Their number, happily, is increasing.

India's discord was England's strength. The Hindu religion opposed the Mohammedan religion, the Hindus numerically strong but not belligerent, the Mohammedans belligerent but numerically weak. But to-day there are issues in India more

[1] The royal pledge (of 1858) is as follows: "It is our further will that, so far as may be, our subjects, of whatever race or creed, be freely and impartially admitted to offices in our service, the duties of which they may be qualified, by their education, ability, and integrity, duly to discharge." The saving clause is *so far as may be*, which is apparently interpreted to mean, "so far as is wise to bestow offices on those who might oppose the policy of the government." Little has been done to redeem this qualified promise, partly because the British fear native opposition in council. Caution in this regard cannot be blamed, but it would mark the desirable beginning of a broader imperial policy to secure some representation for so much taxation. Mr. (Naoroji) Dadabhai's words, cited above, will be found on pp. 201, 202, of his Poverty and Un-British Rule in India.

important than the formulæ of ancient creeds. *Divide et impera* is ceasing to be a useful rule of thumb. The worshipper of Allah and the worshipper of Vishnu-Çiva have found that they have a common ground to stand upon. That ground is national unity. And the more closely the separate parts of India knit themselves together, the more imperative is the necessity for England to let India know definitively whether the good she has done in India in the past is but the earnest of what she will do for her hereafter.

May the heart of that nation which has done so much for India's welfare and yet wrought her, not always unwittingly, so many injuries, be moved to unite with her for the permanent good of both. For, thanks to England, there is a New India, no longer enslaved but free, no longer blinded but enlightened, not perfect but striving for perfection, weak but great, potentially strong, awaking to-day to the full consciousness of a glorious past and the possibility of a still more glorious future. Old India endured and dreamed of God. Her bastards revile and dream of themselves. But New India thinks, her dream is of the future. And what is this noble dream? She dreams not of independence, but of political equality based on moral likeness. She seeks to prove that in fiscal and judicial administration all native officials can, without European supervision, be as incorruptible as are British officials, claiming that to proved ability and integrity is due a recognition of the Indian's right to share in the government of the Indian's country. So may her dream be accomplished, and may England, even at some seeming cost, be ready to meet her halfway, proving in her turn, and before it is too late, that she cares less for revenue than for righteousness.

# INDEX.

# INDEX.

Long vowels in Sanskrit words are here covered with a makron, in other words with a circumflex. Short *a* is pronounced like *u* in punch; the corresponding long vowel, like *aw*, Pañjâb and Mahābhārata, for example, being pronounced *punjawb*, and *muhawb-hawrata*, respectively. Short *a* is frequently transcribed by *e* or *o* as well as by *a* and *u*. Thus B*e*ngâl and b*u*ngalow, b*o*stân and b*u*stân (garden), M*e*nu and M*a*nu, b*u*nia, and v*a*nia. Europeans usually mispronounce long *ā*, for example in Rāja, which should be pronounced *rawja*, the *u* sound (compare dance, 'daunce') being antique as well as modern, as shown by the interchange of *dvā*, *dvāu* (duo), dadā, dadāu (dedi) in Vedic forms. Sanskrit *e* and *o* are always long.